J. LIEBER

LITTLE LOWER
Than the Angels

LITTLE LOWER *Than the Angels*

by RABBI ROLAND B. GITTELSOHN

Illustrated by Jacob Landau

UNION OF AMERICAN HEBREW CONGREGATIONS
New York, N. Y.

Printed in U. S. of America

Second Printing, 1958

To
RUTH

Editor's Introduction

THIS IS AN UNUSUAL BOOK. MANY BOOKS ON RELIGION IN GENERAL and on Judaism in particular discuss the basic problems of life. Questions on how the world came to be, questions on right and wrong, problems of the relation of man to man and man to God are treated. These are usually given to students as "material to be accepted," to be learned and then to be "re-presented" to the teachers on examination day. This book is entirely different from all the others on the subject, especially from all the books written for young people.

Here, the great problems of life, the puzzling issues on which men have reflected throughout the centuries are presented, as far as possible, in a manner to stimulate thought and to arouse discussion, rather than to shut minds off and prevent discussion. The questions, the doubts concerning religion which have agitated men throughout the ages, which the author of that great literary classic of all time, the Book of Job, did not hesitate to express, are here introduced again and again. The presentation, though modern, is so written as to give young people a feeling of the abiding spiritual values inherent in life.

The Workbook which accompanies the volume reinforces the goal of the textbook to stimulate thought and discussion, and provides as well exciting activity on the part of the students. Because this is so, it is important that the book should be used for the right age group. Rabbis who confirm their children at age thirteen are requested not to use this book. It is definitely a book on religion for boys and girls in the high school department.

They should be fifteen or sixteen years old, certainly not younger, when pursuing this course of study.

We are grateful to the rabbis and teachers who have been kind enough to send us their critical and appreciative suggestions after using the experimental edition of this book.

EMANUEL GAMORAN

Acknowledgments

IT WOULD BE FOOLISH TO SUPPOSE THAT I COULD THANK ADEquately all those whose cooperation and help have gone into the making of this volume. The most—and the least—I can do is to express my heartfelt gratitude

. . . to Dr. Emanuel Gamoran, without whose constant counsel, encouragement, and advice this material could never have been completed; and to Dr. Abraham N. Franzblau, who first stimulated me to think in terms of teaching religion by pedagogically-sound methods.

. . . to my friends and colleagues, Rabbis Samuel Glasner and Mordecai M. Kaplan, each of whom helped immeasurably by commenting on the manuscript in its early stages.

. . . to Dr. David Dietz and Dr. Andries Voet for their invaluable aid in the chapters dealing with matters scientific.

. . . to the Reading Committee of the Commission on Jewish Education: Rabbis Solomon B. Freehof, David I. Cedarbaum, and Leon Fram.

. . . to Mr. Ralph Davis for his skilful designing of the book and for seeing it through the press.

. . . to Bessie R. Berman, Helen Hertsch, Natalie Jacoff, Mitzi Moscou, and Belle Steinberg, all of whom typed parts of the manuscript as it developed.

. . . to the many publishers who generously granted permission to quote from volumes issued by them.

. . . to the many organizations who gave us permission to use their photographs. The photographs in Group I all came from the American Museum of Natural History. Group II, pages 1 and 2, Wide World Photos; page 3, Hooker Electrochemical Co.; page 4, top, New Directions; bottom, Philadelphia Museum of Art. Group III, page 1, Wide World Photos; page 2, American Museum of Natural History; page 3, Union of American Hebrew Congregations; page 4, top, Temple Israel of Boston; bottom, Cathedral of the Pines. Group IV, page 1, Religious News Service; pages 2 and 3, from the UAHC filmstrip, "Within the Family of Liberal Judaism," produced by William P. Gottlieb; page 4, Ewing Galloway.

. . . and most of all, to the boys and girls in my own confirmation classes since 1936, whose interest and curiosity have been a source of encouragement in my efforts to bring them an understanding of why they are but *Little Lower than the Angels.*

ROLAND B. GITTELSOHN

Table of Contents

A Letter for You

Dear Student:

Most of the instructions necessary for an enjoyable year together will be found in the first chapter of this book. There are just a few helpful hints, however, which should be called to your attention even before opening Chapter One.

The most interesting and pleasurable part of our course should be the discussions we shall have in class. These discussions can be successful only if every member of the class reads each chapter carefully from beginning to end and does the workbook assignment to the very best of his ability in advance of our class session. In doing so, it is important that you answer all questions in your own words rather than by copying the language of the book.

To make it unnecessary for you to consult a great many additional books at the library, we have added to each chapter a series of readings from other authors. Where there are difficult words or phrases in these readings, a simpler explanation follows in brackets. The readings are an important part of the chapter; you will be unable to complete the workbook assignment properly or to participate in our class discussion without understanding them.

With these suggestions, plus the information to be found in Chapter One, we hope you will be ready for a stimulating year together as we consider some of the most important and puzzling questions human beings have wondered about through the ages. My hope is that you will enjoy reading this book and discussing it as much as I have enjoyed preparing it.

Sincerely yours,

Roland B. Gittelsohn

ROLAND B. GITTELSOHN

LITTLE LOWER
Than the Angels

1. In Which We Get Acquainted

SUPPOSE you were told that in the next ten minutes you could miraculously be given the answer to any *one* question you might wish to ask. Which question would you select as the most puzzling and important one in your life?

Would you ask for the answer you weren't sure of last week in that exam at school? Would you want to know if the weather will be good next Sunday for the picnic you and the family have planned? Would you choose as the most important question in your life who will win this year's World Series? Or—what college should you attend? . . . which girl (or fellow) should you date? . . . for what career do you want to prepare? . . .

Or would you ask an entirely different kind of question as the most important one you wanted answered? One that had to do with the deep, hidden meanings of human life—something like how the world and human beings first began; or what happens to us after we die; or what makes us want to be better than we are; or what was the purpose of our being born and how can we fulfill that purpose?

You recognize, of course, that in the above two paragraphs we have two altogether different kinds of questions. In the year we are about to spend together it is the second type—questions about religion—in which we shall be interested. Most intelligent people, if really faced with our imaginary choice of receiving the answer to any one question, would probably choose it from among these. If anyone could discover the final, complete answer even to a few of them, he would indeed be the wisest man ever to live on this earth.

For these are questions which have been asked by every group of men since the beginning of human history. And every group has had its religion or religions in which answers were attempted. Someone has said that if every kind of religion we know were suddenly to be erased, if all synagogues, churches and shrines were to be destroyed and even the very word *religion* were to be wiped out of man's memory, within a few generations men would have begun to build up some kind of religion again. This is because the old, puzzling, significant questions which we and our ancestors have asked for so many uncounted centuries would remain in our minds and we would still be eager to discover answers for them.

Why have these problems continued to bother every generation of men and women in every part of the world? Primarily for three reasons. *First,* because there has always been so much about life which people were unable to understand. True, we today know much more about many things than our primitive ancestors did; but even we by no means understand everything. Thousands of years ago people had no scientific knowledge at all of how our earth began. Today we believe that in the beginning this planet was a mass of gas that gradually cooled and condensed as it whirled through space, until finally it was cool enough for plants and animals and human beings to live on; or perhaps that it originated in a terrific explosion, after which it proceeded to cool to its present temperature. But these explanations leave us still with millions of unanswered questions. We still don't know for sure how or why the earth began; or what caused the first forms of life to appear after this planet had cooled; or whether the earth will some day become too cool for anyone to live on. Sometimes it seems the more we know about such things, the more there is we still do not know. So we turn to science for more information of this kind and to religion for explanations of why life developed as it did and what the purpose of life is.

In the second place, primitive men also greatly feared much about nature. The crash of thunder, the sharp, sudden crackle of lightning, the brutal blast of hurricane and tornado—these things frightened them far more than they sometimes do us, because they didn't understand what caused them. This sense of fear, this feeling of being weak and powerless against the forces of nature, was a second reason why they asked religious questions.

A third reason why people have always wondered about these things is their need for assurance that life is worth while, that it has some purpose. So far as we know, animals don't worry about such things. They just live, without asking why they were born, or what purpose there is to life. But human beings are different from animals in this respect. We need the feeling that our existence is more than that of an ant, which can be stepped on at any moment and destroyed before it knows what has happened, and is then forgotten. We need to feel that we were born for a reason, that there is a purpose to our lives, and that this purpose will somehow be fulfilled even though we can't live forever.

Most people feel this need especially when they experience tragedy or sorrow in their lives and want an explanation for such unhappiness. But this is not the only time in life we ask such questions. The more intelligent a person is, the more likely it is that he will want to know why and for what purpose he was born, and what he can do to make his life really valuable.

For all these reasons—but especially in our case the third—we, like all those who have preceded us, continue to ask questions about religion.

For Example

> How and when did this world first begin its existence? . . . Out of what material or substance was the first human being made? . . . Will the world ever end? . . . Why do people have to die? . . . What happens to us after we die? . . . Why do some people seem to have nothing but good luck and happiness, while others suffer one misfortune after the other? . . . What keeps all the planets and stars in our universe from colliding with each other? . . . Is there a God? . . . What does God look like? . . . Does He know everything that happens to us? . . . Does He know that I am reading this book now? . . . Can He perform miracles? . . . If He wanted to, could He make a river flow backward, from its mouth to its source? . . . What good does it do to pray?

You'll certainly agree that we have asked some extremely important questions here. Yet these are only a few of the things people have wondered about. In your workbook for this chapter, your first task will be to add at least three other religious problems or questions of your own to this list. Try to choose specific questions about which you have actually wondered yourself. Your rabbi or teacher will then try to include your questions in class discussions later.

Two and Two Is Always Four

Would you like to try an interesting experiment? Tonight at the dinner table, or any time when five or more people are together, ask each one to express in a sentence or two his definition of God or his description of what God is like. Or better yet, give each person pencil and paper, ask your question about God, then let each one think for a few minutes silently before writing his own answer. When all have finished, read and compare the answers they have given. No matter where or with whom you try this, we can almost guarantee you will have almost as many different ideas about God as the number of people who try to answer. And what is more important, if the people you question are intelligent, few of them will be positive they have the right answer.

Some questions are easy to answer. If you ask any person of school age or older, "How much is two and two?" the answer will always be Four. But no one knows definitely or exactly what God is like. The first important thing for you to learn here at the very beginning of our course is the impossibility of any human being knowing all about God.

Once there was an ancient scholar who thought he could. He decided to give a public lecture in which he would tell people everything there was to know about God. While preparing his thoughts for this lecture he happened to walk along the bank of a nearby river, where he saw a child digging in the sand. Puzzled by the fact that the child was carrying water from the river in a spoon and putting it in a hole he had dug in the sand, the scholar asked what he was doing. The child replied, "I am going to take all the water out of the river and put it in this hole." "But that is impossible!" exclaimed the scholar. Only then did he realize that it was just as impossible for any human being to know everything about God.

Another ancient wise man was once asked by his king how long it would take him to give a definition of God. He answered that one day ought to be enough. At the end of the day, still without a definition which satisfied him, he asked for a week. When the week had ended he still had not succeeded, so he asked for a month, and after the month, for a year. Finally, when the whole year had passed and the wise man was still without his definition, he came before the king and said, "O king, the more I think of God, the less I know of Him."

Our Jewish ancestors had many ways of expressing their understanding of the fact that no human being can possibly know all about God. An ancient Jewish poet, whose words are in our Bible, after thinking about God for a long time, wrote:

> Such knowledge is too wonderful for me;
> Too high, I cannot attain unto it. . . .

You have probably heard about Job, the most tragic and unfortunate person described in the Bible. One of Job's friends expressed pretty much the same thing in these words:

> Canst thou find out the deep things of God?
> Canst thou attain unto the purpose of the Almighty?
> It is as high as heaven; what canst thou do?

But long before either Job's friend or the poet, Moses himself knew that it is impossible for human beings to discover all the truth about God. A passage in the Bible which was probably part of a speech delivered by Moses to the ancient Jews reads: "The hidden things belong unto the Lord our God; but the known things belong unto us and to our children for ever."

We certainly don't expect you to answer all the questions we shall deal with this year. But we do expect you to think about them, to discover some of the tentative answers given by wise men and women through the ages, to decide which of these answers seem helpful to you. What little we do know about God and religion has come to us because in every generation there were people brave and enterprising enough to think new thoughts for themselves, people who weren't satisfied just to accept the opinions of others, but who expressed ideas of their own, too. Sometimes it requires more courage to think new thoughts than it does to fight battles in a war. People who think for themselves in politics and economics are often accused of being radicals. Those who think new thoughts in religion are frequently branded as heretics or unbelievers.

Yet no progress would ever be made in religion if there weren't always some people in every generation who, after learning what others had thought before them, proceeded to work out new ideas of their own. They are like the early American settlers, or the first chalutsim (pioneers) in modern Palestine who braved the terrors of the unknown to make progress possible.

It is our hope that some of you in this class will be stimulated by our discussions, not to discover *everything*, but rather to do your own serious thinking and perhaps to come just a little closer to the truth about God than anyone before you has. We won't expect you necessarily to agree with everything your rabbi or teacher says or with everything this book says. But we will expect you to have mighty good reasons for any opinion you express. Probably the most important and frequent question you'll hear in these discussions will be Why? Almost everything you say will be challenged with Why? And you'll have to be prepared to give your reasons. By the same token, however, you have the right also to ask anyone else for reasons supporting whatever he may say.

This will be true both in our class discussions and in the written answers you will be expected to give in your workbook. For each chapter in this text, there is a corresponding chapter in your workbook. To answer some of the questions asked there, all you need do is read your text carefully. Other questions, however, will require serious thinking and reasoning on your part; this book will give you the material with which to think, but it will not always give you the direct answer.

As you begin your quest for religious truth, you are most fortunate in being a Jew, for our Jewish religion is one of the very few which gives its people freedom to think for themselves on such matters. Most religions have a creed consisting of the exact things a person must believe in order to follow that faith. Furthermore, in most religions the priest or minister or leader is supposed to do the thinking and then tell the people what to believe. In our Jewish religion the rabbi doesn't tell you what to believe; he teaches you what other Jews have believed before you, and tries to help and guide you in thinking for yourself.

Today Isn't Yesterday

Of course it isn't, you say. But what is more important is that today's ideas aren't the same as yesterday's either. In our search for religious ideas which will help us live better lives today, we shall be greatly aided by discovering what Jews have believed about God and religion through the ages. Many of the ideas first suggested by Moses about 3,200 years ago or by the great Jewish prophets about 2,500 years ago will still be helpful to us. But some of their thoughts are no longer valid for us.

This shouldn't be surprising at all. Our ideas about most important things have changed quite a bit in the last 2,000 years. We wouldn't think much of a person who still believed that the earth is flat or that trees and stones have spirits inside them, would we? As civilization grows older, as each generation learns what has been discovered in the past and then searches for new truths itself, its ideas change. So we must expect our ideas about God and religion to be different from those of our ancestors also. Let us recognize right here, however, that there is a difference between saying that God changes and saying that people's *ideas about God* change. This earth didn't change any when people stopped supposing it to be flat and began to understand it must be round. It was always round, even when people thought it to be flat. In much the same way, God has probably always been the same; it is our ideas about God that have changed. But we're getting a little ahead of our story.

Some religions insist that people's ideas about God should be the same today as they always were. Judaism does not. Thousands of years ago our religious teachers understood that just as their religious ideas differed from those of previous generations, so they must expect the religious thinking of their descendants to differ from theirs. Do you remember the phrase which appears a number of times in our prayer book, "God of Abraham, God of Isaac, and God of Jacob"? Have you ever wondered why it was necessary to repeat the word "God" before each of these names? The Rabbis who lived many centuries ago wondered about that too. After much serious thinking, they said we repeat it because the God of Isaac was not exactly the same as the God of Abraham, while the God of Jacob was not in all respects identical with that of Isaac! In other words, they meant to tell us that each generation's idea of God can be an improvement over that of the previous generation. Judaism recognizes that and approves it.

Other Rabbis in ancient times had different ways of expressing the same idea. They noticed, for example, that in the Bible God appears in different ways to different individuals and at different times. At the Red Sea, for example, Moses and his people thought of God as a warrior who had saved them from the Egyptians, while some years later they thought of Him as a teacher who was giving them the Ten Commandments at Mt. Sinai. To some people in the Bible God seemed to be a stern, harsh deity who punished them for their sins, while to others He was a kind, considerate God who forgave them. Noticing all these differences, the old Rabbis pictured God as saying to them, "I am the one who appears in all these places and ways." In other words, they, too, recognized that our ideas about God, or the ways in which we think of Him, can change.

Let's look at our Bible for one more example of the same thing. According to the story told in the Book of Exodus, when God first told Moses to lead his people out of Egyptian slavery, Moses said, "Behold, when I come unto the children of Israel, and shall say unto them: The God of your fathers hath sent me unto you; and they shall say to me: What is His name? What shall I say unto them?" God then answered Moses with three Hebrew words: E-h'yeh asher e-h'yeh, אֶהְיֶה אֲשֶׁר אֶהְיֶה. These words can be translated: *I shall be what I shall be*. In other words, as long ago as when this part of our Bible was written, men understood that God does not seem to be the same to every generation. They did not think of God as saying: *I am what I always was;* but rather, *I shall be what I shall be*. That is to say, I shall change in the minds of men from generation to generation.

It is clear, therefore, that we are following good Jewish tradition in expecting that our own ideas about God today may differ from the ideas of our ancestors or perhaps even of our parents. They may also differ from the ideas we ourselves held a few years ago. When you were a little child, your notions about most things were quite different from what they are now. Once you may have thought that the music coming from your radio was actually being played inside the cabinet itself or that there were real people behind the motion picture screen in the theater, acting and speaking their parts. As you grew older, you acquired a more adult, mature understanding of these things.

Exactly the same thing is true concerning your own personal idea of God. At one time or another many of us probably thought of God as a dignified old man, sitting on a throne somewhere in heaven. We may not be sure what God is like today, but we certainly don't think any more that He is an old man, do we? So we must expect our ideas to be different not only from those of our ancestors, but also from those we held ourselves when we were little children.

Looking Ahead

Putting together the most important things in this introductory chapter, we may say that our task through the rest of this book will be threefold:

1. We shall try to ask many of the important religious questions human beings have asked through the centuries.

2. We shall examine the answers given by those who have lived before us, especially by our own Jewish wise men.

3. Using these tentative answers as a guide, we shall search for ideas which can help us live better lives as modern Jews.

Before embarking on this triple task in the next chapter, be sure you have answered all the questions in your workbook for this introduction. And if there is anything in this chapter thus far which you do not clearly understand, don't hesitate to ask your rabbi or teacher for an explanation.

The final part of your workbook assignment for this chapter

will be to answer the "true and false" questions in Section V. The purpose of doing this now is to indicate your opinions on a number of important religious matters. You will be given another opportunity to answer the same questions at the end of our course; by comparing your attitudes now and then, you will be able to see how your opinions have changed as a result of our year together.

SOMETHING FOR YOU TO READ

A. That modern Jews, however, cannot conceive of God in the same way as their fathers did does not mean that they can dispense with the belief in God. Our conception of all things changes with the growth of our experience and knowledge. In this age of electricity our conception of lightning is very different from the conception of it held in all ancient mythologies, which viewed it as a weapon of the gods. Nevertheless, lightning is as much a fact as it ever was. Similarly, the reality of God is as true as ever, despite the dissipation [disappearance] of the thick clouds of miracle with which tradition enveloped it.—Mordecai Kaplan, *Future of the American Jew,* The Macmillan Co.

B. Though the belief in . . . God always has been central in Judaism, it was not always conceived in the same way. Like every other product of human experience, so the idea of God has been subject to continuous development. In response to the growing needs of men and with the advancement of knowledge and of moral refinement, certain notions once held regarding the Divine were later found unworthy . . . and were replaced by more suitable ideas.—Samuel S. Cohon, *The Jewish Idea of God,* Union of American Hebrew Congregations.

C. Many people . . . contend that you have no right to change the meaning of the word "God."

One wonders what these people would say about the word "atom." An atom used to be defined as "the smallest portion into which matter can be divided. . . . An atom is an uncuttable portion of matter."

But now, with the beginning of the "atomic" age, we have learned to cut or split the atom.

Shall we give up the word "atom"?

Of course we won't. We shall . . . go on speaking about the inauguration of the "atomic" age, when an atom is no longer an atom, because it can be split.

Why not extend the same privilege to the word "God". . . ?—Mordecai Kaplan, *The Reconstructionist*, Nov. 29, 1946.

D. The ideas of religion we entertain, the forms we follow, the institutions we cherish, and the prayers we offer must be grounded in present knowledge and experience. We must learn to love God with our own hearts and minds rather than with those of our forefathers.—Samuel S. Cohon, *Judaism—A Way of Life*, Union of American Hebrew Congregations.

2. *In Which We Look Around*

PREPARE yourself for a surprise! . . .

You are about to read an entire chapter of a book about Jewish religion, without even once seeing the word "God." (That is, after these first two paragraphs, and not counting the Reading Selections at the end of the chapter.) Does that sound strange to you? Of course, we have a purpose in following so unusual a procedure, and it is only fair to tell you at once what that purpose is. In the last chapter we mentioned the fact that every people on this earth, in all the centuries of human experience, has developed some kind of religion. There must be something about the environment in which we live—about the larger universe, about our own earth, and in fact even about ourselves as human beings—which led so many different kinds of people, some primitive and some civilized, to develop a belief in God. So let's try, if we can, to retrace in this chapter many centuries of human experience. To be sure, we have the advantage of much scientific knowledge which wasn't even suspected by those who first developed religion; but aside from that, let's try to put ourselves in their position.

Or better yet, let's suppose we just arrived here from some other planet where the earth words, *Religion* and *God*, aren't even known. The first thing we want to do after arriving here is to become acquainted with our new home. What kind of planet is this on which we are now to live? Is it a place where things happen in some kind of orderly manner, or do things just "pop" at any old time so that we never know what's going to happen next?

Let's make a survey of the universe in which we live and of which we're a part. To do that, we'll make two lists, putting under each heading all the evidence we can find. As our heading for one list we shall think of such words as Law, Order, Purpose, Plan, Harmony, Intelligence, and Design. On this first list we shall place whatever evidence we can find which indicates that this is a regular, dependable, trustworthy universe, that things happen according to a definite, intelligent plan and seem to make sense. Our second heading will consist of words like Disorder, Confusion, and Accident. There we shall list those items which seem to occur at random, irregularly, one way one time and another way the next time, so that we cannot depend upon them and we never know what's apt to occur next.

Do you fully understand the distinction now between these two kinds of evidence? Perhaps it will be a little clearer to you if we take another moment to explain what we mean here by the word *Accident*. Usually when you hear that word, you think of two cars colliding. But that's not an accident at all in the sense in which we are using the word here. By *Accident* in this book we mean something that happens without a proper cause or in a way which is undependable. If seven and four added up to eleven today, but totaled thirteen tomorrow, that would be an *Accident*. If the same piece of cork that floated on top of the water yesterday sank to the bottom today, that would be an *Accident*. If the identical causes which produced one result this week yielded an altogether different and unpredictable result next week, that too would be an *Accident*.

If one time when you threw a ball into the air it came down again, but the next time it just kept on going up and never fell back to the ground, that would be an *Accident*. If two cars, approaching an intersection at right angles to each other, starting at the same rate of speed and the same distance from the crossing, both proceeded in a perfectly straight line and when they reached the middle of the intersection at the same instant, they didn't collide but one passed through the other without any crash, *that* would be an *Accident* in the sense in which we are using the word here. The fact that they would *always* crash under such circumstances would be the very opposite of *Accident*.

Well, we hope the meaning of our two headings and lists is perfectly clear to you now. If not, perhaps as we commence our survey you will understand better.

One more word of introduction before we proceed: some of you, who have a greater interest in science and who have read a number of scientific articles and books, may find that you are already familiar with much of the evidence we are about to examine; in that case we hope you will pardon the repetition. Others of you, however, whose interests in the past have not been scientific, may find the material which follows slightly difficult. We have attempted to present it in a way which would maintain the interest of both groups. And now we are ready for the meat of this chapter, "In Which We Look Around."

At the Universe

What kind of universe is this, of which our earth is a part and in which you and I live? What evidence can we find in it to put on either of our lists? Let's find out!

1. The first impressive fact to note about our universe is its immense size and the enormous number of stars and planets moving about within it at incredible speed. The universe is so large

that we find it difficult even to comprehend its size. Perhaps it will help if we imagine it reduced to a much smaller scale. If our earth were reduced to the size of the period at the end of this sentence, and if the rest of the universe were reduced proportionately, the sun would be nineteen and a half feet away from the earth. The nearest star would be 1,005 miles away. The furthest known galaxy of stars would be 81,830,000,000 miles away. Remember:—all this, *if* our earth were only the size of a printed period!

The rapid motion within the universe is perhaps even more impressive than its size.

We know that our earth moves swiftly around the sun, while the moon in turn revolves around our earth. We know also that every other planet in this solar system is constantly in motion, and that indeed the entire solar system is moving rapidly through space. Furthermore, that ours is probably only one of many such solar systems, all of them in swift, perpetual motion. What strikes you as the most impressive thing about all this motion? Isn't it that the planets and stars never seem to collide with each other? Sir James Jeans, one of the most prominent of modern physicists, once estimated that mathematically, a collision between two stars could occur once in 600,000,000,000,000,000 (600 quadrillion) years.

This is remarkable, especially when we consider the number of planets and stars moving through space and the breath-taking speeds at which they move.

Furthermore, each of the planets operates on a time-table. An astronomer can tell us exactly where one of the planets will be at any given moment in the future, or precisely at what day, hour and minute it will return to the spot it is in now. The time-table of the planets is far more regular than that of any railroad or airline. Each planet has its own special orbit or path from which it never departs, and its rate of speed, which it always maintains.

On which of our lists will we place this item? Why? Under what circumstances would we place it on the other list? Be sure you understand this first example very clearly before proceeding; if you do, you will have less trouble with the other items to follow.

2. Occasionally a meteorite hits our earth. Scientists use the term *meteor* or *shooting star* for the bright trail caused by such an object streaking across the heavens; you have undoubtedly seen many such, especially in the summer sky. When such an object actually reaches our earth it is called a *meteorite*. There is no way to predict when this is going to happen, how big the meteorite will be, or just where it will fall on the earth's surface. What happens is that apparently material from outer space comes within the gravitational pull of the earth, and is then drawn toward us by gravity until it hits this planet.

In most such cases we are not even aware of the incident, because the friction between the meteor and the air through which it passes as it comes within the earth's atmosphere causes the meteor to disintegrate and evaporate. Even when the object falling toward the earth is originally a very large one, usually by the time it actually reaches us it has been reduced to a size which can cause only minor damage, if any.

Would you call this an example of Law and Order, or of Confusion and Disorder? Why? Is it an accident in the sense we are using here? Does it demonstrate that our universe is a dependable one, or one in which things just happen without reason or purpose?

3. While it is true that so far as we know the stars and planets do not collide with each other, it is also true that occasionally a star explodes. Astronomers call this kind of thing a *nova*, and tell us that about ten *novae* occur each year in our own Milky Way. Scientists do not know what causes a *nova* nor can they predict in advance when one will occur.

Ask yourself the same questions here that were listed after the example of the meteorite. Continue with the next illustration only after you have thought through this one.

4. If you live near the seashore, or have ever spent a summer on the ocean, you know about the tides. Fishermen, sailors, swimmers, captains of ships, in fact, everyone who has anything to do with the ocean either for business or for pleasure must consider whether it is high tide or low tide. Twice a day the tide reaches its highest point, at which time the beach is very much smaller than otherwise, and twice a day we have the lowest tide level, when the beach is its largest. You probably know already that the tides are caused by the force of gravity of the moon acting on the earth. The most interesting thing about the tide is that it can be timed exactly. Scientists can figure out in advance the exact minute of any particular day when low tide or high tide will be reached. Fishermen know just when the tide will start moving "in" or "out." In cities which are located near the seashore, newspapers announce, along with their weather predictions, exactly when low and high tide respectively are to occur that day.

By now you know what questions to expect after this example. Is this evidence of Order or Disorder, of Purpose or Accident, of something which happens dependably or by chance in the universe? Be sure to give reasons for your answer, and try to indicate under what circumstances you would change your mind and list this under the opposite heading. When you are sure about this example, go on to the next.

Sun and Earth

5. The sun always "rises" in the east and "sets" in the west. It doesn't make its morning appearance in the east on Mondays, Wednesdays, Thursdays and Saturdays, and in the west on Tuesdays, Fridays and Sundays. It always takes the earth 365¼ days to make one complete revolution around the sun. It always takes

the moon the same number of days to make a complete circuit around the earth. It always takes the earth the same number of hours to rotate fully on its axis.

> There isn't much point in repeating the same questions after each of these examples, especially since there are so many more of them to come. So suppose you read over carefully again all the questions listed after the items above, then apply them to this one and to all those listed on the pages to follow. Without repeating them, we'll just assume that after reading each example, you will stop for a moment to think, applying these questions to each of them before proceeding to the next. Doing that carefully now, as you read the text, will make it easier for you later to do your workbook assignment for this chapter.

6. An earthquake is something which practically always occurs as a surprise, to say the least. We know pretty well by now what causes earthquakes, but it isn't very often that we can predict in advance just when or where one will occur. That's why earthquakes are among the greatest natural catastrophes, causing not only tremendous property damage, but also the loss of countless lives. The people of China can certainly testify that earthquakes generally come suddenly, without warning, and that they do enormous damage.

7. The law of gravity works all the time, not just during certain hours or on certain days. A ball thrown into the air *always* falls down again, though, to be sure, it may fall where we can't catch or reach it. If you jump off a ladder, you'll *always* fall toward the earth, never away from it. Even when we fly in a plane or float gently in a parachute, we haven't defied the law of gravity; we've just found a way to adjust to it or to make use of it.

Furthermore, scientists can always determine the extent of the gravitational pull or how fast any object will fall toward the earth at a given time and place. They are able to do this because repeated experiments have shown them how to figure the amount of pull between any two objects or bodies in our universe. This pull or attraction *increases* directly in proportion to the size and weight of the two bodies concerned, and *decreases* in proportion to the square of the distance between them. Scientists are able to express this in the form of a definite law, to which they have found no exceptions. If we tell them the size and weight of any two objects in the universe and the distance between them, they can figure out the exact attraction or pull those two objects will exert on each other.

8. A few pages back we gave the example of the tides. At that point, perhaps someone in the class felt like saying, "Aha, but how about a tidal wave?" A tidal wave, as you most probably know, is a huge wave or series of waves of exceptional power and force, which occurs from time to time, particularly in the Pacific, and which often causes great destruction. It is an altogether different thing from the normal tide, which, as we have already noted, is caused by the gravitational pull of the moon. A tidal wave is usually caused by an earthquake on the bottom of the ocean, sometimes also by a terrific windstorm.

You may have heard of the tidal wave which struck the town of Hilo, Hawaii, back in 1947. It reached inland a distance of about a quarter of a mile, flooding several blocks of houses and stores and wreaking havoc in the business section of the city. It doesn't seem to be possible in any way to predict when a tidal wave is about to commence. True, after one has started and been observed, we are able to predict about where and when it may strike, but the origin of such a wave is beyond our power to anticipate.

9. Most of us just take the planet on which we live for granted. Unless we happen to be scientists, we don't often stop to consider how many things about this earth must be exactly right in order for us to live. For example: the distance of this earth from the sun means the difference between life and death for all of us. If our earth were too close to the sun, the heat would immediately kill us; if, on the other hand, it were too far,

there would not be enough heat to keep us alive. Though none of us had anything to do with it—nor, for that matter, did any human being—it is our good fortune that the distance between earth and sun is just right for plants, animals, and human beings to be able to live here.

The same is true regarding the amount of oxygen surrounding our planet. You know, of course, that oxygen is essential for all forms of life. What you may not have known is that the atmosphere surrounding this earth, which is a combination of many gases, is about 78 per cent nitrogen and 21 per cent oxygen. Now the fascinating thing to note is that only a proportion very close to 21 per cent of oxygen would permit land life as we know it to exist on this planet. If oxygen were about 50 per cent of the atmosphere, the earth would be dangerously inflammable. One stroke of lightning might then explode a whole forest. If, on the other hand, the proportion of oxygen in our atmosphere were only 10 per cent, that would not be sufficient to maintain or permit the forms of life we know.

Many similar examples could be given. For instance, if there were much less water than we now have on the surface of the earth, life on this planet would be impossible. In this and many other respects, it almost seems as if everything that ever happened on this earth from its beginning had been intended to make it possible for life, especially human life, to develop and grow here. Thousands of factors and combinations of factors had to be "just right" as a preparation, before the adventure of human life could occur on this planet. You will be able to appreciate just a small part of this necessary preparation after studying Reading Selections E and F at the end of this chapter.

10. Here is an interesting example, which we give you in the form of a newspaper clipping from several years back. Read it, and then decide on which of your two lists it belongs:

> In Grand Rapids, Michigan, lightning struck an electric transformer in a manufacturing plant, started a fire. Soon after, another bolt of lightning struck a nearby fire alarm box, summoned firemen.

Could this be listed as an example of Law, Order, and Purpose in the universe? Why?

11. Another kind of evidence may be found in the action of chemical elements in our universe. The science of chemistry is possible only because chemists can depend upon chemical elements to "behave" the same way in every experiment. Two chemical elements which produce a certain reaction or result the first time they are placed together will produce the same result whenever they are united in the same quantity under the same circumstances. For example: whenever two parts of hydrogen are combined with one part of oxygen, we have water. Similarly, whenever we analyze the chemical content of water, we find that it consists of two parts hydrogen to each one part oxygen. We can depend upon this always being true.

Unfinished Business

We shall continue our survey in Chapter Three. In the meantime you should find the Reading Selections below both interesting and helpful in doing the workbook assignment. The first three were written by three of the most eminent scientists of our generation.

SOMETHING FOR YOU TO READ

A. One thus cannot be satisfied with any explanation of our world which does not postulate [assume] an intelligence working in nature.—Dr. Arthur H. Compton, *The Religion of a Scientist,* Institute for Religious and Social Studies of the Jewish Theological Seminary of America.

B. We discover that the universe shows evidence of a designing or controlling power that has something in common with our own individual minds. . . .—Sir James Jeans, quoted in Samuel S. Cohon's *Judaism—A Way of Life,* Union of American Hebrew Congregations.

C. I believe that intelligence is manifested [shown] throughout all nature. . . . The basis of all scientific work is the conviction that the world is an ordered and comprehensible [understandable] entity [unit] and not a thing of chance.—Dr. Albert Einstein, quoted in William E. Hocking, *Science and the Idea of God*, University of North Carolina Press.

D. (Our Bible contains an interesting little passage which belongs among the readings for this chapter. The Book of Genesis pictures God speaking the following words to Noah after he and his family had been saved from the flood):

I will not again curse the ground any more . . . ; neither will I again smite any more every thing living, as I have done. While the earth remaineth, seedtime and harvest, and cold and heat, and summer and winter, and day and night shall not cease.

E. So many essential conditions are necessary for life to exist on our earth that it is mathematically impossible that all of them could exist in proper relationship by chance on any one earth at one time. Therefore, there must be in nature some form of intelligent direction. If this be true, then there must be a purpose. . . .

. . . had the crust of the earth been . . . thicker, there would be no oxygen, without which animal life is impossible; and had the ocean been . . . deeper, carbon dioxide and oxygen would have been absorbed and vegetable life on the surface of the land could not exist. . . . If the atmosphere had been much thinner, some of the meteors which are now burned in the outer atmosphere by the millions every day would strike all parts of the earth. . . . The atmosphere is just thick enough to let in the actinic rays [heat and light rays from the sun] needed for vegetation and to kill bacteria, produce vitamins, and not harm man unless he exposes himself too long.—A. Cressy Morrison, *Man Does Not Stand Alone*, Fleming H. Revell Co.

F. We have found that the world is in the right place, that the crust is adjusted . . . and that if the ocean were . . . deeper we would have no oxygen or vegetation. We have found that the earth rotates in twenty-four hours and that were this revolution delayed, life would be impossible. If the speed of the earth around the sun were increased or decreased materially, the history of life, if any, would be entirely different. We find that the sun is the one among thousands which could make our sort of life possible on earth, its size, density, temperature and the character of its rays all must be right, and are right. We find that the gases of the atmosphere are adjusted to each other and that a very slight change would be fatal. . . .

. . . The existence of these facts cannot, therefore, be reconciled with any of the laws of chance. It is impossible, then, to escape the conclusion that the adjustments of nature to man are far more amazing than the adjustments of man to nature. A review of the wonders of nature demonstrates beyond question that there are design and purpose in it all.—A. Cressy Morrison, *Man Does Not Stand Alone*, Fleming H. Revell Co.

G. To an astronomer the most remarkable thing about the universe is not its immense size, its great age, or even the violence of the forces operating within its borders. The thing which strikes an astronomer with awe is the element of perfect orderliness. From the tiny satellites of our solar system to the vast galaxies far beyond our own there is no trace of confusion. There is nothing haphazard, nothing capricious. The orderliness of the universe is the supreme discovery of science.—F. R. Moulton, *The Nature of the World and of Man*, University of Chicago Press.

3. *We Look Further and Closer*

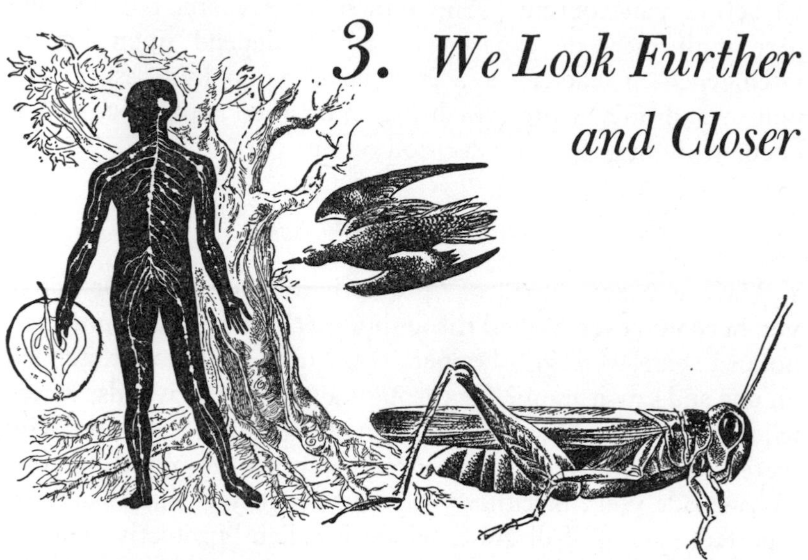

HAVE you ever seen a motion picture which commenced with a wide panorama shot of a whole city, then narrowed down to one building, gradually to one window of that building, and finally gave us a close-up shot of the room in which the story opened? In a sense, we're going to use that technique of moving the camera closer in this chapter. Having examined the whole, vast, unmeasured universe in our last chapter, we're now going to occupy ourselves with a smaller (but in many respects, a far more interesting) part of that universe, namely, with certain animals and our own bodies as they exist here on this earth. When we speak of nature, we include everything from the hugest planet millions and millions of miles away to the tiniest insect right in our own backyard. We ourselves are a part of nature too. So, having already discovered something about the Order or Disorder, the Plan or Confusion in the larger universe, we now want to examine the same thing on a smaller scale of nature. We shall still use the two lists started in the last chapter; if you don't remember all the words we used there for headings, it might be a good idea to review them quickly now on page 16 before you continue. And remember, we aren't concerned here with facts or experiences which depend upon human intelligence or choice. We just want to look at aspects of human and animal life which are altogether automatic, which occur without any act or decision on our part.

"*Creatures Great and Small*"

1. Have you ever heard of "protective coloration"? Or better yet, have you ever walked through a patch of grass and not even noticed there were grasshoppers there until you almost stepped on one and saw it jump? Or through a path in the woods, where it looked like there was nothing on the ground at all until you were suddenly startled when a toad jumped out ahead of you? What made you think there was nothing there? The answer is: a perfect system of disguise, which is called "protective coloration."

Certain insects and animals have developed a skin or outer coating which blends in so perfectly with their surroundings that it is almost impossible to see them. Sometimes it is a green covering which makes it difficult to see them against a background of green leaves; sometimes it is a brown or speckled covering which makes them indistinguishable on a tree trunk. Some animals are permanently colored to resemble their customary environment, while others, like the chameleon, have the further capacity to change color from one moment to the next, as they pass from one kind of background to another. Of course the animals themselves have nothing to do with the whole thing. They themselves don't decide to change color; they aren't even aware of the fact that their coloring is their best protection because it prevents hunters and other animals from seeing them. But the phenomenon of protective coloration occurs so frequently that it is one of the most fascinating things about the animal world. Two of your readings for this chapter describe particularly interesting cases of protective coloration.

> We'll repeat once more in this chapter the kind of question you should ask yourself after each of these examples. Does this illustration seem like something which has been planned or something which "just happened"? Does it impress you as being regular and dependable, or irregular and accidental? Would you list it under Purpose and Order, or under Accident and Disorder? Why? For the rest of this chapter, after each example refer back to this group of questions and think about them in order to be prepared properly for your workbook assignment at the end of the chapter.

2. If we were to place the seeds of ten different flowers on a table, could you distinguish one from the other? Unless you're an expert gardener, it is highly doubtful whether you'd be able to tell the difference even after close examination. But the seed itself always "knows" the difference. By that we mean to say that a rose seed always produces a rose bush, a carnation seed always yields a carnation plant, and a tomato seed always grows a tomato plant. True, there are sometimes unexpected changes or novelties developing out of a seed; these are known in biology as "mutations" or "sports." But whatever grows from a given seed is always identifiable as belonging to the same species. There are never any exceptions. The seed of one plant or tree or flower never "double-crosses" us by producing some other variety of growth.

The same is true, of course, with reference to animals. Two lions mating always produce a baby lion, never a dog or mouse. The sperm of a male cat and the egg of a female cat always result in a baby kitten, never in a squirrel. When a male and a female human being mate, the result is always an infant human being, never a mule.

> What does this show us about the world of nature? How does it help us make up our minds concerning the major interest of this chapter and the last?

While on this subject it is interesting to observe that a seed somehow always knows in which direction to grow. If it is planted upside down, the root reverses itself to grow downward while the stem curls around to grow upward. The root grows toward water; should there be a dry region in the direction of its normal growth, it then limits its growth to the area of moisture. The stem grows toward the light; but if it cannot find light there, it will, if necessary, change its direction in order to reach it elsewhere. A seed thus almost gives the appearance of knowing the purpose it is supposed to serve.

3. Despite the truth of what has just been said, with both plants and animals scientists have long ago learned how to mix breeds. Luther Burbank, for example, "created" many altogether new varieties of fruits or flowers by taking the "male" of one variety and "mating" it with the "female" of another. In this way he produced the first grapefruit by "crossing" the lemon with the orange. By this process new breeds of horses and certain other animals have been established. This is technically known as "cross-breeding."

> Wouldn't this seem to be a direct contradiction of number 2 above? Wouldn't it, therefore, have to be placed on the opposite list from number 2? Be prepared to explain your answer in full.

4. There is an interesting occurrence in plant life to which scientists have given the name "heliotropism," which means "turning toward the light." You know, of course, that sufficient energy from sunlight is necessary for the proper growth of both plants and animals. Many types of plants, if placed, for example, in a window, will grow only toward the light, all the leaves and buds turning in that direction for energy. There are even some plants which follow the sun across the sky during the day, their blossoms facing east in the morning and west at night. Obviously this occurs automatically.

5. At the World's Fair of 1939 in New York one of the exhibits was a cow or bull with five legs. Another exhibit showed an animal of some kind that had been born with two heads. We usually refer to such animals as freaks.

How would they fit into this discussion? What would they show us about the world of nature?

From time to time human beings also are born with unusual features or characteristics. You have probably heard of (or perhaps even seen) such things as Siamese twins, a baby born with only three fingers on one hand, or a child born with a harelip or clubfoot. The writer of this book has a friend who was born with no arms. It is particularly interesting to note (even though it may be a little off our subject at the moment) that despite his handicap he studied for the ministry, became a Protestant clergyman, and served as a civilian chaplain in one of our largest Veterans' Administration hospitals. He has learned to do with his feet almost everything you and I normally do with our hands. This includes dialing the telephone, writing, typing, turning the pages of a book, etc. We may want to mention him again later in this book; for the time being we refer to him only as an example of the kind of extraordinary human birth being described here. On which of our lists should such incidents as these be placed? Why? What do they prove about the orderliness of nature?

Intelligence and Inventions

6. Some of our most useful and advanced modern scientific inventions are really nothing but artificial ways of copying what various animals do naturally or automatically. These examples almost give us the impression that such insects and animals have intelligence similar to ours, so that they consciously know and plan their behavior. The praying mantis, for example, protects her eggs against damage in extremely hot weather by surrounding them with a frothy mass of bubbles. They serve as an insulating material and operate exactly as a thermos bottle does to maintain a cool inner temperature no matter how hot the air gets outside. Without some such protection as this, the eggs of the praying mantis would be destroyed by heat and the entire species might in time become extinct.

Honey bees have a method of air-conditioning. In order for their larvae to be reared and the honey successfully cured, it is necessary to have a constant temperature and proper flow of air through the hive. To secure this, certain bees keep moving so that their muscular motion produces the necessary heat, while others called "the fanners" anchor themselves to the floor of the hive and vibrate their wings just enough to produce the necessary circulation of air.

Nor is air-conditioning the only modern invention anticipated long centuries ago by insects or animals. Certain types of spiders have their own "burglar alarm" system. After weaving its web, a spider of this type attaches a tightly-pulled thread to the center of its web, then carries the other end of the line to a hiding place where it goes to sleep. As soon as an insect strikes the web, the line vibrates, awakening the spider, which then uses the line to reach its web in a hurry and destroy the captive insect.

Something very much like our modern invention of radar may also be found in nature. Radar operates by transmitting radio waves which are then reflected back from a given object to the transmitter. In this way a ship or plane can be "seen" on the radar screen while still hundreds of miles away. The bat has been called "nature's radar expert." He has a natural "radar set" which enables him to hear the echo of his own squeaks and chirps as they are reflected back to him by all objects in the vicinity. In this manner the bat can fly about even in pitch blackness without hitting anything. The bat thus uses sound waves in the same way we use radio waves in our radar sets.

In addition to the usual questions we have been applying to all these cases, it would be helpful here to consider the following: Are these animals or insects aware of what they are doing? Do they consciously plan their air-conditioning or burglar alarm systems? Would these examples indicate that they have intelligence? Would they belong on the same list with similar inventions of human beings? Why?

7. One of the most remarkable examples of this kind is to be found in the life-cycle of the salmon. After a young salmon has spent his maturing years at sea and is ready to fertilize the eggs of a female he swims from the ocean to the quiet and safety of a river. But the amazing thing is that he always manages to swim against the current to the river in which he himself was born, and if he was born in a tributary stream, he swims to that very stream. If he is removed and placed in another tributary of the same river, he immediately realizes that he is not in the right place, fights his way back to the river, and finds the right tributary in which to play his role in spawning a new generation of salmon.

> How can we explain this? How does the salmon recognize the river or stream in which he was born? Does he have intelligence? Memory? What can his behavior teach us in our survey of nature?

Similar to this is the case of a bird called the golden plover which takes off from Alaska, sets itself a course directly for Hawaii, 2,000 miles away across open sea, and without any of our modern instruments or calculations, always arrives precisely at its destination.

In Reading Selections F and G for this chapter you will find two other examples similar to those of the salmon and the golden plover. They are the eel and the wasp. Be sure to read both of them carefully.

8. Here is another interesting example from fish life: it concerns a species of fish called *anableps*, which possesses a most unusual type of eye. The eyes of these fish are divided into two parts, an upper part adjusted for viewing objects through air, and a lower part for seeing things through water. As you may already have suspected, these fish spend most of their time swimming along the surface of the water, only half submerged, with part of their eyes above and part below the water.

> How do you suppose the *anableps* developed such unusual eyes? Do you think that: (a) they swim

along the surface because they have such eyes; or (b) they developed this type of eye because they were in the habit of swimming half out of the water?

9. Reading Selection L at the end of this chapter gives you a different kind of example from the animal world. Read it carefully. What do you think of it? Does it have anything to do with order or disorder in nature? Be prepared to explain your answer in class discussion.

We Look at Us

It's always more fun to talk about ourselves than anything else in the world, so this should be the most interesting part of these chapters. Having considered quite a bit of evidence concerning (a) the universe, including this earth, and (b) certain plants and animals, we are now ready to see whether there is Order or Disorder as far as the automatic functioning of our own bodies is concerned. Up to this point we have used only one incidental example from human life. Now we shall deal only with human beings, using the same two lists, the same questions, and the same procedure we have followed previously.

The human body is one of the most remarkable phenomena in the entire universe. Unfortunately, we usually take our bodies and the way they operate for granted. We overlook such facts as that our central nervous system alone contains something like twelve billion cells, almost all of them present in a tiny, newborn infant. This system is more complicated than the largest of telephone switchboards, yet for the most part, it operates smoothly and automatically throughout the greater part of our lives.

10. Here again we shall find many of our modern inventions are actually copied after devices which occur automatically in the human body. You know how the lens of a fine camera works, do you not? It is adjustable. An expert photographer uses a light meter before taking a picture. He measures the amount of light on the object he wants to "shoot." If there is a great deal

"THE HEAVENS DECLARE THE GLORY OF GOD" (See page 18)

PROTECTIVE COLORATION—
CAN YOU FIND THE TOAD? (See page 28)

FROM HUMAN EGG TO
HUMAN BEING (See page 39)

MAN TODAY

(See page *53*)

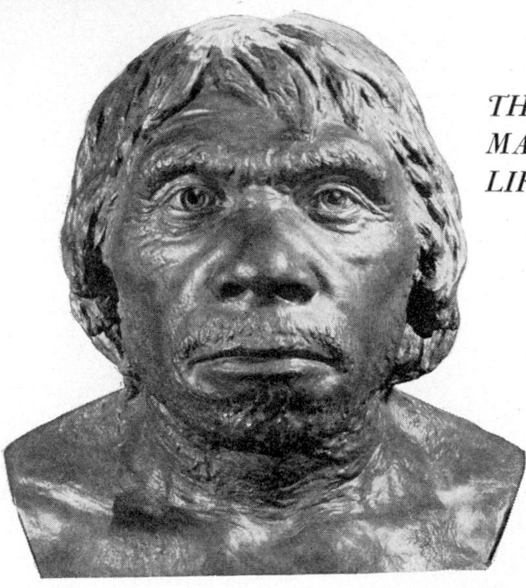

*THE FIRST MAN
MAY HAVE LOOKE
LIKE THIS*

*BEFORE THERE
WERE MEN*

of light, he partially closes the lens; if there is little light, he opens the lens wider; his purpose is to admit through the lens just enough light to make a good picture without damaging the film through overexposure. From this description it shouldn't be too difficult for you to figure out that the inventors of the camera got their idea from the operation of the human eye.

When you walk from a very light room into a very dark room (or into a movie theater), you've noticed that at first you can't see anything. After you stand for a while, however, slowly the objects in the theater or room become visible. What happens is that the pupil of your eye gradually opens wider, admitting more light, in order for you to see. Then, when you walk from the darkened place out again into a bright light which at first dazzles you and makes you blink, the pupil of your eye immediately begins to contract or close, admitting just enough light for you to see, keeping out the excess light which might damage your eye. This happens dozens of times a day—as many times as you walk from a light room to a dark one or the opposite. You yourself have nothing to do with it; you don't press a button to close or open the pupil of your eye; neither do you say to yourself, "I'm walking into a bright light now, I'd better adjust my eyes to admit less light." It all happens automatically. Nature does it for you every time it is necessary.

11. When was the last time you had an infected finger or an abscess? (We hope you'll pardon us for recalling such painful memories.) No doubt you remember the pus. Did you know that if your body hadn't produced pus then, the infection might very well have killed you? Your blood, as you probably know, consists of both red and white corpuscles. The white corpuscles act as an army of defense, guarding your body against poison and infection. Whenever an infection commences in any part of your body, immediately millions upon millions of white corpuscles rush to the point of invasion and try to wall off the infection to prevent it from spreading and especially from getting into your blood stream. Once an infection gets into your blood stream, it is carried throughout your body and you become very

critically ill. Only the fast defense action of your white corpuscles keeps you alive when you have an infection of any kind. But, like any other soldiers of defense, many of the white corpuscles die in waging their war against invasion. Pus consists of the dead bodies of the white corpuscles which have defended you and your health.

> Once again, it is important to note that we ourselves have nothing to do with this defense. It just happens automatically, with no conscious act or decision on our part. It happens in the body of a little child or of an adult, in the body of brilliant people as well as stupid people, in the blood of good people and wicked people alike. Of what importance, if any, is this in determining on which list we are going to place this illustration?

12. If there were no exceptions to the illustration just given, probably no one would ever die of infection. But we know that many people do. The white corpuscles don't always succeed in their defense of our bodies. Sometimes the invading infection overpowers them, and despite the pus accumulated, the individual dies; so we can't always, in every instance, count on being fully protected by our white corpuscles.

> Before proceeding, try to make up your mind whether this doesn't belong on the opposite list from number 11 above. Be sure to have good reasons for your opinion.

13. There are exceptions also to the example of our eyes given in number 10 above. In some people the muscles which control the opening and closing of the pupils don't work properly, with the result that they either find it impossible to see in a darkened room or they never get accustomed to bright lights. You may have seen people who find it necessary always to wear dark glasses because their eyes cannot stand the strain even of ordinary daylight. This may be due to the fact that their eye muscles don't function properly.

Wouldn't this illustration necessarily be placed on the opposite list from the one you used for number 10? Explain your answer.

14. The red corpuscles in our blood also provide an example which is useful here. Their chief function is to carry oxygen from our lungs to all parts of our bodies. Ordinarily there are about five million of these red corpuscles in each drop of human blood. If a person ascends to an altitude of more than 5,000 feet above sea-level, however, it is difficult for his body to obtain enough oxygen because the air at such a height is rarified or thinned. One way for a person high in the mountains to get enough oxygen would be to wear a mask attached to an oxygen tank, the way high-altitude pilots sometimes do. But that would be greatly inconvenient. Fortunately, the red corpuscles in our blood automatically provide for such situations without our carrying heavy tanks with us wherever we go.

As soon as the air becomes thin, the number of red corpuscles automatically begins to increase. After a person has been in a high altitude for several weeks, there are six million red corpuscles in every drop of his blood. If he climbs even higher and remains there long enough, he may have seven million. There have even been cases known where nine million red corpuscles were counted in one drop of a person's blood. In other words, as the air becomes thinner, so that each red corpuscle is able to carry less oxygen from one's lungs to the rest of his body, automatically the number of corpuscles increases, making it possible for the necessary amount of oxygen to be provided for every part of the body. When we return to lower altitudes, of course, many of the extra "oxygen trucks" are destroyed, and their number returns to the normal quantity.

In Sickness and in Health

15. Usually we know when we are sick. A sharp pain, an upset stomach, an achey feeling in our bones—these are symptoms which leave no doubt that we aren't well. But doctors tell us that

many times in his life every human being is afflicted with a disease of some sort—sometimes even a very serious one—without even knowing it, because his body has so effectively fought off the disease germs. Most of us, for example, have suffered mild attacks of infantile paralysis without knowing it and without after-effects. Similarly most of us have had tuberculosis germs in our lungs; chest x-rays show tuberculosis scar tissue in the average person's lungs, indicating that at some time in the past the disease had attacked him, but his body took care of things and walled off the affected part of the lung so quietly and efficiently that he didn't even know he had been sick.

One of the clearest examples of this sort of thing occurs in certain liver conditions when the liver becomes hardened so that blood can no longer flow through its normal channels. But it is essential for our health that blood pass through the liver. When that becomes impossible in the usual way, automatically the blood seeks and finds a new route, much as a mountain stream, if its path is blocked, will make a new route for itself. In these liver conditions a detour is established for the blood, in some cases via new blood vessels, in others through enlarging old blood vessels. Obviously, this too is a change which occurs without our knowing or consciously willing it.

16. You know, of course, that when blood leaves your heart it is pumped through arteries to reach all parts of your body. Very often as people age their arteries become hardened. Instead of the artery walls remaining flexible and thin, so that blood can flow through them easily, they become hardened and thick, leaving little space for the flow of blood. When that happens, the heart automatically begins to enlarge, working much harder than it did before in an effort to pump sufficient blood through the arteries and to keep the body alive in reasonably good health.

17. Perhaps the most dramatic example of how the human body operates automatically may be found in the wonderful way in which the body of a woman prepares itself automatically for motherhood. The very moment a woman becomes pregnant her body begins to ready itself for the time when her baby is to be

born. The skin of her abdomen stretches to enable her to carry the baby in her womb. Her posture changes to distribute the additional weight properly. As the time for her baby's birth arrives, her vagina is enlarged so that the baby can be delivered, and as soon as the baby is born her breasts fill with milk for its nourishment. Through the nine months of her pregnancy, her entire body acts almost as if it knew what was about to happen and consciously wanted to prepare itself for the wonderful event. Of course we had to use the words "almost as if" because there isn't anything conscious about it at all. A woman who is pregnant doesn't decide herself that her body should in every respect prepare itself for the birth of a child. All this happens automatically.

18. While speaking of pregnancy and birth, we should also note the remarkable way in which a human being develops from two cells so tiny they can't even be seen without a microscope. In these two cells—one from the father and one from the mother—are potentially all the physical, mental, emotional, and spiritual characteristics of an adult human being. You yourself were once a combination of two such infinitesimal cells, invisible to the unaided human eye. Yet, in those cells was already contained the ultimate color of your hair and eyes, the general bone structure of your body, and in part, at least, something of your disposition and special abilities. Of course, your environment—which means to say, your surroundings and experiences since birth—also affected your development greatly. But whatever you are today—or will be at any time in the future—grew out of the tiny combination of two cells in which your life began.

* * *

Even though this has been a long chapter, we have given here only a very few of the many, many instances which can be seen in the behavior of our bodies. There are so many of them that a well-known physician, Dr. Walter B. Cannon, has written an entire book of such illustrations, called *The Wisdom of the Body*. You may be interested in securing this book from the library if you want to become familiar with other examples.

You will also find additional illustrations of this type in the Reading Selections which follow. To do the workbook questions for Chapter Three properly it will be necessary for you to read all these items carefully.

Before closing this chapter, it is important to add that we have by no means exhausted the subject of ourselves. At best we have considered here only one phase of our lives. In the next chapter we shall say a little more about how human beings live. For the present, however, this will suffice. Time now to put together all the things we've covered in this chapter by doing your workbook assignment.

SOMETHING FOR YOU TO READ

A. In the laboratories . . . we use an instrument called a thermostat, that is, an instrument which keeps the temperature stable. In growing bacteria we have to arrange that the temperature around them shall not vary more than a few degrees. If it rises or falls more than that the bacteria that we are trying to study die. A thermostat is a difficult instrument to manage. It seldom works perfectly, and it never works nearly as well as that extraordinary instrument, the human body.

Most of us know that if our temperature is taken with a clinical thermometer it is approximately 98° Fahrenheit, varying only a few tenths of a degree during the twenty-four hours. But we do not realize perhaps that when a person goes into a temperature of 40° below zero, or when, as used to be the case with the stokers in steamships, he has to live minutes or hours in temperatures of 130° to 150° Fahrenheit, still his body keeps its temperature the same. A piece of metal and most substances that can become heated or chilled will respond to the temperature around them. The human body has the extraordinary capacity to keep its balance in terms of heat. Unless that were the case death would occur whenever one went into a cold temperature or into a hot temperature. . . .

By a number of ingenious, clever devices the body ordinarily preserves its temperature at a point between 98° and 99° Fahrenheit. These devices are not familiar to everyone. For instance, if we are cold we often shiver, and we think of shivering, perhaps, as an inevitable misfortune. As a matter of fact, by shivering we keep ourselves warmer than we should be if we did not shiver. Shivering is a muscular action; and the action of any muscle tends to create warmth. . . .

B. A second example . . . is the balance of moisture in the body. The human body is about four-fifths water, and it must preserve nearly that proportion of water, or life cannot go on. We are giving out water and taking in water all the time, and yet the body by its own intelligent arrangements preserves almost exactly the same proportion of water in itself at all times. . . .

Imagine a bank with its receiving and paying tellers; imagine that thousands and thousands of dollars are being poured into that bank in various amounts, large and small, and at various times of the day, without any rule or order. Then at the same time imagine that large amounts or small amounts are being taken out of the bank by depositors. This is what is usually going on in fact. Now imagine what, of course, never happens, that the balance of money in that bank is preserved within a few dollars of the same amount at all times. Imagine that if the balance in the bank varied more than a few dollars the bank would break. Then you have a picture of what is actually going on at the present moment in your body and the bodies of all human beings. It seems too strange to be true, but it is true.

C. When heart disease takes the form of valvular inflammation and deforms the valve [which means, when the valve through which the heart pumps blood becomes inflamed] . . . the situation is like what would happen if one of the doors of a room were stuck halfway open, so that it would neither open nor close fully. That is what happens to the heart valve when the germ of rheumatism attacks it. The individual could not live if it were not that, as the deformity gradually occurs in the valve, the heart gradually thickens and so strengthens its own muscle. A heart that is ordinarily the size of an individual's fist will become as big as two or three or even four fists, because it must. In no other way can it push the blood along hard enough to maintain the circulation when the openings into the heart and out of it are narrowed.

D. When we cut into a lung at autopsy we often find evidence of a healed tuberculosis which during his life the person never knew he had. The knife with which we cut may be broken across a stone, a mass of lime deposited there by the blood so as to wall in a group of tubercle bacilli [tuberculosis germs], as in the Middle Ages they sometimes walled in a human being in the wall of a castle and left him to die. So the healing powers of the body wall in the tubercle bacilli in the lung so that they are harmless. We cut through this stone and sometimes find the tubercle bacilli still alive but harmless, because they are shut off from the lung.

E. The facts are before us. Every doctor knows them. There is nothing new or doubtful about them. The conclusions are for each to draw for himself. The conclusion which I draw is a greater confidence in life. However we may fall short, a gigantic healing power fights on our side. . . . The thing I am speaking of here is that great power in ourselves that makes for health, and that works day and night, when we are asleep and when we are awake, when we are good and when we are bad. . . .

. . . The powers which carry on the work of our body are not neutral in the battle between us and the enemies of our health. A great healing power fights on our side and wins most of our battles for us.

. . . If we look at that portion of nature which concerns us most, our own bodies, we see no indifference, no neutrality, but an extraordinary bias in our favor. On the basis of these healing powers our intelligence and our will get their opportunity.

(All the Reading Selections given above are taken from Chapter Nine of a book called *The Art of Ministering to the Sick*, written by Richard C. Cabot, a physician, and Russel L. Dicks, a minister. Copyright, 1936 by The Macmillan Co. and used with their permission.)

F. These amazing creatures (eels) migrate at maturity from all the ponds and rivers everywhere—those from Europe across thousands of miles of ocean—all go to the abysmal deeps south of Bermuda. There they breed and die. The little ones, with no apparent means of knowing anything except that they are in a wilderness of water, start back and find their way to the shore from which their parents came and thence to every river, lake and little pond, so that each body of water is always populated with eels. They have braved the mighty currents, storms, and tides, and have conquered the beating waves on every shore. They can now grow and when they are mature, they will, by some mysterious law, go back through it all to complete the cycle. Where does the directing impulse originate? No American eel has ever been caught in European waters and no European eel has ever been caught in American waters. Nature has always delayed the maturity of the European eel by a year or more to make up for its much greater journey. Do atoms and molecules when combined in an eel have a sense of direction and will power to exercise it?—A. Cressy Morrison, *Man Does Not Stand Alone,* Fleming H. Revell Co.

G. The wasp catches the grasshopper, digs a hole in the earth, stings the grasshopper in exactly the right place so that he becomes unconscious but lives as a form of preserved meat. The wasp lays her eggs exactly in the right place, perhaps not knowing that when they hatch, her children can eat without killing the insect on which they feed, which would be fatal to them. The wasp must have done all this right the first and every time, or there would be no wasps. Science cannot explain this mystery, and yet it cannot be attributed to chance. The wasp covers a hole in the earth, departs cheerfully, and dies. Neither she nor her ancestors have reasoned out the process, nor does she know what happens to her offspring or that there are such things as offspring. She doesn't even know that she has worked and lived her life for the preservation of the race.—A. Cressy Morrison, *Man Does Not Stand Alone,* Fleming H. Revell Co.

H. Much farther down in the body, atop the kidneys, lie two yellowish glands which are called the adrenals. (The word means simply "near the kidneys.") The inner core of the adrenal glands is a tiny factory for the secretion of adrenalin, a most powerful drug. One writer has calculated that a row of street sprinklers twenty miles long, with two hundred sprinklers to the mile and each one containing six hundred and twenty-five gallons, would supply just enough water to weaken one ounce of pure adrenalin to the right strength for body use. The adrenals are the emergency glands of the body. We might almost call them the Department of Personal Defense.

When we become angry or afraid, adrenalin pours into the body and a great many things happen all at once. The heart speeds up. (Have you ever felt your heart pounding when you got angry or when you stood before a large audience to make a speech?) The blood pressure rises. Sugar is released from the liver to provide additional energy. Digestion slows down or stops entirely, for the reason that, when a dinosaur or a ten-ton truck is approaching, the important thing is not to digest a recent meal but to get away—and fast! (This is why a person may have a spell of indigestion after a quarrel at the dinner table.) The breathing rate increases, so as to insure an adequate supply of oxygen. The blood that is drawn away from the digestive tract is channeled into the large muscles of the body, where it will do the most good for fighting or running. At the same time it is drained out of the surface blood vessels. (This is the explanation of a person's paleness when he is "scared white.") The subject is now less likely to bleed to death if wounded, especially since adrenalin helps to coagulate the blood. In animals, such as a cat, hair stands on end to make the intended victim seem larger and more formidable. There may be a relic of this even in humans in the prickly skin which we call "goose flesh." Thus in a variety of ways the whole organism adapts itself to a crisis.

These adjustments were quite helpful in getting primitive man out of the reach of a saber-toothed tiger. They are still useful in many modern emergencies, such as an automobile accident. A passenger may be able to lift one end of the car to free a badly wounded person, whereas an hour before he would not have been able to budge it. Unfortunately, the same procedure goes on its tireless way when a concert pianist appears on the stage for the first time. His body is still back in the forests of the Old World, trying to get away from that tiger. But the adjustments which once saved many a life now merely serve to make the pianist miserable. Perhaps in fifty thousand years from now our adrenals will have caught up with the requirements of civilized life.—Nevin C. Harner, *About Myself*, Christian Education Press.

I. Some animals, particularly wild sheep, deer, and bears, have developed the sense of smell to an astonishing degree. In the Altai Mountains of Mongolia, where I hunted giant bighorn sheep, I was provided with an excellent example. A herd of sheep, containing some magnificent rams, usually fed on a steep slope in the early morning. When the sun was high, they retired to a narrow ridge connecting two peaks, with deep ravines on either side, to sleep away the midday hours in plain sight. Always an old ewe acted as a sentinel. For an hour or more, after the sheep were lying down, she would stand on a rocky spire above the saddle, gazing in every direction over the plains and mountain slopes. At last, satisfied that it was safe, she would settle herself with the rest of the herd. Then my Mongol hunter and I would begin the stalk, being sure that the wind was blowing from them to us. But never could we approach near enough for a shot. Always the herd was up and off. At last we realized that the reason they selected this particular ridge day after day, and attempted no concealment, was because the air eddied in a peculiar way about the saddle and brought odors to their noses no matter from what direction the wind was blowing. On that saddle the sheep were as safe from wolves, their only natural enemy, as from man.

J. . . . the octopus (or devil-fish) has still another method of concealment. In its skin are various pigment cells, which can, by contracting or enlarging, produce a wonderful series of color changes. These cells are of many hues—orange, yellow, blue-green, or brown—and have muscular walls which enable them to contract until almost invisible and then expand to many times their former size. The different color cells can expand alone or in combination with the other colors, and enable the animal to produce flashes of rainbow hues over its whole surface. As a devil-fish crawls about on the sea bottom, it may change its color instantly from deep chocolate through dull red and brown to gray.

K. The Ceylonese walking leaf is a very remarkable insect. Unlike his ferocious cousin, the praying mantis, he is a gentle leaf-eater and has no special equipment with which to defend himself against enemies.

But the walking leaf is usually in little danger of attack.

A tree dweller, his camouflage is one of the most extraordinary found among insects. It protects him in all stages of his existence.

His eggs look exactly like shriveled, spiny seeds. When the young walking leaves emerge, they are wingless, reddish, and glossy, nearly impossible to distinguish from buds at the ends of branches, where they usually feed.

The green body of a full-grown walking leaf is shaped and veined in precise replica [exact copy] of a leaf. The legs are flattened to appear like smaller leaves and are even stained yellow, with ragged edges, as if injured by nibbling insects.

Yet despite this elaborate disguise, the walking leaf has another habit which may serve as an additional precaution for safety. When a wind stirs the tree, he often wiggles himself back and forth in perfect imitation of the agitated leaves.

(Selections I, J and K are taken from Roy Chapman Andrews, *Nature's Ways*, published by Crown Publishers.)

L. Our attention has been drawn to yet more horrible forms of destruction, such as that practiced by the paralysing wasps, whose formula for a particularly horrible kind of slaughter is to paralyse without killing by inflicting upon their victim at key points several paralysing stings whose ultimate effect is a slow and probably quite dreadful death. There is a further instance which we may use to illustrate the point that in the animal world the stronger forms of life prey upon the weaker quite mercilessly. A scientific worker told the story of his expedition into a side valley of the Amazon basin.

He was in a lightly built canoe of the kind used by the natives. Suddenly, on the bank, he saw something which gripped his attention and which he will never be able to forget. A llama was quenching its thirst at the river's edge, and the explorer saw a leopard crouching in the bush above it ready to spring on the peaceful beast and tear it apart. The leopard sprang, and the two animals were locked in battle, when suddenly they fell apart and both let out a scream of terror. What had happened was that shoals of small fish which abound in those southern waters, their teeth sharp as razors, had suddenly come up from the depths of the river and fallen upon the two fighting animals to strip the flesh from them both. They finished their murderous work in a quarter of an hour. The terrible cries were silenced and the uncanny stillness of death lay over the dark water. The scientist was so shocked by the whole episode that he could not suppress the awful thought that if his canoe were to be smashed against a rock he too would share the fate of the two animals whose death struggles he had witnessed.—Karl Heim, *The Transformation of the Scientific World View*, Harper and Bros.

4. *How Did We Get This Way?*

SAY, what are we supposed to be studying in this class anyway —religion or science?"

That's a good question someone in the back of the room just asked (or felt like asking). We thought, when we began writing the last couple of chapters, that sooner or later someone would come up with that one. It shows that some of you at any rate have already commenced to understand one of the most important truths we shall discover in this entire course, that intelligent modern people just can't completely separate religion from science. Religion is part of human life, just as science is. The two are closely related. We are actually studying both in this course, because it is impossible to study either thoroughly without giving some consideration to the other. In a later chapter we shall have more to say about the relationship between religion and science. For the time being, suffice it to say that this is certainly a book about religion, and that in looking around us as we are now doing—at the universe, at this earth, and at our own bodies—we are most definitely talking about religion and preparing for some mighty important conclusions about religion which we shall reach before long.

No doubt you noticed that in the last chapter we gave examples and evidence not only from the human body, but also from certain animals. If there had been more time, you would have been able to see even more clearly through additional illustrations how many similarities there are between the bodies of human beings and those of animals. This is particularly so with reference to such animals as apes. All of us have observed in the zoo how an ape can sometimes act almost like a human being. In fact, several years ago at a large zoo there was an ape that had been taught to obey certain commands, to sit on a chair as you and I would, and even to hold a spoon in her hand and eat from a dish. Now don't get us wrong; we don't mean to say or even to imply that under any circumstances an ape can be as intelligent as a person or that any person is exactly like an ape. But you yourself must have said more than once, as you stood before the cage of a monkey or an ape, "My, he looks almost like a human being, doesn't he?"

In this chapter we want to inquire into the reasons for this similarity, and to learn, if we can, just how our bodies developed into the truly wonderful things we have already discovered them to be. There is a rather long word used to describe the sort of thing we shall talk about in this chapter; it is the word *evolution*. You may already have studied something about evolution in your science or biology classes, but we are going to assume no one in the class has heard about it yet. If you have, you're that much ahead of the game and can help in explaining it to the rest of the class.

The dictionary defines evolution as "development or growth" and as "a process in which something complex is developed from simple beginnings." As used in biology and in this chapter, evolution refers to the story of how life on this planet developed from its earliest beginnings many millions of years ago to the present moment.

"Did you say 'many millions of years ago'?"

"Yes, that's exactly what we said."

"But, I thought that according to the Jewish calendar the world has existed only for a little less than six thousand years."

"You're quite right that our ancestors thought they were counting the number of years since earth's beginning. Many Orthodox Jews even now would say that this chapter is being written 5715 years after the creation of the world. Most of us, however, relying on scientific facts and discoveries, know that this planet is very much older than our ancestors supposed. When we say that it is the year 5715 (or whatever the year is as you read this), we simply mean that this is the number of years since our people first began counting time by the calendar."

"I see; but there is still something that bothers me about that 'millions of years' business. Sometimes it's hard for me to understand how we know so much about people who lived even two or three thousand years ago, before books were printed or films made. But how can we be so sure this earth is *millions of years* old when we haven't any written record going back that far? I'm afraid you'll have to do a little convincing. . . ."

This imaginary conversation probably reflects some of the questions in your mind. So let's proceed to the story of evolution, beginning with a "little convincing" on how we can know so much about things which happened long before there was any printing or indeed any human beings. The record of events which transpired so long ago is preserved for us in nature's own history book—the rocks! You know, of course, that archeologists are able to tell us much about ancient human civilization because of the remains they have found buried under the earth, especially in graves and tombs. But they and the geologists can go back still farther, to pre-human times, by examining some of the skeletons and bones which were covered thousands and millions of years ago by lava or mud which then hardened into rock. Some of these early remains exist today, preserved in rock, exactly as they were when they were first covered shortly after the death of a particular animal. From such remains as these we can uncover the fascinating story of evolution, through which we trace the development of life from earliest times to this day.

The Story of Evolution

Unfortunately, we haven't time here to give you more than the briefest outline of that story. Here are a few of the most interesting things the rocks tell us about evolution:

We cannot tell for sure exactly how old our earth is. Scientists vary in their estimates from two billion years to four and a half billion years.

For about half that time—or until the earth was between one billion and two and a quarter billion years old—there was no kind of plant, animal or fish life on it at all. It's hard to imagine the earth existing for so long without even a blade of grass or a weed on it, but that's exactly what happened.

It was, then, about one billion or two billion years ago that the very first form of life appeared on this earth. But that first life wasn't even remotely like a human being, or for that matter, like any plant or animal we see around us today. The very first human being to appear on this earth lived about one *million* years ago. Even he, however, was considerably different from people as we know them today. He probably looked and acted more like that ape we were speaking of a moment ago than like a person living today. The first human being more nearly like ourselves probably appeared on earth about a quarter of a million years ago. But we're getting ahead of our story. What has happened during the last billion years or so, since the first life appeared on this planet?

There is much we still do not know. We still haven't the faintest idea, for example, just how or why the first form of life developed, after a billion years or more without any life. We do have reason to believe, however, that the first living thing was a one-celled form of life which couldn't even be seen by the human eye; that is, if there had been any such thing as a human eye then. This one-celled living thing is a protozoan.

Gradually, in the course of time (meaning tens of thousands of years), the protozoa developed from one-celled creatures to two cells, then four, then eight, and so on. Some protozoa remained forever on that level, that is to say, their "children" and "grandchildren" down through the ages were exactly the same, unchanged and undeveloped. What makes the story of evolution so fascinating, however, is that some seemed to be restless protozoa; they kept changing and developing until they became a kind of water worm which in the course of time developed eyes. This didn't happen, of course, as quickly as it sounds here. It wasn't a case of a protozoan suddenly giving birth to a water worm. But very slowly—we wouldn't even have been able to notice the changes had we been alive then—certain protozoa began to show tiny changes in their development from generation to generation, until finally these little changes led to the development of water worms with eyes. We call these changes, which make evolution possible, mutations.

After the passing of more millions of years some of the water worms developed into forms of sponge and shell-fish. Then came fish with backbones, as we know them today. The next stage of life consisted of the so-called amphibians—fish that could also live on land. This was perhaps the most important change that had yet occurred, and it wasn't an easy one. Up to this time life had existed only in water. But the surface of the earth was gradually drying off, with more and more dry land appearing. Unless some fish would develop the ability to live on dry land, many of them would perish, and the whole thrilling adventure of evolution might end right there.

Meanwhile, however, even before it became necessary for some fish to live on land, a most interesting thing had begun to occur. In addition to their gills, through which they obtained oxygen from the water, some fish began also to develop lungs, which would for the first time enable them to obtain their oxygen from the air. By the time it became necessary for them to live on land at least part of the time, they had already (through slow development which must have taken millions of years) acquired the lung apparatus they would need to survive and to continue their development. We owe a great deal to these amphibians who developed the necessary equipment to begin life on land. Had it not been for them, you and I wouldn't have been here today—or at least as fish we wouldn't be studying about religion.

We are able to gain a clear picture of how amphibians developed by watching the growth of frogs which are born as fish, able to live only in water, but which gradually develop legs and the ability to live on land as well as water. A frog retraces in a few weeks the development of fish into amphibians, which took hundreds of thousands of years in the course of evolution.

After the amphibians came the age of reptiles. You have probably seen pictures or reconstructed skeletons of the dinosaurs, giant lizards that lived at that time. On route U. S. 5 near Springfield, Massachusetts, there is a place where dinosaur footprints can still be seen, preserved in rock which must have been mud several million years ago when a dinosaur stopped there.

Somewhere along the line some of the smaller reptiles developed wings and the ability to fly. This, however, wasn't the "main-line" of evolution; it was a kind of "side-excursion." The "main-line" developed further when some of the creatures, much smaller than the giant reptiles, began to develop larger brains. When the earth's surface was covered by enormous glaciers, the huge reptiles, despite their greater strength and power, weren't able to survive. Some of the smaller creatures could flee from the ice-sheets, and, because of their greater brain power, could find ways of getting food and maintaining life despite the glaciers. So the road of the dinosaurs became a dead-end road in the story of evolution. It was the smaller creatures with the larger brains who continued the story to its next chapter, making it possible for still higher forms of life to develop.

The First Man

Some of them slowly developed into what are known as mammals, which means animals that carry their young inside their bodies while they are developing (instead of laying eggs outside) and which nurse their young after they are born. Little by little these mammals developed into various kinds of apes, and about a million years ago the highest level of ape had developed hands and feet, had lost enough of his outer hair covering, and had developed his brain-power or thinking-power to the point where he could be considered the first human being! Of course much has happened during these last million years too; we aren't the same today by any means as that first man. The chief direction in which we have changed is that more and more our brain has become the most important part of us.

So here we are—human beings who can look back through the rocks and figure out pretty well just how we got this way. If, in some respects, we seem to be very much like animals, that's because, after all, we have developed through various animal stages to what we are today. And if, in other respects, we're quite different from animals, that's because we're the latest and highest development up to this moment on the "main-road" of evolution.

In what respects, specifically, are we superior to all other forms of life which have developed through evolution? We're not the strongest (witness the lion) nor the fastest (a slow race horse could beat the fastest human runner without half trying) nor the most graceful (you never saw a human being as graceful as a deer). So in what way or ways are we superior?

First, we're the only form of life which is aware of what is going on through evolution. Not only don't plants and animals have anything to do consciously with the changes and developments which occur in them, they don't even know about those changes or the relationship between themselves and other forms of life. We human beings are the only actors in the drama of evolution who know what the score is—who are aware of how we got this way.

Second, we are the only ones who can control the processes of evolution or speed them up to some extent. When we cross-breed plants or animals, for example, we are creating in the course of a few months or years changes which might never have occurred or which might have taken millions of years to occur by themselves. Likewise, through the science of medicine we have learned to help nature along by eliminating some of the diseases which would kill people and thereby interfere with the further development of evolution.

Third, the forms of life which developed before us were limited to adapting themselves to their environment. They could not change the physical facts of the world in which they lived, but could only—unconsciously, automatically, and gradually—change themselves to fit the environment more suitably. Human beings, however, are the first form of life able to adapt the environment to themselves. We are able, for example, in part, to alter our climate, the weather, the purity of the air we breathe, etc.

Fourth, so far as we know, evolution in plants and animals below the human level is on a purely physical basis. That is to say, the changes which take place are all changes in body structure, like the development of lungs in place of gills, or of arms and hands in place of forefeet. In man alone has evolution reached the point where it occurs on a higher level, too. Only human beings have developed a conscience, for example, and the ability to distinguish and choose between acts that we consider morally right and others that we consider morally wrong. Only human beings can consciously create great art, beautiful music or eloquent poetry. And precisely these aspects of human life, the very things in which we differ from plants and animals, are the most important phases of our lives. One of your Reading Selections for this chapter expresses very clearly the principal difference between human beings and all other creatures in evolution.

A paragraph or so ago we used the phrase "the further development of evolution." Will there be changes in life forms in the future as there have been in the past? This is another of the important questions to which none of us can give a definite answer. There is every reason to believe, however, that the course of evolution is by no means completed.

Just as there have been constant though slow changes since the first life-form appeared, so it is more than reasonable to suppose that a million years from now there will be life-forms we now know nothing about. It is also reasonable to assume that more and more in the future the changes wrought by evolution will be in the direction of man's special distinction over other forms of life. There may or may not be substantial changes in the physical forms of our bodies. But there will probably be great improvements in our minds, our thinking ability, our creative and artistic powers, etc. This seems to be the direction of tomorrow's evolution. It would be fascinating if we could return to earth, say a half million years from now, just for a glimpse into the kind of beings who will have been developed by that time through evolution, helped along by man's ability to think. Which of this chapter's Reading Selections seems to agree most closely with these thoughts about the future of evolution?

It might be helpful to us, in summarizing the story of evolution, to think of it as a road which seems to be traveling in a consistent direction; see (A) in the diagram on page 56. Off that road, in the course of time, have branched many side roads. Some of them have continued to develop in their own direction (B), producing interesting experiments which, however, seem to have little or nothing to do with the main highway. Others of them, like the dinosaur, have reached a dead-end (C). But the main road (A), reaching in the direction of man, has continued, and will doubtless go on into the future.

We have been able here to give only a small part of the whole story. You will find a summary of it as Reading Selection C at the end of this chapter. If you are interested in a still more complete picture, see the full account from which that summary has been taken on pages 53 through 89 of a book called *Beginnings of Life and Death,* written by Fahs and Spoerl.

. . . How or why did the whole adventure of evolution take place? Who or what caused the very first one-celled protozoan to appear? What caused some fish to begin developing lungs, almost as if they knew in advance they would need them to keep the story going?

The only honest answer to these questions is that we don't know. No one knows. But we can use the brain and the sense of reasoning which have come to us through evolution in an effort to understand it, and we can suggest some tentative answers which are consistent with whatever facts we have. Actually, there are only two possible answers. Either (a) the appearance of the first protozoan on this earth and the whole glorious, exciting, thrilling adventure of evolution over the last billion years has been an accident—something which "just happened" by coincidence; or (b) there is a plan or purpose or law or order of some kind behind it, which means there is something about evolution that pushes it in a certain direction and prepares at each step in the story for the next one. If the first answer is true, then obviously evolution would go on the Accident side of the list we have been making. If the second answer is correct, then evolution is the most important piece of evidence yet on the Purpose and Order side.

Most intelligent people would agree, we think, that evolution couldn't possibly be just an accident, without meaning or direction. The story we have told in this chapter is far too wonderful for that. There have been literally thousands if not millions of times and places where the whole experiment of evolution could have failed, or where the main road might have been permanently detoured, preventing the development of any higher forms of life. If fish had not begun to develop the ability to breathe on land long before the environment made that ability necessary, if forefeet had not commenced slowly to develop into arms and hands, if apes had not assumed a stand-up posture instead of walking on all fours—if these and countless other changes (over which plants and animals had no conscious control themselves) had not taken place in the right way, at the right time, humanity could not have developed as it did. It is too much to ask us to believe that at each one of these places the right thing happened just through sheer chance or accident. It is far more reasonable and logical to conclude that, even though we are far from understanding everything, there must be something which is working through evolution in a consistent direction to attain a specific purpose. Several of your readings at the conclusion of this chapter will express this thought. A, B, and E are taken from the writings of famous scientists.

SOMETHING FOR YOU TO READ

A. Everything always takes place as if a goal had to be attained, and as if this goal was the real reason, the inspiration of evolution. All the attempts which did not bring the goal nearer were forgotten or eliminated.—Lecomte du Nouy, *Human Destiny*, Longmans, Green and Co.

B. It is . . . difficult to avoid an interpretation which sees underlying these evolutionary processes an intelligent power, directing it with some great purpose.—Arthur H. Compton, *The Religion of a Scientist*, Institute for Religious and Social Studies of the Jewish Theological Seminary of America.

C. The amazing story of evolution goes on and on. There is much in the story about which we are still uncertain. What we know is but a hundredth part of what we wish we might know. Yet with all our ignorance, there are a few things which seem quite clear.

First of all, the scientists have shown us that living creatures have changed as the years have gone by. New ways of living have been tried. New powers have been gained. Children have not always been just like their parents. From the first simple one-celled creatures have been born all the varieties of plants and animals in the world today. Somehow, this power to change has been in the very nature of living things. It must be in us.

In the second place, the higher up the Ladder of Life we have climbed—and the more of mind-stuff we have acquired—the faster we are able to learn and the greater becomes our power to change. Like the first men-who-stood-up-straight we, too, need to think harder, and to try out new ways of living. Who can imagine the greatness possible for mankind in the years to come?

In the third place, scientists have taught us that all living things that are on the earth or that ever have been on the earth are related. We all have had the same first parents—the first simple one-celled growing specks that lived a thousand million years ago. Seaweeds, amoebas, worms, fish, frogs, dragon-flies, dinosaurs, birds, tigers, horses, people—all of us are members of one great family. Something in our natures we all have in common. We scarcely know what to call it. It is something we can feel rather than talk of. We have it in just being alive—in our strong desire to live and to grow and to have children live after us.

We who are human folk think we are the most gifted of all this family. We think we have climbed the highest up the Ladder of Life, for we are better able to think and to understand ourselves and our universe. . . .

. . . Such great changes as we have described could not have happened merely by chance. When we see a piano, for example, and we hear music as someone plays on the keys, we know that all the many pieces of wood and ivory and iron and copper that go to make up so marvelous an instrument did not just happen to fly together into the shape of a piano. We are sure that some thinking being planned the piano and put it together.

So it is also when we find that all mankind has evolved or grown from simple one-celled protozoa, we are not satisfied to say that so great achievements have come by mere chance. All living creatures seem united in some sort of common urge or purpose. We all share the power to climb up the Ladder of Life into more intelligent ways of living. That power seems to have been in living things from the beginning. We are part of an unspeakable Greatness—in us, around us, and moving in the life of the ages. . . .—Fahs and Spoerl, *Beginnings of Life and Death*, The Beacon Press.

D. (The following interesting selections are taken from the Talmud and Midrash, written many centuries before science had developed the theory of evolution):

1. Rabbi Judah taught: "Man was first created with a tail like an animal, but God afterwards removed this tail from him for his honor, not to put him to shame."

2. It was said: "Up to the generation of Enosh the faces of the people . . . resembled those of monkeys."

3. The pre-eminence [superiority] of man over the beast is nought, for all is vanity, save only the pure soul.

E. As we view our evolution from life's primitive beginnings, we can see, though dimly, the outline of a great plan. Its end we do not see, but we know that we are part of it, and we feel that we can share in promoting it. . . .

. . . It is possible to see the whole great drama of evolution as leading toward the goal of the making of persons, with free, intelligent wills, capable of learning nature's laws, of seeing dimly (the) purpose in nature, and of working . . . to make that purpose effective.—Arthur H. Compton, *Man's Destiny in Eternity*, The Beacon Press.

F. Man is a creature in the process of becoming. This is true of the individual here and now. It is true of the specie over the long history of human evolution. This is obvious for the past. I believe it is just as true for the future. The future of man's development lies not, however, in acquiring a third eye or a sixth finger or wings. The pattern of his continued evolution must lie in the realm of mental and spiritual evolution. In order to attain that development he must see himself as still being in process. He has come a long way—from one pattern to a higher pattern to a still higher pattern of life—but there is a continuum [continuation] beyond this present stage.—Julius Stulman, *A Pattern for Life*.

G. Man is different from all other known creatures, not primarily in his body, which is similar to many others, and not absolutely in his intellectual processes, which some others share in degree, but in his capacity as a moral agent. Various higher animals use intelligence to secure ends which are dictated by appetite, but man has the unique capacity to choose between ends. Man is the creature who can say no to his appetites and often does so on the basis of moral considerations. The higher animals sometimes show genuine intelligence by the way they ask and answer the question, "How can I get it?" But man shows something beyond mere intelligence by his capacity to ask and answer the vastly different question, "Ought I to get it?" This is a difference so crucial that it must be termed a difference in kind rather than merely a difference in degree.—Elton Trueblood, *The Life We Prize*, Harper and Bros.

5. *Adding Up*

ANYONE who has read the last three chapters carefully must by now have reached the conclusion that this is a truly wonderful universe in which we live, and that life of all kinds, most especially human life, is more fascinating than most of us had ever suspected. Our survey of the universe is almost completed. This chapter, which finishes that survey, will attempt to accomplish three things:

1. One more look at ourselves as human beings.
2. A brief inquiry into another kind of evolution.
3. Adding up all the data of these last chapters and reaching some mighty important conclusions.

One More Look at Us—As Individuals

We have already suggested that the most important part of man's evolution, as well as the probable direction of his development in the future, lies in his brain, his creativity and his conscience. In the first part of this chapter we want to deal a little further with these non-physical aspects of man's nature. Someone once actually figured out what the average human body is worth in chemicals. It contains enough fat to make about seven bars of soap, enough iron for one medium-size nail, sugar enough to fill one shaker, sufficient lime to whitewash a chicken coop, etc. At market prices prevailing when this was figured out, a human being's body was worth just ninety-eight cents in chemicals. Even with prices much higher today, it is easy to see that you and I aren't worth very much if we think of ourselves as just collections of chemicals.

Obviously, however, a human being is a great deal more than a dollar's worth of physical material. Ninety-eight cents' worth of chemicals couldn't have written the Gettysburg Address or the Book of Amos. Ninety-eight cents' worth of chemicals could never have given us the Ten Commandments or the Four Freedoms. There is obviously something in a human being which goes far beyond his physical body, which cannot be measured in dollars but is extremely worth while.

Let's look at just a very few examples; thousands upon thousands could be given easily.

Take the case of the German Jewish poet, Heinrich Heine. During the latter years of his life Heine was critically and hopelessly ill. He was afflicted with an incurable disease which was literally eating away his brain. He lay on his mattress of straw, his body ravished and consumed by disease, racked with endless pain—even his brilliant mind wasting away—without enough strength to stand on his feet. But during that terrible time of physical weakness and pain, Heinrich Heine wrote some of his most magnificent poems and songs—poetry which will live forever.

What made it possible for him to do that? Courage? Stubbornness? Will-power? A strong urge to create things of beauty? No one knows exactly what to call it, but all of us must agree that in Heine there was something over and above his ninety-eight cents' worth of chemicals—something no one could see or touch or identify—which made a bundle of pain into a great poet.

* * *

The same "something" has enabled countless other human beings to live lives that will never be forgotten, to create great beauty of every kind, to sacrifice things they may have selfishly wanted for themselves in favor of doing good for others.

The great Jewish philosopher Spinoza wrote his finest discussions of ethics at a time when he was gravely ill and so poor that he scarcely had enough to eat.

Franz Rosenzweig, one of the outstanding modern Jewish thinkers, was stricken with a form of paralysis when he was only thirty-four years old. Gradually he became so incapacitated that he was no longer able to speak at all and could move but one finger. He had to be placed in an armchair, his head propped up with a cushion. With his arm in a sling, he would slowly move his right thumb over an alphabet chart pointing to one letter at a time so that his wife could combine these letters into words and sentences. Most of the important books Rosenzweig wrote were done in this unbelievable way. They included books on biology, philosophy, the Bible, Jewish law and Jewish music! His accomplishments during this period of illness and pain outweighed by far everything he had done before.

The great Indian religious leader, Mohandas K. Gandhi, is another outstanding example. Your teacher or rabbi can tell you where to read the full story of Gandhi's remarkable life if you are interested. For present purposes all we need tell you is that at one time he was earning $25,000 a year as a very successful attorney in London. He could have continued doing so all his life. Instead, he gave up his professional life there, returned to his native India, dressed only in a simple loin-cloth, renounced all the luxuries of life, and taught his people religious ideals which ultimately led to the freedom of India and which brought meaning and comfort into the lives of millions.

> What made Gandhi and Rosenzweig do what they did? The chemicals in their bodies? The fact that they had developed two hands in place of a second pair of feet? Their lungs, which had developed millions of years ago in their "ancestors" instead of gills? Obviously, none of these is the answer. It must have been that "something" which we have already met in Heine.

* * *

Marie Curie is another good example. She, and her husband, Pierre, were the discoverers of radium, a remarkable radioactive substance which has cured or relieved thousands of cancer patients. At the time of their discovery they could easily have taken out a patent on radium; in that event, anyone using it would have had to pay Marie and Pierre Curie, the discoverers. There would have been nothing wrong in that; after all, it was through their long, patient hours of experimentation and research that radium had been discovered. Furthermore, the Curies could well have used the money; they lived in utmost poverty. Even their laboratory was inadequately equipped due to insufficient funds. Radium, which they had discovered, was worth $100,000 a gram. Yet they refused to apply for a patent, which would have limited its use and increased their wealth. When asked why, Marie Curie replied, "Radium was not to enrich anyone. Radium is an element. It belongs to all people."

> What made these great scientists place the health and welfare of their fellow man above all personal gain? Was it because they didn't like or want luxuries and comforts for themselves? Was it because they preferred to live in poverty? Did they have in their bodies or brains chemicals superior to those

> of people who might have behaved selfishly under such circumstances? Or was it due to something that was not physical at all, that could never be counted or weighed?

* * *

Here is one more example of the same kind: one of the key scientists in the development of the atom bomb was Dr. Louis A. Slotin, a Canadian Jew who died in May, 1946, at the age of thirty-five. He had worked on the atom bomb project since 1942, had been responsible for assembling and delivering the first atom bomb actually tested by the American army. Three days before leaving government work to join the physics faculty at the University of Chicago, Dr. Slotin was working in his laboratory when an accident touched off a plutonium chain reaction in the next room. Dr. Slotin knew that unless someone pulled the material apart, seven people working in that room would be doomed to death. He also knew that if he dashed in to save them, it would inevitably mean his own death.

He could have rationalized quite convincingly by telling himself that his life as an outstanding scientist was worth more than theirs, that he had to save himself for future work in atomic energy which would benefit millions of other people, not just seven. But in less time than it would have taken him to reason all this out, Louis Slotin dashed into the next room, pulled the material apart, saved seven lives, drenched himself with death-dealing radioactive charges, and died nine days later. Several of the doctors who had worked with him wrote: "Those of us who worked with Slotin loved him for his selflessness, his modesty and his sure and quiet competence. His death, like his life, was quiet, brave and clear."

> What part of the chemicals in Dr. Slotin's body was responsible for his selflessness? Does each of us have the same chemical? Would all of us have done the same thing? Why? Was Dr. Slotin worth more, physically, than some other person who would have chosen to save himself? What kind of heroism

is more praiseworthy, Dr. Slotin's or that of a soldier who saved his comrades in combat? Why?

A less heroic but equally valid way of noting the non-physical aspect of a human being is to think of a man's personality. While we shall have more to say on the subject later, the important thing to observe here is that your personality is not something material or physical. You can touch and see your hands, your nose, your knees, and all other physical parts of yourself. You cannot touch or see your personality, yet it is the most important thing that distinguishes you from other people.

A person who unfortunately loses a leg or arm in an accident is just as real and whole a person thereafter as he was before, even though he is obviously lessened physically. Clearly, therefore, the intangible or non-physical part of an individual is even more important in making him a unique human being than is the physical part.

—In Groups

Thus far we have given examples only of individuals. The same kind of thing can also be found in the life of groups. And no group has shown more of this "something" we've been discussing than our own Jewish people. How else can we explain the fact that for more than 3,000 years we have lived through persecution and trouble as a small minority, yet have survived? Every ancient people that lived with our ancestors at the time of Moses has either disappeared from the stage of history or become totally insignificant. If we were to examine scientifically all the physical factors which caused these other peoples to perish, it would be easy to prove that we Jews should have vanished long ago, too. For two thousand years we had no land of our own—no government, no state, no parliament—none of the physical requirements for survival as a people. Yet we survived. Only we Jews have remained without interruption an important and surviving people through so many centuries, a people which has clung to its religious and ethical ideals even in the face of torture and death.

> Is there something in our physical make-up which accounts for that? Do we have in our bodies some factor or chemical which other peoples did not have? Or has it been something which isn't physical that accounts for our survival?

Nor need we limit ourselves just to Jews who lived in the past. The story of Jewish survival in our own day is equally exciting. Nowhere on this earth in our generation has there been greater heroism than that of Jews who managed to survive World War II; who found their way—it almost seems miraculously—to Israel; who defeated the combined armies of six Arab nations, any one of which was numerically much stronger than they; and who are now performing the almost impossible task of setting up a new nation. You are probably already familiar with the heroic story of the Warsaw ghetto. If not, read about it in Marie Syrkin's thrilling book, *Blessed Is the Match.* She tells how the head of the Jewish Council in the Warsaw ghetto, when ordered by the Nazis to give them lists of Jews to be deported to extermination camps, steadfastly refused and in the end committed suicide rather than betray his fellow Jews. Finally, even though they knew their immediate cause was hopeless and could only end in defeat and death, the handful of Jews left in Warsaw organized a heroic resistance which took the German army weeks to subdue.

> What drives a man like the head of the Warsaw Jewish Council to be so stubborn? What good could be accomplished by resistance such as that in the Warsaw ghetto? Any immediate good? Any good in the long run? Was it just "animal instinct" or "self-preservation" which stimulated these people to fight? Was it something physical or chemical?

A Name for It

Well, we could easily go on like this for many more pages. These examples should be enough, however, to make our point. And you will be given an opportunity in your workbook assignment to suggest additional illustrations. Right now we're interested in knowing just what this "something" extra in human beings is or by what name we can call it. The truth of the matter is, of course, that no one knows exactly what it is. The word usually used to express it, however, is *Soul*.

That part of a human being which isn't physical or material—which we can't see, hear, touch, smell or measure—is called his soul or the spiritual part of him. It includes his conscience, his courage, his creative ability in music or literature or art, his emotions, his thoughts, and his ideas. It is the margin of superiority man has over all the other animals produced by evolution—the important difference between human life and animal life. We spoke of all this in our last chapter without using the word *Soul* to describe it. Now we have a name for it. Physically our bodies are very similar to the bodies of the animals through whom we developed to our present condition. Spiritually, however (that is, as far as our souls are concerned), we differ from the animals vastly. Which of the Reading Selections at the end of this chapter show that our ancestors understood this many centuries ago?

You recognize by now that a person's soul is the most highly developed and important part of him. It is the most recent development of evolution, pointing the way to the future. It is the part of a human being which most clearly distinguishes him from animals and plants. In amphibians, lungs were the latest and highest development of evolution; had we lived then, with our modern scientific knowledge, we could have predicted that along the line of further lung development would lie the future of evolution. In mammals, the womb, which meant carrying and protecting the young inside the mother's body, was the highest stage, anticipating the direction of future development. In much the same way, as far as human beings today are concerned, the soul seems to be the most exciting and valuable development of evolution for the future.

Unfortunately not all of us are like Gandhi or the Curies or Louis Slotin in our conduct. There are in this world many extremely selfish people, too, probably more selfish ones than individuals like those just named. There are also many men and women who don't seem to have developed their souls very much, who live life chiefly or only on a physical, material level, without paying much heed to conscience, without using their creative ability at all, without thinking great thoughts. All this is a way of saying that some human beings are farther advanced than others in the development of evolution. In this connection, and before we permit this fact to discourage us, it is important to keep two things clearly in mind:

1. Our spiritual evolution is very recent. It began not more than 10,000 years ago at most. If you had before you a piece of graph paper containing 100,000 squares to represent the entire course of evolution, the period of man's spiritual development would be covered only by one tiny square! If we think of the time since the first protozoan as one day, the development of the human soul started about four-fifths of one second ago! It is remarkable that so many people have developed souls in so short a time.

Or we might think in terms of the book mentioned in the workbook assignment of Chapter Four—a book of 2,000 pages representing the age of our planet. How much of it would then cover approximately the time during which our souls may be said to have developed?

2. Remember also what was said in Chapter Four: that human beings, unlike animals, know what has happened through the long centuries of evolution, and furthermore are able themselves to hasten the speed of future evolution. This is especially true regarding the spiritual part of our evolution. The ape had nothing to do consciously with the gradual development of arms in place of forefeet. He simply had to wait patiently over hundreds of generations for the Force behind evolution to work out its plan of development. When it comes to our human souls, however—to the beauty we create, the music we compose, the inspiring thoughts we think, the ethical ideals we conceive—each one of us can hasten or retard his own rate of development.

Judaism has some very interesting and important things to say about the soul. Perhaps the most important is that in human beings the body and soul work together indivisibly. There are some religions which teach that only man's soul is important, and anything connected with his body is evil. Judaism says that the body and the soul work together and belong together. One of our ancient rabbis illustrated this by telling the story of a blind man and a lame man who conspired to steal fruit from an orchard. The blind man lifted the lame man onto his shoulders. The lame man then directed the blind man where to carry him in order to pick the fruit. Now then, asked the ancient Rabbi, who was guilty of the crime—the blind man or the lame man? The answer he gives is that both are guilty because neither could have committed the crime without the other. In the same way, he said, man's soul and body together are guilty of whatever sin he commits. To which we might add that man's body and soul together deserve the credit for the fine things he does.

The conclusion of this first part of our chapter, then, is that man has a soul, which consists of the non-physical phases of his life, and which drives him to do most of the fine, courageous, heroic things he does.

More about Evolution

We have said quite a bit about *evolution* already. There is one other meaning of the word we want to discuss before closing the subject. In its biological sense, we have seen that evolution means slow but steady progress from simple to higher and more complicated forms of life. Is there any similar progress to be found in the history of human ethics and ideals? In other words, can we find something very much like evolution in the development of the soul as well as the body of man? You realize, we hope, that discussing this we are dealing with only the last and most recent part of the whole picture of evolution. Out of the billions of years the earth has existed, out of the billion years since life first appeared, out of the million years since the first man, we are dealing only with the last five or ten thousand years when we talk here about the development of the ethical ideals which are an important part of the soul. Has there been any progress in the development of these ideals?

Sometimes it seems not. It is 2,500 years since the ancient Jewish prophet Isaiah urged the nations to "beat their swords into plowshares and their spears into pruning-hooks," but civilization is still plagued with war. It is longer than that since Moses first taught "thou shalt not murder" and "thou shalt not steal," but every day's newspaper still carries stories of burglary and killing. And sometimes when we look at periods of history we also become discouraged. After the French Revolution people thought great progress had been made, but very shortly a dictator named Napoleon arose to erase much of that progress. After World War I the League of Nations was established to end war, but it failed and the Second World War was more terrible by far than the First. How can we speak of human progress in ethics when we see such things as these?

Actually, it is only a quick glance at history which gives us such a discouraging picture. True, Napoleon was a disappointment after the French Revolution, but after a time Napoleon was destroyed, and many of the most important benefits of the Revolution were maintained. Hitler certainly didn't represent progress either, but Hitler too was destroyed, making ethical progress possible again. Though the League of Nations failed, the United Nations, which followed World War II, was a great improvement on the League and has, we hope, a better chance to avert war in the future. The mistake made by many people is to expect that progress in ethics will always be smooth and steady. They expect a line representing such progress to look like the upper illustration on page 72.

Actually, however, ethical progress through history has always occurred in spurts. A time of progress would be followed by a period of retrogression; a period of ethical growth would often give way to one of decline and decay. The line would really look more like the lower illustration on page 72.

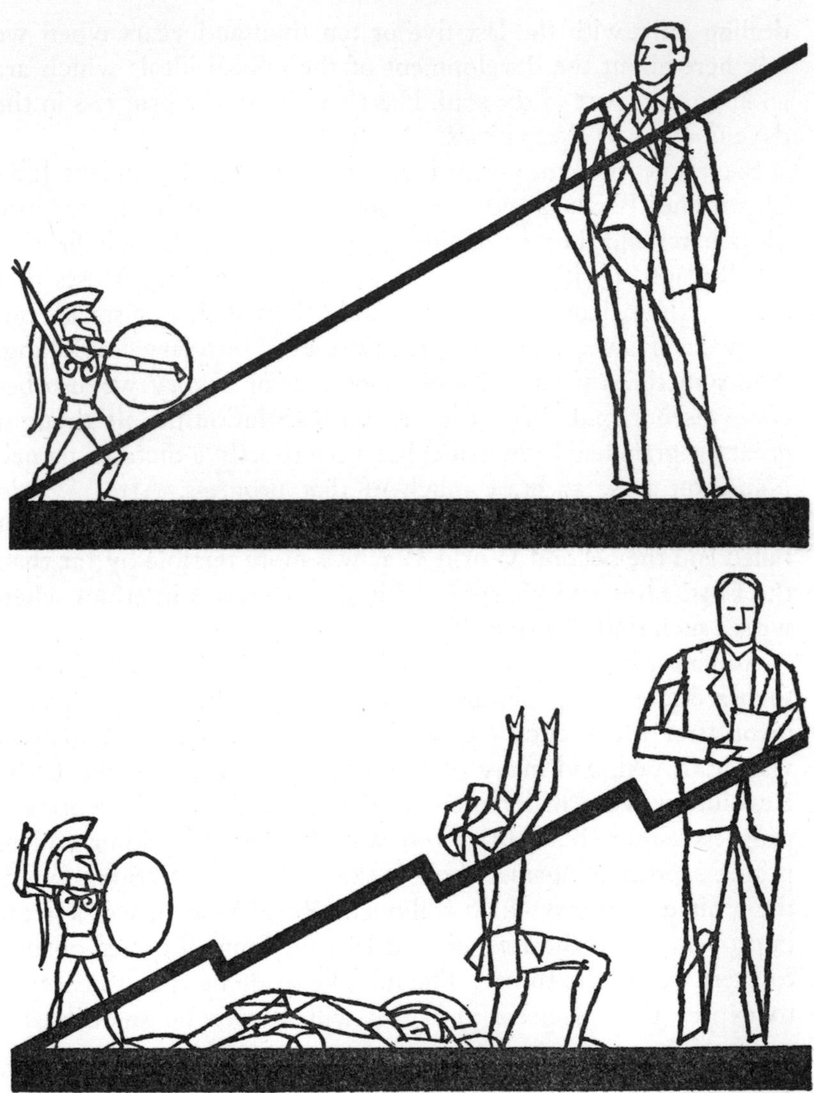

The important thing to note is that, on the whole, each low point on the line is a little higher or better than the last low point, while each high point of progress is a bit higher than the last high point also. That is the way progress has been made.

As a matter of fact, we might almost use the lower illustration on page 72 to represent biological evolution, too. Though the line of development there may seem from our description to be sure and steady, there must have been many times and places when a human being (if there had been any), watching evolution, would have felt sure the whole thing was bound to fail. When the water first began to recede from the land, for example, and before it was certain whether enough fish had developed lungs to keep alive on dry land, our imaginary human being might easily have represented such a crisis by placing a downward line on his graph.

Another way of inquiring into pretty much the same sort of thing is to stop for a moment to think of times in human history when a group representing good was opposed by a group representing moral wickedness or evil, and when the evil group seemed about to vanquish the group which, on the whole, represented good. It is easy to think of examples from history like those pictured on page 74.

> In each of these cases, which group was the stronger physically? Which, therefore, might have been expected to triumph? Which actually won out? How can we explain this victory? In your workbook for this chapter you will be given an opportunity to answer these questions as well as to add other examples of your own.

The fact that we have divided these examples into "good" and "evil" does not necessarily mean that any group was entirely good or bad. Human beings individually as well as groups of human beings are without exception mixtures and combinations of good and bad. No person or group is apt to be either 100 per cent good or 100 per cent evil. Nevertheless, having agreed to this, the fact remains that the groups used in our illustration above can be divided into those, which, at a given time and on the whole, represented "good" and those that were generally "evil."

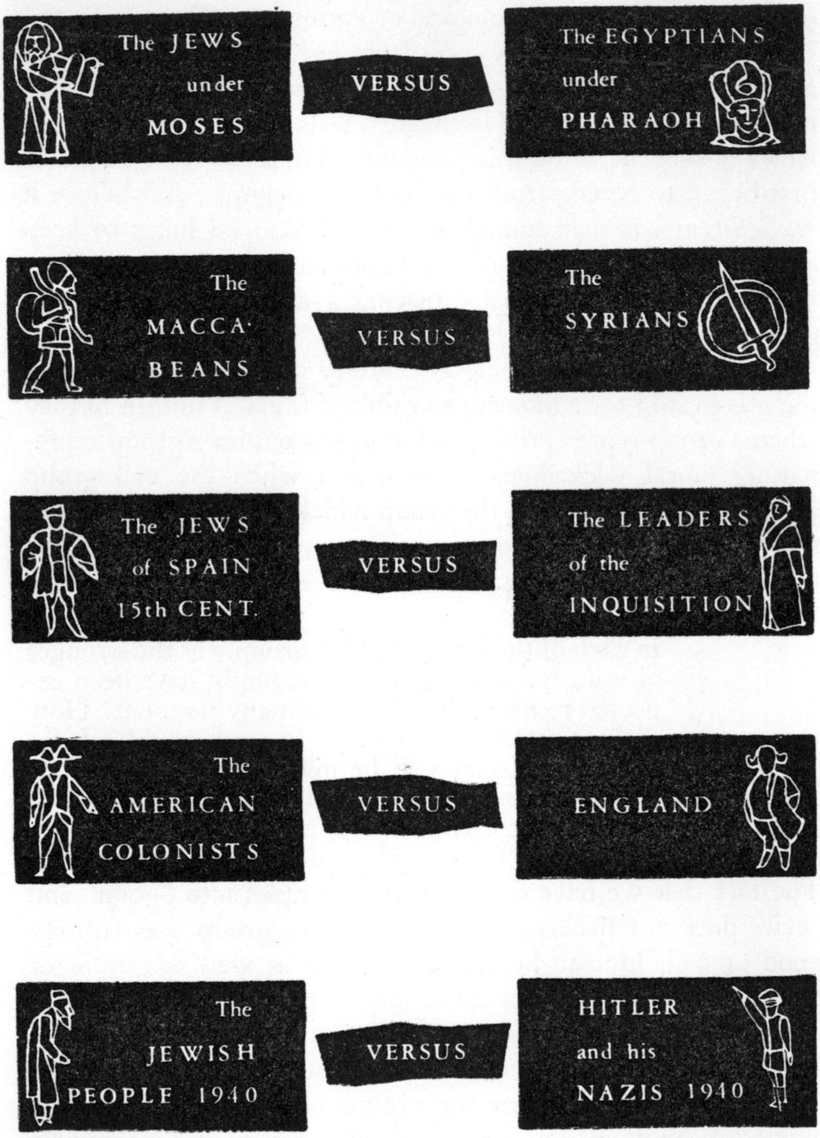

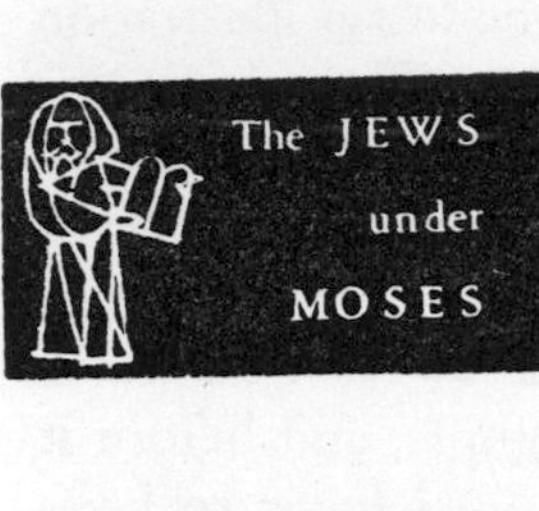

The JEWS under MOSES
VERSUS
The EGYPTIANS under PHARAOH
The MACCA-BEANS
VERSUS
The SYRIANS
The JEWS of SPAIN 15th CENT.
VERSUS
The LEADERS of the INQUISITION
The AMERICAN COLONISTS
VERSUS
ENGLAND
The JEWISH PEOPLE 1940
VERSUS
HITLER and his NAZIS 1940

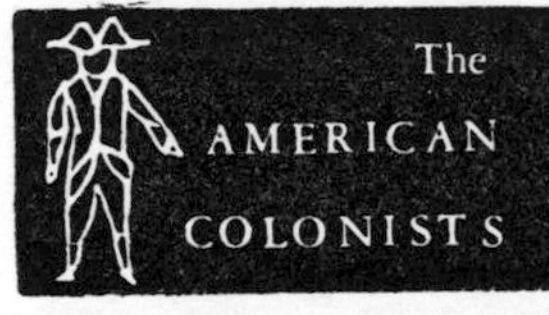

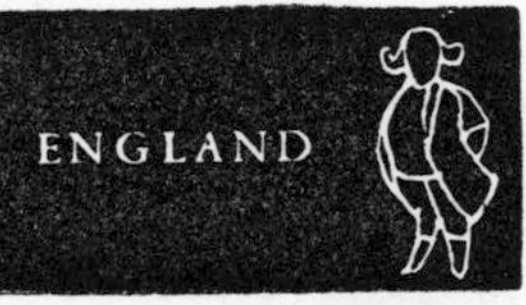

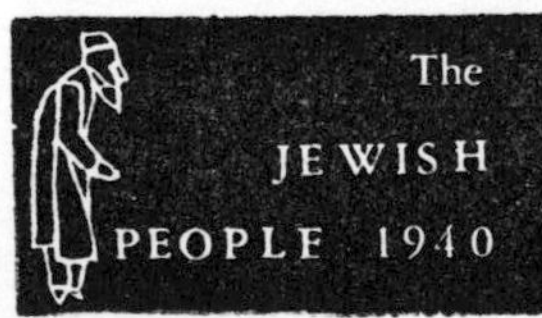

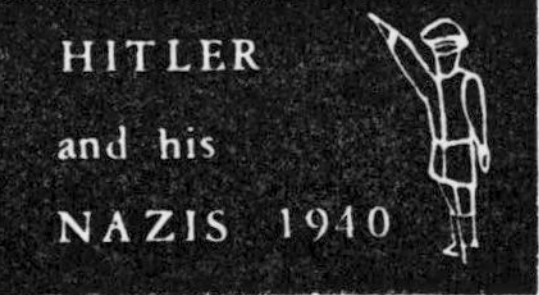

Furthermore, it would be a mistake to gain from these examples the impression that a weak "good" group always and automatically wins out over a strong "evil" group. Usually a long bitter struggle is necessary first. To illustrate by means of the last of the examples used above, it is true that Hitler killed 6,000,000 Jews before he himself was destroyed. The fact that the Jewish people as a group triumphed over him and outlasted him may be small comfort to the victims and their families but it is enormously important in the light of history.

It would likewise be an error to assume that any individual or group which, at a given moment, seems to be winning a contest or battle, is therefore morally right. It is the final outcome of the struggle in history rather than each temporary victory that counts.

The point we wish to make here is that in the long run the groups we have recognized as being on the whole good have triumphed and survived though they were physically weak. If this were a universe and world governed only by physical factors, the stronger group would *always* triumph, whether or not it was the ethical group also. Even though there may be temporary exceptions, the fact that usually and in the long run the ethical group wins out leads us to believe that human history and experience are governed largely by factors that are not purely physical.

When you have finished this assignment, you will have seen that in the history of ethical ideals also (or, to say the same thing in a somewhat different way, in the development of the soul), there has been progress quite similar to that which we noticed in biological evolution. In Chapter Four we reached the conclusion that evolution could not have occurred merely as a series of accidents, that there must be some sort of Power working out a plan through evolution. The same thing would apply here too. When we see that both individuals and groups are capable of living life spiritually as well as physically, and that moral right so often triumphs over mere physical strength, we conclude that this is another evidence of a Power in the universe which isn't merely physical, chemical, or material.

And Now

We have at long last completed the "look around" which we commenced at the beginning of Chapter Two. It is time now for a quick summary of our discoveries, before turning to our next important task. Wherever we have looked—at the planets, at this earth on which we live, at the bodies of animals as well as human beings, at evolution, and at man's soul—we have discovered the same things:

1. Everywhere there are signs of Order, Design, Purpose, Plan, and Law. There is very little evidence of Disorder, Confusion or Accident. Even some of the examples which at first seem to belong under this second category may actually be due to the fact that we have not yet learned what causes them or how to explain them; they are not necessarily convincing illustrations of Accident.

2. The universe, our earth, and the development of life do not look like things which "just happened" without any meaning or purpose behind them. No one in his right mind, seeing a watch, would suppose for an instant that the various pieces of metal "just happened" to be the right size and shape or "just happened" to arrange themselves in such order as to be a functioning watch. The minute we see any working piece of mechanism like a watch, we know at once there must have been intelligence and purpose applied to make it. What we have seen here of the universe and life is more complicated and wonderful by far than any mechanism ever created by human intelligence. We must assume, therefore—even though we by no means are able to understand it fully—that there is some great purpose or intelligence behind all this, too.

3. We are—or ought to be—particularly impressed by the non-physical part of man which we have called his soul. It is wonderful almost beyond belief to think of the tiniest one-celled protozoan developing through the ages into a creature which can create so much beauty, think such inspiring thoughts, and live so courageously as a human being at his best. This too cannot be

just an accident or a coincidence. It is reasonable to suppose, moreover, that if man has both a physical and a non-physical life, there must also be something non-physical (spiritual is the word for something which is important but which isn't physical or tangible) about the universe in which he lives.

4. There seems to be something in this universe which helps man when he tries to develop his soul, when he lives up to the best possibilities within him. Because of the soul within himself and this "something" which apparently helps him, time and again in history a small, weak group representing the right has been able to vanquish and survive a large, strong group which hadn't developed as far in human evolution and which therefore didn't represent high ethical ideals.

We are not the first by any means either to look so curiously around us for signs of meaning or to reach the conclusions stated here. Men and women through the ages have asked the same questions, and almost without exception have reached the conclusion that there is more to this universe than meets the eye. Though much—very much—remains in the realm of mystery, we know enough to understand that there must be something which accounts for all the order and beauty we have seen. In the next few chapters our task will be to see how ancient people, including our own Jewish ancestors, explained these things, and then to find an explanation which will be satisfactory for us today.

SOMETHING FOR YOU TO READ

A. (The following excerpts are taken from Psalm 8 in our Bible):

O Lord, our Lord,
How glorious is Thy name in all the earth!
Whose majesty is rehearsed above the heavens.
. . . When I behold Thy heavens, the work of Thy fingers,
The moon and the stars, which Thou hast established;
What is man, that Thou art mindful of him?
And the son of man, that Thou thinkest of him?

Yet Thou hast made him but little lower than the angels,
And hast crowned him with glory and honour. . . .

B. True enough, history moves in cycles of development and decay! But the total movement is ever upward, however slow and tortuous. . . .—Jay William Hudson, *Religious Liberals Reply*, The Beacon Press.

C. Bachya ibn Pakuda, one of the greatest of our medieval Jewish religious thinkers, once wrote the following, which is of interest in connection with our discussion in this chapter:

If one should bring an ordered manuscript and claim that the writing was produced by the accidental spilling of ink upon the paper, would he be believed?

D. After all the creatures were made, God said to them, "Let us make one more creature in partnership. Each of you shall have a share in him, and I will give him a portion of myself."—Zohar (a medieval Jewish book).

6. *Old Ideas and Older*

FROM the first moment that men, evolving from earlier life forms, developed a brain with which to think, they have wondered about many if not all the things we have observed in the last several chapters. *Their answers*—the explanations and interpretations they gave for all this—constituted *their religions.* Although we are, of course, primarily interested in *modern* Jewish religion which can serve those of us who are living today, it should be both interesting and helpful to notice first what kind of religious theories were developed in ancient times.

The earliest forms of religion we know much about were called *animism.* Primitive peoples, recognizing as we do that there seems to be "something" in the world and the universe beyond what we ourselves know and can see, developed the idea that this "something" consisted of spirits dwelling in every object of nature. They believed that each tree, each river, every rock possessed such a spirit. One had to be very careful, therefore, about chopping down a tree or kicking a rock. If the spirit dwelling in that particular object took offense, it might well seek revenge against a person. The way to get along in life, therefore, and to avoid serious trouble, was to find ways of pleasing and appeasing the spirits which were in all such natural objects.

This kind of explanation sounds very simple and childish to us now. Yet it is interesting to note that occasionally we, too, act almost as if we still believed in animism. Have you ever stubbed your toe against a rock while swimming or hit your "crazy bone" against the corner of a table and then addressed a few unkind comments either to the rock or the table, as if it were a person instead of a thing, and could properly be blamed for being in your way? When we unthinkingly do things like that we seem for a moment to believe in animism, much as primitive folk did thousands of years ago. This practice of acting as if an inanimate object were a person is called *personification.* Sometimes we *personify* things in a poetic sense, as when we refer to a ship as "she" though we know it isn't a person. But when ancient men personified, they believed literally that the object they were dealing with was a person or had a personal spirit of some kind within it.

Soon, however, religion developed beyond the stage of animism to a belief in gods rather than in spirits. To explain all the things they couldn't understand but which deeply impressed them about nature, to calm their fears, and to reassure them that the high ideals they had glimpsed could be attained, giving meaning and purpose to their lives, men began to think in terms of gods very much greater than themselves, who controlled everything. Whether we look at the ancient Romans, Greeks, Egyptians, or American Indians, we shall find great similarities in their early god beliefs.

Because our space is limited, we shall consider here only the ancient Greeks; members of the class may bring in additional reports if they wish, showing how the religion of other ancient groups resembled that of the Greeks.

The Greeks, as you no doubt know, believed in many gods. Zeus, their chief god, was god of the sky and the weather. Athena was the goddess of wisdom, Apollo the god of youth, and Demeter the goddess of agriculture. In addition, there was Ares, the god of war; Hercules, the god of strength and endurance; Hermes, god of commerce and invention; and many others. It is obvious that these were "departmentalized" gods; each was in charge of a specific area of life. They were like a president's cabinet, each directing one particular department under the general supervision of Zeus, their chief. For each of these Greek gods the Romans had almost the exact equivalent under a different name. In place of Zeus, for example, their chief god was named Jupiter, and so on.

Though there were some differences from people to people, the following four characteristics, true of the Greek ideas, were likewise true of most ancient ideas about the gods:

1. They all believed in many gods rather than one God. That is why we spell the word "god" with a small "g" when referring to their religions.

2. Their gods were very much like human beings. It would not be going too far afield to say that most ancients thought of their gods much as a modern child thinks of Superman. Among some peoples the gods were believed to be actual human beings who became gods after their death. Among all of them the gods were in human form, lived like human beings, had human desires and faults, but were so powerful they could do or get anything they wanted. One of your readings for this chapter will give you interesting details on this point.

3. Some of their gods represented or *personified* phases of *nature*. This helped primitive men understand all the strange, wonderful, and fearful things they saw in the world of nature. Most ancient peoples, for example, believed in a god of thunder and a god of the wind, who were responsible respectively for the crash of the thunder and the howl of the wind.

4. Others of their gods symbolized ethical ideals which the people wanted to achieve. A person who wanted to improve himself in a particular field would concentrate on worshipping the god who happened to represent perfection in that field. One who wanted to be a track star would be particularly careful about serving and pleasing the god of speed. A man who desired to paint beautiful pictures or to carve great statues would be especially zealous in his devotion to the goddess of beauty.

Religion was a very *practical thing* to these ancient peoples. It had to meet certain very real needs which they felt, or it was no good to them. Throughout the ages, only those religions which continued to meet people's needs survived. The same thing is true today. If religion is to mean anything to us as modern Jews, we shall have to find a religious interpretation of life which will meet our needs, which will adequately explain for us the things we have observed in the first part of this book and will help us to live better lives. Whatever we find in our ancestors' beliefs which meets our needs today we shall keep. Whatever in their religion no longer helps us live better lives today we shall have to change. But once more we are getting ahead of our story.

The religious ideas outlined above had all been developed before the first Jews appeared in the world. It would have been easy for our ancestors just to accept the ideas they found among other peoples. But they didn't. Like the fish which wasn't "satisfied" just to remain a fish and which therefore developed the ability to live on land; like the ape which wasn't "satisfied" to remain an animal with four legs and which therefore developed two hands; so, in a different meaning of evolution, our Jewish forefathers weren't satisfied just to accept the religion of the past. Instead, they developed altogether new insights into religious problems, as a result of which we Jews are known in civilization as the people whose greatest genius has been in the realm of religion. Of course, neither the fish nor the ape had anything to do with the change or was even aware that it was taking place. That is why we placed the word "satisfied" in quotes. Our Jewish ancestors, on the other hand, expressed their conscious and deliberate choice in developing new ideas of religion.

The ancient Greeks are most famous for their contributions to sculpture, art, and philosophy. The Romans made their greatest contributions to civilization in the fields of law and engineering. In much the same way, we Jews contributed more than any other people to religion, chiefly because we weren't satisfied just to go on thinking and believing the way others had before us. A great difference, incidentally, between our contributions to civilization and those of the Greeks and Romans is that these other groups made their contribution and then passed out of existence; what they had to give to the world was given, period. But there has been no "period" after our Jewish contribution to religion. Without interruption through the centuries and to this very day, Judaism has kept contributing to the development of new ideas in religion.

What were the great contributions our Jewish ancestors made to the idea of God? Where shall we look to discover what they believed? The answer to this last question is obvious. In the Bible, of course! We don't have to examine skeletons in rocks or inscriptions in tombs to know about the religion of ancient Jews; we can find it written plainly in our Bible. Since the Bible is our greatest source of information, we ought to know something about it before starting to use it. If your teacher or rabbi feels that you already have enough knowledge about the Bible, he can give you permission to skip this next section. Otherwise, consider the following a kind of parenthesis, after which we shall continue our search for ancient Jewish ideas of religion.

Quick Facts about the Bible

Pick up a copy of our Bible. The translation we shall use is that of the Jewish Publication Society. The title, as you can easily see, is The Holy Scriptures. You probably know that "scriptures" means "writings." So another title for the Bible would be The Holy Writings. But what does the word "holy" mean? Something holy is something which is *extremely precious or valuable in a spiritual sense,* that is, in more than a physical or a material sense. A gold watch is valuable, but in a material sense. A diamond ring is even more valuable, but still in a physical or material sense. A great symphony composition or poem is not only more valuable than the watch or the ring, but it is valuable in a different way, in a spiritual way. It isn't the financial cost of the paper on which it is written that makes it valuable, but the fact that it can bring beauty and comfort into so many people's lives. A great symphony or poem is so valuable that it might even be considered holy.

The Ten Commandments are holy because (1) they are about as valuable as anything can be; (2) they are valuable purely in a spiritual sense; (3) they add greatly to man's further evolution in a spiritual direction. In other words, something which is among the most valuable things in the world in a spiritual sense is called holy. We call our Bible The Holy Scriptures because it contains so many passages and selections which meet this description.

Although many people think of our Bible as *a book,* it is actually a collection of thirty-nine books bound together. The Bible is an anthology—a collection of books on a particular subject. And, of course, in this case the anthology is primarily on religion. To be sure, there are other types of literature in the Bible, too. There is a great deal of history, and there are many legal passages which form the foundation of much law known in the world today. But the Bible is most especially known as an anthology of religion. It is within the covers of this great anthology that our Jewish ancestors wrote their impressions of religion.

Who wrote the Bible? The answer you get to that question depends on whom you ask. An Orthodox Jew would say that the first five books of it at any rate were all written by Moses. Most other Jews would say that even the first five books, which constitute the Torah, were written only in part by Moses, that many men had something to do with the writing of them. Most scholars are agreed today that the Bible was written over a period of ten to fifteen centuries, and that it contains the writings and ideas of hundreds of individuals, only a few of whom are known to us by name. This is an important fact to keep in mind.

Are the Christian and Jewish Bibles the same? Only in part. You have heard our Jewish Bible referred to as the Old Testament. We Jews don't like that description, because it implies that our Bible somehow is inferior to the New Testament, which, incidentally, is exactly what Christians believe. They say that our Bible never really reached the heights of noblest religion, that it was necessary for the early Christians to add to it the New Testament as a higher development of Jewish religious teaching.

Our answer to that is that every important religious or ethical idea found in the New Testament was stated centuries earlier in our Jewish Bible. The important thing to keep in mind here, however, is that when we say "Bible" we mean what Christians refer to as the Old Testament. The Christian Bible consists of both the Old and the New Testaments, with very much greater emphasis placed on the New. Christians believe that our Bible is, so to speak, but the foundation or base of a pyramid, the apex of which is the New Testament. We Jews, on the other hand, believe that the so-called Old Testament is the entire pyramid, with no need for another Bible to complete it.

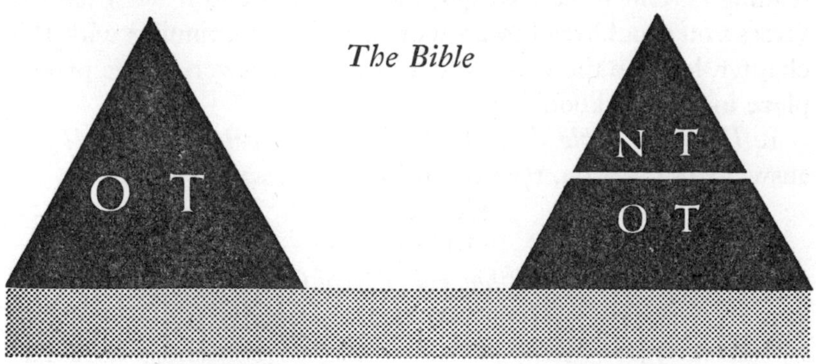

The Bible

There are three main divisions of our Jewish Bible. The first, called the Torah, תּוֹרָה ("Law"), we have mentioned already; it contains the first five books of the Bible, telling the early history of the Jewish people and giving some of our great religious laws like the Ten Commandments. Opposite page xvi of your English Bible you will find listed the titles of these five books.

The second section of the Bible is called N'vi-im, נְבִיאִים ("Prophets"), because it consists for the most part of volumes and speeches written by the ancient prophets; you will find the individual book titles on page 259.

The third and final section is called K'suvim, כְּתוּבִים ("Writings"); it is a kind of miscellaneous collection, including all the books which do not belong in either of the previous sections. The titles of books in this section may be found on page 775.

And now, with this very brief introduction to the Bible for those of you who may not have had it before, we are ready to begin our inquiry into the changes our ancestors made in the ideas of God they found among the other early peoples on the stage of history.

Three Questions

We could tell you what the Bible says about God, but it will be more fun for you to find out for yourself. So we're going to give you three questions, the answers to which can be discovered by reading certain Bible passages; after each question we'll list the verses you should read to answer it. Before continuing with this chapter, look up the verses and write your answers in the proper place in the workbook.

1. *Does the Bible describe God as physical or spiritual?* To answer this question, read the following passages:

Gen. 3:7–8	Gen. 8:20–21	Exod. 33:11
Exod. 31:18	Deut. 4:12–15	Job 23:8–9

2. *According to the Bible, where was God to be found?* What was His "address"? To answer this, read:

Exod. 25:8	Exod. 25:22	1 Kings 8:22–24
1 Kings 8:26–27	Ps. 139:7–12	Exod. 3:1–6

3. *What did God require of man?* How could human beings serve or please God? Read these passages:

Lev. 1:1–2	Micah 6:6–8	Ps. 51:17–19
Amos 5:15	Amos 5:21–24	Lev. 6:1–6
I Sam. 15:22	Isa. 1:11–17	

Since you will not be able properly to understand the contributions which our Jewish ancestors were the first to make to the idea of God until after you have read and considered all these Bible passages, do them now, writing your answers under III of your workbook for this chapter. Then you will be ready to go on.

Reading Selection F has something to say about question 2 of this section. While it comes from a time very much later than Bible days, it shows us how Jewish thought on this subject developed.

The Jewish Contribution

Now, by looking back again at our list of the four characteristics common to very nearly all ancient pre-Jewish ideas of God (see pages 81 and 82) and by keeping in mind the answers we have just discovered to the three questions above, we should be able to list the three most important ideas first contributed by the ancient Jewish people to the idea of God. Any one of them alone would be considered a very major improvement. The three together constituted nothing less than a revolution in mankind's religious thinking.

1. *The idea that God is one.* You must have noticed that in every one of the Bible passages you read a moment ago, mention is made only of one God, not of several or many. This is obviously different from the thought of the Greeks, the Romans, and all other ancient folk. Today most of the civilized world professes a belief in only one God. Our people was the first to teach this. Indeed, the very watchword of our faith has always been Sh'ma Yisroel Adonoi Elohenu Adonoi Echod, שְׁמַע יִשְׂרָאֵל יְהוָֹה אֱלֹהֵינוּ יְהוָֹה אֶחָד "Hear, O Israel, the Lord our God,

the Lord is One." Instead of thinking in terms of many departmentalized gods, serving under the direction of one chief god, ancient Jews thought and taught about only one God. What real difference does that make?

a. In the first place, belief in the unity of God results in greater unity among the people who worship Him. If a group of people worship many gods, some of them will have their favorites whom they especially want to please, and before long the people will be split into different factions, based on their preference of gods. When the entire people worship only one God, this possible cause of conflict is removed.

b. But belief in one God can create unity in an even deeper sense. In our review of evolution we have already seen a strong relationship among all forms of life on this earth. The statement was made in one of your readings that in a sense all the animals, plants, and human beings on earth are together members of one family. Believing in one God means understanding that one God is responsible for all the human beings living on earth, whether they be black, white, yellow or red—American, European or Asiatic—brilliant or stupid. It is easy to see that this would increase our feeling of family or kinship, and would therefore increase the possibility of peace and brotherhood on this earth.

c. There is a third great difference too. We have already seen that among ancient peoples like the Romans and Greeks various gods were thought of as symbolizing different ideals the people wanted to follow. There was, for example, a god of love, a different god of wisdom, and still a different god of strength. This meant actually that each ideal was followed separately, as each god was served separately.

Now then, very often we find ourselves in a situation or facing a problem where two or more very fine ideals conflict. For example, a number of years ago the writer of this book was making regular visits to a dear friend who was slowly dying of an incurable disease. During the period of her illness, her father, whom she had not seen in many years, died. Her doctor advised that if she were to be told of her father's death, the shock would unquestionably kill her at once. On the occasion of each visit over a long period of time she would inquire about her father's health. What should the writer have answered? To follow the ideal of *truth* would have meant to kill her by ignoring the dictates of *mercy*. To be merciful would mean prolonging her life at the expense of truth. It was humanly impossible completely to follow both mercy and truth in that situation. What would you have done?

It would be of considerable help to you in such a situation to know that according to Talmudic law one is not allowed to tell a seriously sick person about the death of a close relative, lest this news disturb him mentally and thus aggravate his illness. Jewish law in this respect is a direct outgrowth of Jewish belief in one God who symbolizes all our ethical ideals together.

If you had to face this dilemma as an ancient Greek, believing in a different god for each ideal, there would be no solution. Each separate ideal would then have been for you the equal of each other ideal, and each god would have been zealous about your strict adherence to the ideal he represented. Under those circumstances to choose either mercy or truth as the ideal of greater importance would have meant to please one god at the risk of offending the other. As a Jew, however, believing in one God who symbolizes or represents all ideals in one, you would have realized that each of life's ideals is valuable and important, not by or for itself, but only together with all other important ideals. Believing in one God means that neither truth nor mercy nor any other fine, high ideal is to be pursued alone, but that the goal of life should be to follow all of them together, each tempered and colored by all the others.

There may have been times when you recited the Sh'ma halfheartedly or mechanically, without thinking much of its meaning. Later we shall say more about this important declaration, but even now, whenever you hear or recite it, you should think of its true meaning in terms of these last few pages.

2. *The idea that God is purely spiritual, not physical.* All other ancient peoples, you will recall, thought of their gods very much as if they were supermen—human beings with unlimited power. To be sure, some of the very early Bible passages we read for this chapter sound as if the ancient Jews thought the same way. Unless we interpret poetically the passages referring to God writing with His finger, or smelling the odor of sacrifices, these references sound very much like a physical deity, do they not? It is possible, of course, that in the very earliest beginnings of our Jewish religion there was still some confusion on this point. But before long the teachers and leaders of Judaism made it clear that to them God was in no sense a human being of exaggerated power. Nor was He at all physical or material. Even some of the Bible passages which sound as if the writers thought of God as a human being do not necessarily mean exactly that. In some cases the Bible writers were using language poetically. They referred to God in human terms much as we call a ship or our country "she." Two of your readings for this chapter (D and E) will make this clear.

No doubt you remember the story of Abraham destroying the idols of his father, Terach, then blaming the destruction on the biggest idol to show his father how ridiculous it was to believe in physical gods. Abraham, remember, was the *first* Jew. Whether or not this particular incident actually occurred in his life, the fact that our ancestors ascribed it to him shows that at a very early stage of our people's history we had advanced beyond the idea of a physical deity. To be sure, from time to time ancient Jews had to be reminded of this great truth. The story of the Golden Calf (if you have forgotten it, take a quick look at Exodus 32:1-26) shows that sometimes Jews, too, sank back into a belief in a tangible, physical God. But our great religious teachers in every generation constantly reminded their fellow Jews that God is spiritual. We have already noted the advantages of our first contribution to the idea of God. In what respects was this too an improvement?

a. The first answer is obvious from the two stories mentioned above. A people which believes in physical or material gods is a people which sooner or later will make images or idols to represent those gods and which will then begin to worship the idols. Because our Jewish religion has always taught that God is spiritual, it has never permitted idolatry. It is one of the very few religions of which that can be said without reservation. Maimonides, perhaps the greatest of all Jewish philosophers and teachers, said as long as eight centuries ago that belief in an anthropomorphic god, that is, a god thought of as possessing human characteristics, leads to the danger of idolatry.

b. There is a second, and perhaps an even greater advantage to the Jewish belief in a purely spiritual God. It will be understandable to you if you recall now our earlier discussion in which we said that man is superior to all lower forms of life precisely because he has developed above the material into the spiritual area, and that it is in the further development of his soul that the great future unquestionably lies. To believe that God is spiritual means we recognize which are the most important phases of human life, and in which direction we must strive to hasten our evolution. Someone has said that a people's gods reflect what that people believes to be the most important things in life. Thus a people which believes in material gods is apt to be a group in whose lives material things are the most important. A people, on the other hand, whose God is spiritual, is apt to be one which recognizes that man's conscience, his thinking, his creative ability, are the most important things about him, the things which he must constantly cultivate.

3. *Associating God only with the ethical good.* In observing how much the gods of the Romans and Greeks were like human beings, we have already noticed that their gods were identified both with good and with evil conduct. Just as the ancient pre-

Jewish gods were thought of as having all human virtues greatly magnified, so they also possessed most human faults—likewise greatly magnified. To get around this dilemma some ancient peoples—primarily the Persians, the Norsemen, and the Indians —developed the idea of a double system of gods. One set of gods was responsible for goodness; another set was the sponsor of wickedness. Life then became a constant struggle between the gods of goodness and the gods of evil, with helpless man caught between the two.

Judaism for the first time associated the word "God" only with things which were ethically good and fine. While this may not have been unqualifiedly true in the very early stages of our religious development, it certainly became true even before the Biblical period had ended. For us God represents, sponsors, and upholds only conduct and ideals which are ethically good. As one of our ancient rabbis expressed it in the Midrash: "God never associates His name with evil but only with the good." It may have been somewhat difficult at first for you to recognize the advantages of the other two Jewish contributions to the idea of God, but in this case the great improvement is almost self-evident:

a. In every type of religion people try to pattern themselves after their gods. If a people's gods are conceived as capable of doing great wrong, what incentive is there for the people itself to pursue only goodness? If, on the contrary, God is thought of as a source only of goodness and we human beings are supposed to make ourselves as nearly as possible like Him, we have an incentive or challenge toward ethical improvement in ourselves.

And We? . . .

Here, then, are the ways in which the very early religions of mankind sought to explain the universe and human life. Here also are the great contributions or improvements in religious thinking made by our own Jewish ancestors. If this were a course in religious history, or if we had more than enough time, this chapter might be followed with several others showing how our Jewish religious thinking developed steadily through the centuries from Bible times to our own day. There was never a period when Jews stopped thinking about God or when their ideas remained exactly the same for a long time, without changing. We shall have to skip the story of how and when these changes took place, however, and after doing the workbook assignment for this chapter we shall shift our attention from past to present in order to see whether there is a modern Jewish concept or idea of God which can help us explain the universe and life in a way which will be helpful for us today.

SOMETHING FOR YOU TO READ

A. In Homer's time the gods were completely humanized. Their heavenly home on Olympus was an ideal copy of an . . . earthly court. Zeus ruled as king in a royal palace above the residences of the other immortals. In the great council chamber the gods met to discuss earthly strategy and to quarrel over their own problems. They lived the life of aristocrats, sitting on their thrones with the wine cup passing around. Divine servants attended them, Hebe, the cup-bearer, Themis, in charge of food, Paieon, the doctor, Hephaistos, the smith and builder, Athena, caring for the domestic arts, Iris, the messenger, later supplanted [replaced] by Hermes. . . .

The gods on Olympus became too completely human. In their relations with each other they were quarrelsome, deceitful, unfaithful. . . . The long series of love affairs of the king of the gods became a scandal to later generations. In morality and justice the celestial [heavenly] company fell below the standards of human society. . . .—A. Eustace Hayden, *Biography of the Gods,* The Macmillan Co.

B. In ancient times, and, in fact, until quite recently, people believed that there were many gods and that, although the gods did not look like human beings, they thought and acted just like human beings. The difference was that gods could do *anything they wanted.* Men could carry burdens, but if the burdens were too heavy for them they had to drop those burdens. Gods, however, could carry burdens no matter how heavy. Men could plant crops in their fields and if the rain and the sun and the soil were proper, the crops would come up. Gods, however, could make crops come up no matter what happened; they could *force* the sun and the rain and the soil to do *their* bidding. . . .

We must understand that in olden times people believed that they could get their gods to do difficult things for them, things which they themselves were unable to do. They depended upon the gods. Their main problem was how to win the gods over to them so that these gods would be willing to help them. They solved this problem in their own minds, by feeding the gods and flattering the gods. People believed, as we have said, that in many ways gods were like men, and therefore liked good food. Therefore these people would prepare wonderful feasts, which they would bring to their place of worship and either leave the food there for the gods to eat, or would burn the food, thinking that the sweet smell of the burning food pleased the gods.—Ira Eisenstein, *What We Mean by Religion*, Behrman House.

C. The concept that the one God is so spiritual and pure as to be indescribable by any image made by man must have been realized by certain sages and isolated thinkers in many places at many times. Yet these lofty thoughts disappeared when the thinkers died. But the prophets of Israel were never content with merely thinking of God's pure spirituality. They waged a war of the spirit against images and statues which misled men and coarsened their concept of God. Beginning with Moses they conducted a ceaseless battle against all idolatry. These pioneers wanted to create an entire *nation* of philosophers, a people in which the humblest man should learn to realize God as pure spirit. Thus they fought and struggled and wrestled with their people, forbidding them the joy of the plastic arts at least in relation to depicting God, mocking their human weaknesses, hectoring [bullying] them without respite [rest] until they became the first people on earth to learn to visualize [picture] God, the Great One, without the aid of delimiting images. Israel was the first entire people to think of God as pure spirit; thus, it helped permanently to purify the religion of all men.—Solomon B. Freehof, *The Small Sanctuary*, Union of American Hebrew Congregations.

D. All expressions concerning the description of God must never be taken literally; they are simply due to the inadequacy of human language, or "to make the ear listen to what it can hear."—Talmud.

E. Great Jewish religious philosophers, Maimonides among them, said centuries ago that many of the phrases and expressions in the Bible are visions which people saw. When they say "God walked" or "God talked," these things are dreams or visions and not to be taken literally. The Talmud says that the Bible speaks in the language of man. These ideas should give us a guide as to how we should look upon the Bible. . . .

It is evident that many of the phrases which are used about God in Scripture, such as God "speaking" with human words, or "walking," or "stretching out His hand," are not to be explained as mere primitive ideas of God. It is the natural genius of Scripture to speak of . . . God in language that is vivid to human beings. It is not that they were naive [simple] enough to think of God as having feet or hands; it was simply that God's presence was so real to them that they could not talk of Him in abstract [indefinite] terms. . . . —Solomon B. Freehof, *Preface to Scripture*, Union of American Hebrew Congregations.

F. When Rabbi Yitzhak Meir was a little boy his mother once took him to see the maggid of Koznitz. There someone said to him, "Yitzhak Meir, I'll give you a gulden if you'll tell me where God lives!"

He replied, "And I'll give you two gulden if you tell me where He doesn't!"—Buber, *Tales of the Hasidim*, Schocken Books, Inc.

7. *New Ideas and Newer*

As we turn our attention now to more modern interpretations of God and the meaning of life, it would be well to remember that there are still a great many people, apparently modern in every other respect, whose religious ideas differ very little from those of the ancients. It might surprise you to know how many adults in the world today still act almost as if God were an old man, with superhuman powers, sitting on a throne in heaven—an old man whom we had better please if we want to get along happily in life. True, civilized men and women no longer believe that the way to please God and win His favor is to offer sacrifices of animals or other human beings. But a great many people—perhaps even some whom we ourselves know—believe (or at any rate act as if they believe) that if they say nice things to God in their prayers, if they flatter Him often enough and do the things they think He likes, He will surely reward them with all the things they want.

It would be natural to suppose that the one respect in which no modern people would still subscribe to the ancient idea of God would be in worshipping more than one God; after all, some 4,000 years have passed since the Jewish people first began to teach the idea of *one* God. Yet even here, millions of civilized, modern people today don't seem to be quite sure whether they believe in one or in more than one God.

You have probably heard of the doctrine of the Trinity, accepted by most Christian denominations. This doctrine consists of a belief in God, in Jesus, and in the Holy Ghost. If you have ever attended a Christian religious service, you probably noticed that at times God and Jesus seemed to be two separate beings; at other times there is an apparent confusion between them. When, for example, Christian prayers are directed to "Lord Jesus," it is difficult to know whether it is God or Jesus who is being addressed, or whether the two are the same. Now then, while many Christians have interpreted the doctrine of the Trinity in a way which enables them to believe in only one God who shows Himself in three different ways, and while every Christian would tell you that, of course, he believes only in one God, still the idea of the Trinity is most confusing, at least to us.

Often Christians themselves find it difficult to reconcile a belief in one God with the doctrine of the Trinity. Some years ago, for example, a Catholic priest named Father Ross wrote: "Just how there can be Three Divine Persons and only one God cannot be completely explained."

In his novel, *The Moon Is Down*, John Steinbeck, in describing a military character named Captain Loft, says of him, "If he considered God at all, he thought of Him as an old and honored general, retired and gray, living among remembered battles and putting wreaths on the graves of his lieutenants several times a year." While very few people alive today actually are as crude as this in their thinking, more than a few have similar ideas of God.

Perhaps we ought to add here that the farthest thing in the world from our intentions is to ridicule anyone for his idea of God. As a matter of fact, it isn't necessary at all for everyone to have the same notion of God. The important thing is for each of us to find an interpretation which he can honestly accept, which will help explain for him the universe and human life, and which will inspire him to live a better and more useful life together with his fellow men. Any concept of God which enables a man to do that is for him a good concept. Any concept which doesn't do these things, and particularly which doesn't make him a more unselfish type of person, is not a valid religious belief, no matter how fervently he holds to it.

Through the centuries we Jews have developed our own ideas about God, ideas which have come from our people's experiences and from the religious genius of our ancestors. They differ in many respects from the God ideas of Christianity and of other faiths. This does not mean that all Jews agree in every detail of their interpretation of God. The three basic contributions of Judaism to the idea of God, which we discussed in Chapter Six, are accepted by all religious Jews, but within that framework we differ even among ourselves. When we speak, therefore, of our Jewish concept of God we mean the larger area of agreement within which there are numerous differences on detail. For most Jews today our Jewish concept of God is the most reasonable and the one which helps us live better and more complete lives. But other peoples, with different experiences and ideas, may get more inspiration from their own thoughts about God. Neither modern Jews nor modern Christians, however, can accept the kind of God idea described above or in our discussion of the ancients.

Still Puzzled

Yet we do need some intelligent explanation of the wonderful things we observed in Chapters Two through Five. We are still faced with a world of nature which is characterized by law, order, purpose and design. How shall we explain it? We still thrill to the amazing story of evolution. What causes it? The perfection of our own human bodies and the self-sacrificing courage of those who have learned to live human ideals at their very best uplift and inspire us. Who is responsible for these things?

Let us consider briefly once again our conclusions about the world of nature. We can no longer think in terms of a cabinet of departmentalized gods, each controlling one part of nature, nor can most of us still believe in even one God who decides on Tuesday that it should rain on Wednesday, but upon hearing our prayers for nice weather, decides to postpone the rain until Thursday. Neither, however, can we conclude that there is no answer, that all the order in nature is an accident or a coincidence.

Suppose you had ten pennies, each marked with a number from 1 to 10. Put them in your pocket, shake them well, then start taking them out, one at a time. What would be the likelihood of pulling them out in perfect numerical order? Well, you would obviously have one chance in ten of getting penny number 1 out first. Then your chance of getting number 2 out next, with nine pennies remaining, would be one in nine. At that point your chance of getting number 3 out in proper order would be one in eight. Your total chance of removing all ten pennies from your pocket in perfect order, without seeing them, would be one in 3,628,800. Which means to say, if you tried this trick endlessly you would probably succeed only once in each 3,628,800 attempts!

Now suppose you saw someone actually take ten such pennies and withdraw them from his pocket in proper order. You would be flabbergasted, wouldn't you? You'd say, "That was something that could happen once in a lifetime—or more accurately, once in 3,628,800 tries!" But suppose the same man tried it a second and a third time, each time with the same successful result! Would you believe it possible just through chance? Or would you immediately begin to suspect that somehow there was a plan or an intelligence which was directing or controlling the choice of pennies, that this didn't just happen through accident or coincidence?

Let's take another example. Four people are playing cards; after carefully shuffling, one of them deals the entire deck. When he finishes, each person at the table has a perfect suit! One holds thirteen clubs in his hand, one thirteen spades, one thirteen hearts, and one thirteen diamonds. According to Mr. Charles H. Goren, an expert card player and teacher, the mathematical chance of any one person being dealt thirteen cards in the same suit is one in 158,753,389,899. The odds against all four players receiving perfect hands in any deal would be about 300,000,000,000 to 1. Very rarely does it actually happen that such a perfect deal occurs; when it does, the event is so unusual that it is reported prominently in all our newspapers. Now suppose a man managed to deal perfect hands like that all evening—or even five times in a week. We would all of us immediately conclude that there was something going on here that we didn't fully understand, but obviously it wasn't just chance. Either the dealer or some other person with intelligence and a plan had something to do with the result.

More Wonderful than Pennies and Cards

Do you begin to see our point? The things we observed several chapters back about the universe and ourselves are millions of times more wonderful and unusual than either example above. The probability of this planet breaking from the sun and cooling to exactly the right temperature, of the first protozoan appearing somewhere beneath the water, of evolution developing through thousands of danger points from one cell to the brain of Albert Einstein, of the planets moving in perfect order, of our own bodies operating almost perfectly to keep us alive and developing—the probability of all this happening merely through accident or coincidence is unbelievable. We are forced to conclude that somewhere in this whole, vast, wonderful process there must be some kind of power or spirit or force or intelligence. We have to use so many words for this power or force because none of us knows exactly what it is. But we do know that it must exist, and in order not to use so many different words whenever we think of it, we call this spirit God.

A world-renowned zoologist, Julian Huxley, once tried to calculate statistically the odds against a horse developing in evolution from a protozoan, purely by chance. The figure he arrived at was 1, followed by three million zeros! Just to write that figure down would require three large books of about 500 pages each! And remember—this estimate deals with evolution only up to the appearance of the horse, long before the development of man's soul, the most impressive product of evolution! This is the kind of data which leads many scientists to the conclusion that far from having occurred accidentally or by chance, evolution is a plan being worked out by a force or power too great for the human mind fully to understand.

A few years ago Dr. David Grant, a famous physician, stated pretty much the same conclusion in his own scientific terms. While dissecting a human corpse and lecturing to a class of medical students, he stopped, turned to them, and said, "Gentlemen, here in this human organism is a complete refutation of what is called atheism. No reasonable being can look upon the miraculous construction and arrangement of organs in this body without acknowledging that some Creative Power above and beyond human comprehension must have been responsible for them. . . . It seems to me that doctors, above all others, should be truly religious, dealing constantly as they do with this inexplicable miracle. When I say that doctors should be religious I mean they should be humble, prayerful men who recognize that a Supreme Power operates in human affairs."

Johannes Kepler was one of the greatest of medieval astronomers. He once said that looking through his telescope at the stars as they moved in their courses made him feel as if he were "thinking the thoughts of God after Him." What do you think he meant? How would you say the same thing in your own words?

We have just used the examples of the pennies and the cards to illustrate our meaning. In an earlier chapter we mentioned the examples of a piano, a manuscript and a watch. Others have used different but equally effective illustrations. The story is told, for instance, of the unbeliever who came to Rabbi Akiba nearly two thousand years ago asking for proof that there is a God. Akiba in reply pointed to the man's coat and asked him who made it. The man answered, "Why, a weaver, of course." Akiba said he wouldn't believe him unless he could offer proof. Whereupon the man became greatly impatient and shouted, "Why should I have to prove to you that a weaver made this coat? Isn't it obvious the coat couldn't have made itself?" Then the learned and patient rabbi explained that the same thing must be true of our world and all the wonderful things in it; they too could not have created themselves; there must be a God who is responsible for all this, even as there had to be a weaver responsible for the coat.

A great modern Christian preacher, Dr. Harry Emerson Fosdick, once said that Robinson Crusoe knew there was another human being on his island long before he saw the man Friday. The minute he saw one human footprint on the sand, he knew it couldn't have been caused accidentally by the action of the waves; there *had to be* another human being there to make it. In much the same way, after surveying all the "footprints" we have seen in the universe and in life we conclude that there just *has to be* some force or power which caused and still causes all this.

It isn't just in the realm of religion that we sometimes accept the existence of certain realities which we haven't seen, because we know their consequences or results. If you walked by a pond and saw on its surface a series of freshly-made circles spreading outward from a center, you would know that something had fallen into the water, even though you hadn't seen anything fall. You wouldn't know unless you had been there whether someone had thrown a stone into the water, or an apple had fallen from the overhanging branch of a tree, or just what the object had been. But you would not doubt for an instant that *something* had to fall into that pond to cause the ripples. Similarly, we know that there must be some force or power which has caused all the facts it took us four chapters to describe.

The same is true in science. Science accepts the reality of many things that cannot be seen by the human eye. We are able actually to see only a very small proportion of the light rays existing in our world. Infra-red rays, for example, are too long to be "caught" by our eyes, though their heat can be felt by the nerve endings of the skin. Ultra-violet rays and X-rays, on the other hand, are too short to be seen by the eye, but can be detected by their effects on photographic plates. We are sure of the existence of these long and short light waves, in other words, because we can see or feel their effects. No one has ever seen an electron. Nor has anyone ever seen an atom with his eye. Yet scientists are agreed that there must be such things as electrons and atoms, because assuming that they exist is the only way they can explain other things which they have observed. Similarly in religion, assuming that some kind of power called God exists in this universe is the only way for us to explain the many wonders which we can actually see and prove.

The New and the Old

What, then, is the greatest difference between our way of explaining things and our ancestors' way? This is another way of asking: what is the most outstanding difference between their concept of God and ours? The answer is to be found in that long word we used in the last chapter, the word *personification*. At first, primitive men couldn't think even of stones and trees except as persons of some kind; that was when their religion was one of animism. Each of us has gone through the same stage of development in his own life. Little children think of their dolls and wagons and spinning tops as *persons;* sometimes they even talk to their toys. Later they mature to the point of knowing the difference between a *person* and a *thing*.

When you were little, it was difficult for you to understand words like love or hate or how a thought could exist without being something you could touch or see. As you grew older, you were able to understand these things. After primitive men—in much the same way—had reached the point where they could understand rocks and stones as *things* rather than *persons*, for many centuries they still weren't able to think of the wonderful force or power in this universe as anything but a *Person*. That's why their descriptions of God so often sound like a human being of unlimited power and strength.

There are people today also who think of God in terms of personality, though not as the kind of physical person accepted by primitive men. In an earlier chapter we discussed the difference between body and soul in human beings, recognizing that the body is the physical part of an individual, while the soul is the spiritual or non-physical part of him. Obviously, the soul is just as much part of a man's personality as is his body. My conscience for example—clearly a part of my soul—helps make my personality what it is.

Some modern religious people believe the same thing to be true regarding the universe and God. They would say that all the physical things we can see, touch, hear, or smell in the world of nature constitute the "body," so to speak, of our universe, while God is the non-physical part or the "soul" of the universe. They would add that just as a human being's soul is part of his personality, so God is the personality of the universe, though not a physical person.

Those who today still believe that God has what we generally call personality have reached that conclusion also through a consideration of evolution. They would remind us that the highest development in evolution thus far is conscious personality. A protozoan is not conscious of itself; it does not know that it exists. Neither does a tree. A dog knows that it exists but does not have the same kind of consciousness that a human being has. By this we mean that a dog is not conscious of itself as part of something larger, nor can a dog consciously choose between good and evil, as human beings can. In other words, evolution has developed upward through many, many centuries to the human level, which is the level of conscious personality. This is a somewhat different way of repeating that only human beings have a spiritual aspect, a soul.

Now many people would conclude that if God is the force or power responsible for evolution and if evolution has reached a level which includes personality, then God too must have personality and must be conscious of Himself. They might add that just as every characteristic of a flower must exist potentially in the seed which produces the flower, so every characteristic—past, present or future—of evolution must exist, potentially at least, as a characteristic of God.

Others among us, however, now think of God as a creative force, spirit, or power, without picturing Him as a person or thinking of Him in terms of personality. They would offer electricity as an example. The only form, of course, in which primitive men knew electricity was through lightning. At once they assumed there must be a person in the sky who was responsible for the lightning. Later they developed an understanding that it wasn't a person at all; it was a process. When you were a very little child, every time a light or a radio was turned on you may have thought there was a person in the bulb or the box, directly causing the light or the sound. Little by little you learned that electricity and radio are *processes* or *forces,* not individuals or persons. That didn't make them less valuable or helpful in your life; it merely changed your way of understanding and explaining them.

So there are religious people today who say that it is no longer necessary for them to use the concept either of person or of personality in thinking about God. What is important to them is that they recognize God as an enormous power in the universe and in themselves—a power which they can use and which can help them. Reading Selection E for this chapter will explain this point of view further.

The most important part of this discussion is to remember that even those modern men and women who think of God as a personality no longer believe Him to be a physical person, as primitive people did. This is the most essential difference between the older and newer ways of interpreting God.

We must remember also that recognizing the existence of God is more important than disagreeing on whether or not He possesses personality. Judaism, as a matter of fact, has spent far less time trying to describe or define God than most other religions have. We believe that more important than quarreling about what God is like is recognizing that He exists and that those who believe in Him are obliged to live in a special way.

If there are parts of this discussion which you find difficult to understand, bear in mind that no human being has ever been able to describe exactly what God is like. Each of us is so small a part of the power responsible for our universe that none of us can understand or describe God fully. When we look at the sun with our naked eye, its brightness is so great that it blinds us. We know beyond doubt that the sun is there, but because its light is too intense for the human eye, we cannot see exactly its size or shape. (See Reading Selection K.) Similarly, when we try to describe God our little minds are seeking to comprehend a power far too great for us to see or to know exactly. We know that God exists, but we find it difficult to describe what He is like.

This is something of what the great Jewish philosopher, Maimonides, must have had in mind back in the twelfth century when he said that we can only describe God in negative terms. That is to say, we can describe what God is *not*, but we do not know precisely what He *is*. Maimonides added that there are only two positive descriptions we can give of God. We know definitely (1) that God *lives*, and (2) that He is *one*. If so great a religious teacher as Maimonides found it that difficult to describe God, we need not be too dismayed at our own inability to be exact.

Did God Create the World?

Even if you haven't looked at the first chapter of Genesis for a long time, you undoubtedly remember how the Bible explains the creation of the world. Later in our course we shall actually read the entire story as a class assignment. For the time being, however, all we need keep in mind is the traditional account of how God created the world, all the plants and animals, finally Adam and Eve, then rested on the seventh day. It is easy to understand how God could have created the world if we think of God as an all-powerful person who could make things the way a potter, let us say, takes clay and makes a vase. But how will we explain the creation of the world if our idea of God is that of a force or power?

We simply interpret the Bible story to mean that the creative power called God, which is responsible for all the beauty and wonder and order of the world and its life, existed even before there was a sun or an earth, animals or plants or human beings. Though we are far from understanding all that happened or exactly how it happened, it is our belief that this power caused our earth to begin, that it caused the first protozoan to appear and then to develop through millions and millions of years. We believe not that God is a person who created everything in six days, but that God is a power which has been creating things for billions of years, is still creating today, and will continue to create always.

An ancient Jewish poet came very close to expressing our modern meaning of God creating the world when he wrote in one of the psalms:

> Lord, Thou has been our dwelling-place in all generations.
> Before the mountains were brought forth,
> Or ever Thou hadst formed the earth and the world,
> Even from everlasting to everlasting, Thou art God.

And one of our Jewish morning prayers also expresses the idea of never-ending creation by God: . . . u-v'tuvo m'chadesh b'chol yom tomid ma-asei v'reshis, וּבְטוּבוֹ מְחַדֵּשׁ בְּכָל

יום תָּמִיד מַעֲשֵׂה בְרֵאשִׁית "and in His goodness renews daily the work of creation."

In the early nineteenth century Rabbi Hayim ben Isaac explained this prayer by saying that a man who erects a building does so by taking certain materials and using his own power to arrange them in proper order. Once the building is finished, it remains standing even after the builder removes his power. But God's relationship to the universe is different. His Power, which was necessary for the universe to be created in the first place, is still essential continually for the universe to endure and for evolution to go on developing. This is comparable, we might add, to saying that the power of electricity is necessary not only to turn a light on in the first place, but also to keep it burning. Much the same thought was in the mind of the Chasidic rabbi who wrote: "The universe is always in an uncompleted state. . . . It is not like a vessel at which the master works and he finishes it; it requires continuous labor and unceasing renewal by creative forces. Were there a second's pause by these forces, the universe would return to primeval [original] chaos."

One more kind of question should be raised here before we conclude this chapter. We have been speaking about a modern Jewish interpretation of God with relation to the world of nature. In the next chapter we shall turn our attention to some of the other aspects of God. In connection with nature, however, these questions:

In the White Mountains of New Hampshire there are two remarkable stone formations which you may have seen. One, which is called *Old Man of the Mountains,* is a cliff which exactly resembles the side view of a human face. It has never been touched by anyone to make it look that way; it is entirely a natural formation of rock. The other, nearby, is called *Indian Head;* another natural phenomenon, it looks just like the profile of an Indian, feather hat and all. Now for our question: should we list these as examples of Order and Purpose in our universe? Are they examples of Accident or Disorder? Do you think God deliberately fashioned these rocks in a way that would make them resemble human heads? Think about this and be prepared to give your answer in the workbook.

Farther south in the same state of New Hampshire (you guessed it; this book was written during several summers in that state) is a beautiful spot called Cathedral of the Pines. It was the favorite hill of a young World War II army lieutenant who lived near there. The view from that place, over mountains and forests and lakes, is so perfectly beautiful it leaves one speechless. When he left for the army, Sandy Sloane vowed that upon his return he would build his home on that hill, because whenever he was downhearted or depressed he would go there, sometimes to pray, sometimes just to meditate, and he would always feel inspired. Tragically, Sandy Sloane never returned; he was killed in a bomber over Germany. His parents subsequently built on that spot an outdoor cathedral in his memory. Its altars are built of stones coming from every state in the Union and from most of the battle-fields of the war. Every Sunday people of all denominations come there for religious services under the pine trees. No synagogue or church could be more truly inspiring.

Now then—before the hurricane of 1938 no one even knew what a marvelously inspiring view could be obtained from that spot, because it was completely and thickly covered with pine trees of great height; all one could see were tree trunks and pine needles. The hurricane of 1938 blew down scores of trees, cleared off the plateau at the edge of that cliff as if intentionally to build a cathedral there, and opened the view which so thrilled Sandy Sloane and the thousands who have come there to worship. Our question: Do you think God cleared off that plateau because He wanted to have a place there for people to pray? What makes you answer as you do? What are your reasons? Did God arrange for Sandy to be killed, in order that a cathedral might be built there instead of a home, enabling so many people to be inspired by that beauty instead of only one family?

There are many additional questions to be asked about our modern interpretation of God, but you will be better able to consider them in the next chapter.

SOMETHING FOR YOU TO READ

(Our first three Reading Selections for this chapter consist of excerpts from three psalms in our Bible. You probably know that the Psalms are ancient songs, originally sung in the Temple at Jerusalem. They include some of the most eloquently beautiful religious poetry ever written. You will be asked to interpret these Bible selections in your workbook.)

A. From Psalm 19:

The heavens declare the glory of God,
And the firmament showeth His handiwork;
Day unto day uttereth speech,
And night unto night revealeth knowledge;

B. From Psalm 65:

Thou hast remembered the earth,
and watered her, greatly enriching her,
With the river of God that is full of water;
. . . Thou makest her soft with showers;
Thou blessest the growth thereof.
Thou crownest the year with Thy goodness;
And Thy paths drop fatness.
The pastures of the wilderness do drop;
And the hills are girded with joy.
The meadows are clothed with flocks;
The valleys also are covered over with corn;
They shout for joy, yea, they sing.

C. From Psalm 104:

O Lord my God, Thou art very great;
Thou art clothed with glory and majesty.
Who coverest Thyself with light as with a garment,
Who stretchest out the heavens like a curtain;
Who layest the beams of Thine upper chambers in the waters,
Who makest the clouds Thy chariot,
Who walkest upon the wings of the wind;
Who makest winds Thy messengers,
The flaming fire Thy ministers.

Who didst establish the earth upon its foundations,
That it should not be moved for ever and ever;

Thou didst cover it with the deep as with a vesture;
The waters stood above the mountains.
At Thy rebuke they fled,
At the voice of Thy thunder they hasted away—
The mountains rose, the valleys sank down—
Unto the place which Thou hadst founded for them;
Thou didst set a bound which they should not pass over,
That they might not return to cover the earth.

Who sendest forth springs into the valleys;
They run between the mountains;
They give drink to every beast of the field,
The wild asses quench their thirst.
Beside them dwell the fowl of the heaven,
From among the branches they sing.
Who waterest the mountains from Thine upper chambers;
The earth is full of the fruit of Thy works.

Who causest the grass to spring up for the cattle,
And herb for the service of man;
To bring forth bread out of the earth,
And wine that maketh glad the heart of man,
Making the face brighter than oil,
And bread that stayeth man's heart. . . .

Who appointedst the moon for seasons;
The sun knoweth his going down.
Thou makest darkness, and it is night,
Wherein all the beasts of the forest do creep forth.
The young lions roar after their prey,
And seek their food from God.
The sun ariseth, they slink away,
And couch in their dens.
Man goeth forth unto his work
And to his labour until the evening.
How manifold are Thy works, O Lord!
In wisdom hast Thou made them all;
The earth is full of Thy creatures.

D.

Let Earth unbalanced from her orbit fly,
Planets and Suns run lawless through the sky;
Let ruling angels from their spheres be hurled,

Beings on Beings wrecked, and world on world . . .
So, wondrous creature, mount where Science guides;
Go, measure Earth, weigh air, and state the tides;
Instruct the planets in what orbs to run,
Correct old Time, and regulate the Sun. . . .
—Alexander Pope, *An Essay on Man.*

E. Now, we cannot actually picture *goodness.* It is not a being; it is a force, like electricity. Nobody ever actually saw electricity. We know that it exists. We can see and feel what electricity does. If we have an electric bulb and connect it with an electric wire, we get light. If we have an electric heater and connect it, we get heat. If we have an electric motor and attach it to a vehicle, we get the vehicle to move. In other words, we get to know what electricity is by *what it does.* In the same way, we get to know what God is by what God makes us do: when a person is, so to speak, connected with God, he does good things. We call that person a *godly* person, and his act is a *godly* act. Whenever this force is active, we say that God has exercised influence and power.—Ira Eisenstein, *What We Mean by Religion,* Behrman House.

F. Science cannot yet really "explain" electricity, magnetism, and gravitation; their effects can be measured and predicted, but of their ultimate [final . . . elementary] nature no more is known to the modern scientist than to Thales of Miletus, who first speculated on the electrification of amber around 585 B.C. Most contemporary physicists reject the notion that man can ever discover what these mysterious forces "really" are. "Electricity," Bertrand Russell says, "is not a thing, like St. Paul's Cathedral; it is a way in which things behave. When we have told how things behave when they are electrified, and under what circumstances they are electrified, we have told all there is to tell."—Lincoln Barnett, *The Universe and Dr. Einstein,* William Sloane Associates.

G.

Wheresoe'er I turn mine eyes
Around on earth or toward the skies,
I see Thee in the starry field,
I see Thee in the harvest's yield,
In every breath, in every sound,
An echo of Thy name is found.
The blade of grass, the simple flower,
Bear witness to Thy matchless pow'r.

My every thought, Eternal God of Heaven,
Ascends to Thee, to whom all praise be given.

—Abraham ibn Ezra—Abraham E. Millgram, *An Anthology of Medieval Hebrew Literature*, Associated Talmud Torahs of Philadelphia.

H. Abraham was absorbed by the vastness, the orderliness of the universe. Studying the skies, he thought at first that the sun must be the power to regulate it, and to direct it all. But evening came, and again looking at the skies he saw that the sun had disappeared. Perhaps the moon, he then thought, was this directing force. But again, on the morrow, he observed that the moon was no more and that the sun had again taken its place. Thus contemplating the cosmos [universe], he came to the conclusion that there must be a Power higher and above all these powers visible to the eye who rules and guides the order of the universe.—Louis I. Newman, *Talmudic Anthology*, Behrman House.

I. The Burning Bush:

And the angel of the Lord appeared unto him in a flame
of fire out of the midst of a bush.
A heathen asked Rabbi Joshua ben Karhah:
"Why did the Holy One, blessed be He, choose to speak
to Moses out of the midst of a thornbush?"
The rabbi answered him:
"Had it been out of the midst of a carob tree or out of
the midst of a sycamore, you would have asked the
same question.
Still, I cannot send you away empty-handed.
Well then: Why out of the midst of a thornbush?
To teach you that there is no place void of the
Presence of God, not even a thornbush!"

—Midrash, quoted in Nahum M. Glatzer, *In Time and Eternity*, Schocken Books, Inc.

J. From Psalm 139:

Whither shall I go from Thy spirit?
Or whither shall I flee from Thy presence?
If I ascend up into heaven, Thou art there;
If I make my bed in the nether-world, behold,
Thou art there.
If I take the wings of the morning,
And dwell in the uttermost parts of the sea;

Even there would Thy hand lead me,
And Thy right hand would hold me.
And if I say: "Surely the darkness shall envelop me,
And the light about me shall be night";
Even the darkness is not too dark for Thee,
But the night shineth as the day;
The darkness is even as the light.

K. Thus it is related in a Talmudic anecdote that the emperor had said to Rabbi Joshua ben Hananiah: "I desire to behold your God." Rabbi Joshua explained to him that it was impossible. When the emperor persisted, the rabbi asked him to stand in a fixed gaze at the sun. The emperor found the sun too strong. Thereupon the rabbi exclaimed: "You admit that you are unable to look at the sun, which is only one of the ministering servants of the Holy One, blessed be He; how much more beyond your power of vision is God Himself."—Bokser, *The Wisdom of the Talmud*, Philosophical Library.

8. *God and You*

Does our last chapter make God seem very awesome, very impressive, but also very distant? It wouldn't be surprising in the least if, at this point, you felt like saying, "I'm certainly impressed by this interpretation of God as a wonderful creative power which operates at all times in the planets and stars, through the course of evolution, and even in my own physical body. But God as described here seems to work automatically. Doesn't God have anything to do with my own daily conduct, with my actions, my thoughts and my prayers? I always used to think of God as being very close to me; this discussion makes Him seem far removed."

The answer to such doubts as these is that Chapter Seven discussed only one part of the modern meaning of God. It dealt only with God as the force or power which is responsible for all the order, purpose and design we observed in our survey of the universe. But remember, there were other conclusions we reached also in earlier chapters. We made mention of all the inspiring ethical ideals to be found in human life, of the courage and self-sacrifice with which truly great men and women devote themselves to those ideals, and of the fact that apparently "something" in this universe seems to sustain us or help us as we strive toward our ethical goals. It shouldn't surprise you by now to learn that God is related to all this also.

To begin with, the evidence we have already examined indicates there is a *moral power* operating in human life, which can be compared to such natural laws as the law of gravity. It is this moral power which accounts for the fact that so often in history the nation or group which upheld the right was vindicated, even though it may have been so much weaker and smaller than its opponent group. The moral power of this universe apparently operates in such manner that *in the long run* any individual or group which does not abide by ethical rules and laws is doomed to disaster. Please note carefully that phrase, *in the long run.* Many people make the mistake of thinking that each of us is supposed to be punished for every little individual act of evil we commit. Then, when they see that some person who has been guilty of iniquity seems to have "gotten away" with it, they foolishly conclude that there is no moral power in the world.

Furthermore, we do not mean to imply that every time an individual suffers some tragedy or misfortune, it must be punishment for his wickedness, or that every person who enjoys happiness and good fortune must thereby be assumed to be a righteous individual. The moral power just doesn't operate that way. Sometimes good people suffer a great deal; at other times evil people seem, at least for a time, to be prospering. One never knows, however, what pangs of conscience may be afflicting the person who has done wrong without any apparent punishment. Nor can we always tell what the consequences will be *in the long run.*

Notwithstanding exceptions, however, and despite many questions to which we have no answer at present, the fact remains that in most cases continued disobedience of ethical rules and laws sooner or later brings unhappiness or disaster upon the guilty person or group. This is what our ancestors meant when they spoke of God as "visiting the iniquities of the fathers upon the children unto the third and fourth generation of them that hate Me, and showing mercy unto the thousandth generation of them that love Me and keep My commandments."

Sometimes that statement seems somewhat harsh to us, but sober reflection shows us that it is simply a straightforward description of how the world actually operates. If a man is guilty of sexual immorality, as a result of which he contracts a sex disease, it is literally true that his sins are visited upon his children and perhaps his children's children. If a person murders or cheats or steals, sooner or later not only he but his family and children also are apt to pay the consequences. If an individual carries the weight of serious wrong-doing on his conscience—even though he may apparently be prosperous and happy—sooner or later he is likely to suffer discomfort or mental illness which far exceeds any pleasure or benefit he expected to achieve through his unethical conduct. Reading Selection O for this chapter will help you see how this truth about moral power is valid even in situations which seem to be exceptions.

The well-known Jewish writer, Sholem Asch, has written an interesting novel on the theme of the mental suffering that can be caused by unethical conduct. It is entitled *Passage in the Night*. You may wish to read it.

If a people so far forgets the difference between right and wrong as to support and follow a man like Hitler, even though for a time they may seem to succeed, eventually they will meet disaster and defeat, after which they and their children for several generations may have to pay the price. Or—to illustrate on an even wider scale—if all humanity loses sight of moral truths for an entire generation, as we did between 1918 and 1939, the result of disobeying the moral law is that we must suffer through another terrible war, as we did from 1939 to 1945.

Although the direct cause of World War II was Hitler's aggression, in a sense all the civilized nations were responsible for it. If we had not allowed the conditions which created Hitler to exist in Europe, or if we had cared enough about the difference between right and wrong not to help Hitler and Mussolini remain in power at the beginning, the war would probably have been averted.

The same thing is true regarding the spread of Communism as an evil force in the world. If governments had observed the rules of ethics in treating their peoples justly and fairly, if the richer and the stronger nations had been ethical in providing enough food and clothing and democratic opportunity to the inhabitants of backward colonial areas, Communism could never have grown as it did after World War II.

Sometimes people speak of *ethical* considerations and *practical* considerations as if the two were inconsistent. But those who understand how God operates as the moral power of the universe realize that in actual fact ethical behavior is the only really practical way to survive. An example of this may be seen in the elimination of racial segregation from the United States Armed Forces. Almost without exception, Negroes were segregated in units of their own all the way through World War II. One of the few exceptions occurred in the final stage of the war in Europe, during the so-called Battle of the Bulge, when for a time it appeared that the last desperate lunge of the German armies would succeed.

The situation became so desperate for the American army that it was imperative for Negro troops to be rushed into the breach, to fight alongside white troops. Breaking down the walls of segregation was obviously an instance of cooperating with God's moral power. Had this not been done, many thousands of additional American men would have lost their lives. Because it was done—because our American army did the ethically right thing—the tide was turned in our favor and the European part of World War II soon came to an end.

After our victory the United States army and navy embarked upon a concerted effort to eliminate all segregation. The first large-scale test of racially mixed troops in combat came during the fighting in Korea. There our army learned conclusively that ethical procedure is the only fully practical procedure. For even those officers who at first were opposed to the elimination of segregation had to agree that this cooperation with the moral power has resulted in increased combat efficiency on the part of both Negro and white soldiers.

Gravity and Ethics

This is what we mean by the moral power in our universe. We believe that it operates as firmly—even though not as immediately or obviously—as the law of gravity. No man can defy the law of gravity without paying the consequences. If a person is foolish enough to stand on top of the Empire State Building and say, "I refuse to recognize the law of gravity. I deny and defy it"—and if he then follows through by stepping out into space, you know the inevitable result. It will be his last chance ever to do any defying. Similarly, an individual or group can refuse to recognize the moral power and try to evade it, *but in the long run,* the result will be as disastrous, though in a different way, as jumping from the tallest building in the world. One of your Reading Selections for this chapter expresses the similarity we have referred to here between the operation of natural law and moral law.

A word of caution is necessary before we continue our discussion. Many people, in speaking of the operation of moral power in human life, think exclusively in terms of material "punishment" and "reward." They assume that a person who lives ethically will enjoy good health, long life, a high income, etc. This is not always or necessarily true. The individual who, by and large, lives ethically, is "rewarded" in a far more important sense than material success. He achieves an inner satisfaction and happiness, a sense of fulfilling the purpose of being born as a human being, a feeling that he has helped advance evolution to the next stage ethically and spiritually. Even though this kind of feeling cannot be counted or measured like money, it is one of the greatest sources of happiness in human life. A person who has attained only material wealth without ever having known this kind of happiness has missed one of the most wonderful satisfactions of human existence.

Now then, this moral power we have been discussing couldn't have been just an accident or a coincidence, any more than the other evidences of order and purpose we have noted could be. Judaism teaches that the same great power or intelligence or force which is responsible for all the natural laws of the universe also accounts for this moral power. This is another way in which we see the power of God in operation. Matthew Arnold came very close to expressing this point of view when he described God as "the Power, not ourselves, that makes for righteousness." That's one of the greatest phrases ever written or spoken in the realm of religious truth. It is worth repeating: "—the Power, not ourselves, that makes for righteousness." Here is another modern meaning of God.

It is, then, the power responsible for the moral law which makes it possible for our highest ideals to prevail. If the universe were not properly constructed in terms of air, temperature, oxygen, etc. (which is another way of saying: if there were no God), we human beings would find it physically impossible to live and grow and evolve on this earth. If the universe were not governed by a power which operates the moral law (which is still another way of saying: if there were no God), our striving to live ethically would be difficult and discouraging; we would have no assurance that our ethical ideals can be achieved.

One of the fundamental beliefs of Judaism has always been that because of the moral power, human beings *can* make ethical progress, that we *can* develop to higher and higher levels ethically, even as we have done physically through the millions of years of evolution. Our ancestors expressed this confidence of theirs in the universe—this faith that with our own effort ethical progress is possible—through their belief in the Messiah. Briefly, they held that some day in the future a Messiah (meaning Anointed One) would be born. He would be a descendant of

King David and would miraculously usher in an era of perfect peace and harmony, a time when all our ethical ideals would be realized and there would be no more war or hate or strife. You must be familiar already with one of the most beautiful descriptions of the conditions which the Messiah would bring about, the description of the prophet Micah, which you will find among your Reading Selections for this chapter.

Christianity borrowed the Messiah idea of Judaism; in fact, Christianity is founded upon this belief. The principal difference between Christianity and Orthodox Judaism, as far as belief in the Messiah is concerned, is one of timing. Christians believe the Messiah has already appeared on earth, that his name was Jesus. While no Jews accept Jesus as the Messiah, many Orthodox Jews still confidently await the arrival of one man who will be a miraculous Messiah.

Modern Judaism has significantly changed the old Jewish expectation of a Messiah. Many of us no longer anticipate the actual birth of a miraculous individual who will usher in the realization of all our high ideals. We believe instead in the coming of the Messianic Era; which means to say, we are confident that it is possible for all humanity together, led by our greatest heroes of the spirit, gradually to work in cooperation with the moral power, until the vision of Micah will be realized. Despite discouragement and doubt, we have faith that this is possible. This modern Jewish belief is closely akin to a Chasidic teaching. One of the Chasidic rabbis was asked when he expected the Messiah to arrive. He answered that he did not expect the Messiah at all. When his disciples gave voice to their amazement, he explained that every one of us has within himself a spark of the Messiah. It is only when we all put together our little sparks that the Messiah can be said to have come. This is quite different from both the Christian and the Orthodox Jewish views.

Here, then, in our modern interpretation of the Messiah, we have another of the ways in which the great power of God is seen to operate—in terms of the moral law which makes ethical progress and evolution possible.

God in History

One more word is necessary here before we leave the relationship between God and moral power. Both in this chapter and Chapter Five we have noticed how often in history a weaker group has prevailed over a stronger one because the former was more ethical. What we have actually done in observing examples of this is to note that God can be seen in human history and experience quite as much as in the world of nature. We have turned most of our attention thus far to nature because this is an area easier to observe and closer to the actual life of young people. But it would be a serious mistake to forget that God operates through history just as much as through nature.

It has been a great contribution of Judaism, as a matter of fact, to stress history more than nature in thinking of God. In a way this is understandable, since we Jews have so often had to struggle in history against more powerful groups to uphold that which was ethically right.

The emphasis of Judaism on God in history may be seen in the way our forefathers shifted the major meaning of many Jewish holidays. Take Passover, for example. In the beginning Passover was a nature festival, established to mark the beginning of spring and the planting season. Its celebration, therefore, reminded Jews of God as the power behind nature. In the course of time, however, Passover became more an occasion for commemorating the Exodus of the ancient Hebrew slaves from Egypt. This placed the chief emphasis of its celebration on God as the power behind the moral law which upholds those who strive to live ethically and which helps them achieve freedom.

The same thing is true of Shovuos, which was originally a nature holiday marking the harvest of early spring grains, and of Sukos, which at first celebrated only the fall harvest season. In the course of Judaism's development Shovuos became primarily a holiday on which to remember the giving of the Ten Commandments at Mount Sinai, while Sukos came to remind us of our ancestors' forty-year journey through the wilderness.

To be sure, we have by no means forgotten or ignored the original meanings of these holidays. We still recognize God as the power behind every aspect of nature. But we perceive God also as a great force supporting man's ethical strivings in history.

Our Jewish prophets in Bible times interpreted every important event in the history of their people in terms of God and the operation of His moral power. Thus they said the little band of unarmed Hebrew slaves who escaped from mighty Egypt were able to succeed only because they were cooperating with the moral power of the universe while the Egyptians were not. That is why, in order for them to establish a nation of their own, Moses had to take them first to Mt. Sinai, where they received the Torah, which taught them how to live ethically, in cooperation with God.

Likewise, when Assyria conquered the Northern Kingdom of Israel in 721 B.C.E., the prophets declared this disaster was due to the people's failure to live ethical lives, and warned that if the Southern Kingdom of Judah did not reform, the same thing would happen there. Their prediction came true when Judah was conquered by Babylonia in 586 B.C.E. The prophets insisted that any society or nation which fails to cooperate with God as the moral power of life eventually becomes weakened to the point where it cannot survive. Thus they saw God operating in history no less than in nature.

It is important to remember that despite these several ways of seeing how God exists, the wisest person in the world does not even begin to know everything about God. Our hope in the first nine chapters of this book is to understand as much as we can about God through our experience and our reasoning. But God is in part beyond everything we are able to experience or observe. This is true in other important areas of life too, quite aside from religion. No one can explain fully on a basis of reason and fact alone why he prefers one painting or poem to another or why he is in love with one person in preference to all others. We are able to follow reason and facts only up to a certain point, beyond which we may feel such things as love very strongly in our hearts without being able very fully to explain them.

This is especially true with respect to our belief in God. Reason, experience—the things we see and understand in the universe and in our lives—lead us to the conclusion there must be a God. As Jews we could not believe in God unless reason and experience convinced us of His existence. But our faith in God—like our love of parents now and of sweethearts later—goes much deeper and farther than anything we can "prove" in a laboratory.

The Still, Small Voice

> Well, this idea of a little bit of the Messiah in each of us mentioned a few paragraphs back begins to sound as if God isn't quite so distantly removed from us, doesn't it? Is there any of the power responsible for the moral law in each of us? Did you ever feel anything within yourself which seemed to be helping you live by the moral law? What's that? You say you think you have, but you can't quite identify it. Can anyone give us a name for the "something" inside us which apparently is part of that power? That's it! You're absolutely right—it's *conscience,* of course! You may never have thought of it just that way before, but your conscience is actually part of the "Power . . . that makes for righteousness."

Needless to say, we aren't the first to think of that. You may remember the Bible story of how the prophet Elijah searched for God. He knew that God was the power behind nature, so when a strong wind began to blow, he thought he would find God in it. But the Bible tells us, "the Lord was not in the wind." Then an earthquake came, and Elijah was certain he would find God there. But "the Lord was not in the earthquake" either. Then a fire, but God wasn't in the fire. Finally after the fire, Elijah heard "a still, small voice" and God was there. Having already seen God working many times before as the power behind nature, Elijah now discovered Him also as the still, small voice of his own conscience.

Modern people too have discovered the same truth. A six-year-old boy once told his father he had discovered that "God is what's good in me." A young girl once spoke of the "*have to* that's inside of me." These are both ways of saying that God may be found not only in the planets and in evolution, but also within ourselves, as our conscience. Perhaps it will help you understand how God can be both outside and inside you, if for a moment you think in terms of air. This whole planet is surrounded by air, isn't it? The farther we climb or fly from the earth's surface, the thinner the air becomes. But for miles around the entire planet there is air. At any given moment, however, there is also a quantity of air in your lungs. The air in your lungs isn't different from the air outside; neither does drawing more air into your lungs diminish the amount of air available for others to breathe (unless, of course, you're sitting in a small, crowded room). In the same way, your conscience, as the little bit of God which is within you, is part of the power we find everywhere in the universe.

A slightly different example of the same truth was given by one of the great Rabbis in Talmudic times. After reviewing what he said in your Reading Selections for this chapter, you should be better able to understand how God can at one and the same moment be everywhere in the universe and also inside yourself.

Let's carry this idea of a little bit of God in each of us a step farther. Some time before we are ready to discuss this question in class you will be asked to bring with you a picture of yourself between the ages of one and four. We will have a lot of fun in class passing some of these pictures around trying to identify them. Unless your group is a most unusual one, there will be many pictures which won't look a bit like their proud possessors. All of you will have changed enormously since these pictures were taken. That, obviously, is because all of you have grown.

What caused you to grow since this picture was snapped? Many things, of course. But above all, there seems to be something in each of us which makes us grow, providing (and this is the most important part of the whole idea)—*providing* we cooperate with that "something." By cooperating we mean eating the right foods for nutrition, getting the proper amount of exercise, breathing fresh air, etc. Two babies at the age of two can be exactly the same size and weight. The factor or law of growth is in both of them. But if one is placed in a concentration camp or lives in the slums, while the other lives in the country—where it receives plenty of milk, fresh eggs, sunshine and exercise—obviously one will grow much larger and heavier than the other. So whatever it is that causes growth is found in every human being. If it seems to do more for some people than for others, that's because some are able or willing to cooperate with it, while others either do not or cannot.

But we grow in more ways than one. The illustration given above deals only with physical growth. Each of us grows spiritually as well. For example, listed below, you will find five items.

1. An ice-cream cone
2. A bag of marbles
3. A quarter
4. A college education
5. The Ten Commandments

Now then, in your workbook, where you will find these five items listed again, to the left of them mark the way you would have valued them when you were four years old, numbering the most important 1, etc. Then, to the right of them, number them in their order of importance to you today. Though it is quite possible that we shall differ among ourselves in how we mark these choices, no one in the class will number them exactly the same today as at the age of four. It should be clear from this that we grow also in our sense of values, which is another way of saying that we grow spiritually as well as physically. It is the force within each of us, or the little bit of God within each of us, which is responsible for this growth, too. But remember, the force can make us grow to our maximum possibilities both physically and spiritually *only if we ourselves cooperate!*

The same thing is true of our conscience. It may have occurred to you to ask, a moment ago when we were talking about conscience: Does every human being, without exception, have a little bit of God within him? Did even Adolf Hitler have some God within him? Our answer would be: Yes, *even* Adolf Hitler had a little bit of God within him. To be sure, some individuals have more of God within them than others have, just as some have a higher intelligence or greater artistic ability. And some persons make greater use than others of the portion of God within them, even as some of us develop our intelligence and use our brains more than others. The chief difference in this respect between Hitler and a great man, let us say like Albert Einstein, is that the latter has done his best to cooperate with the bit of God inside him, while Hitler did not.

Shintoism, the early primitive religion of Japan, had something interesting to say about our conclusion here that there is a little bit of God within each human being. The Shinto priests, like our own Jewish ancestors, did not allow any images representing God to be placed in their temples. But high up on the temple wall they placed a large mirror, tilted at such an angle that each worshipper could see himself in it. Thus they meant to impress upon every individual that he could find God within himself.

A good way to summarize this discussion on moral law and conscience would be through the following comparison. All of us know that it is perfectly possible to drive a car from Cleveland to New York. The road is so constructed that we *can* drive from one place to the other. This does not mean, however, that all we need do is drive our car on to the highway, head it in the right direction, and rely on the road to carry us along while we ourselves relax. The road simply makes it *possible* for us to get from Cleveland to New York, *if* we cooperate by keeping our car in good condition and driving it properly. If there were no roads, we couldn't make such a trip by automobile no matter how hard we tried. Similarly, this universe is so constructed (there is a moral power in it) that we can improve and progress ethically *if we want to* and *if we cooperate fully*.

Before proceeding with this chapter, this would be a good place for you to summarize the various respects in which we can recognize a little bit of God within ourselves. In this chapter especially, but also implied in Chapters Three and Four, we have suggested ways in which we can see God working within our own bodies and lives. In your workbook for this chapter you will be asked to list all these indications of God within us.

Far more important and valuable than any such list, however, is the actual experience of having felt something so deep and wonderful within you that only the word God can adequately describe it. You may have stood high on a mountain top watching either a sunrise or a sunset that was so beautiful there were no words to describe it. At such a moment you may have felt something inexpressible within you reaching out to the great beauty you were watching. You may have felt, without putting it into words, that you were a part of the natural beauty you were witnessing and it was a part of you and your life. If so, then you have actually had the experience of the little bit of God within you reaching out toward and relating itself to the power of God in the larger universe.

At other times perhaps you have been so much in love with another human being that you were unable to describe your love or think of yourself as a person different and apart from the one you loved. Or you may have seen people you didn't even know living in such miserable poverty that you wanted at once to do something to help them. Or you may have read about other human beings who showed such courage that you recognized something spiritual that was wonderful within them and felt that the same "something" existed also within you. All these are possible ways of experiencing God deeply within yourself, not just reading about Him in a book.

An even more wonderful way of knowing God ourselves is when we feel the stirring of conscience within us. The writer of this book remembers vividly the early part of World War II when he was trying desperately to decide whether or not to become a chaplain. Thousands of clergymen—both Jewish and Christian—faced the same dilemma. Since they could not be drafted, the choice had to be entirely their own. On the one side they had to think of their natural desire to remain safely at home with their loved ones and of the undeniably important work facing them in civilian life. On the other hand there was the fact that our servicemen, who were sacrificing so very much for their nation, needed religion and religious leadership more desperately than ever before.

This was not an easy decision to reach. The writer remembers so clearly that during the months of debate within himself he felt time and again there was some strength or power that was helping him see above and beyond his own desires of the moment. Later he realized that this power within him was closely related to the same power which was helping others. And when he was in actual combat—an experience to which we shall return later—again he felt a power that was giving him strength. You, too, may already have had moments of difficult decision, moments when you tried hard to hear the voice of conscience and succeeded in feeling something within yourself that was helping you. If so, you have experienced God. You know, then, that there really is such a power within you, that it can help you if you strive to recognize it and cooperate with it.

Are You a Mirror?

That sounds at first like a silly question, doesn't it? But before you turn away, hold on a minute. Maybe it isn't quite so silly after all. A little while ago we mentioned the fact that there is air both inside and outside our lungs, just as there is God both within us and outside us. This brings to mind another reason which has led many people to believe there must be something spiritual about the universe in which we live.

Long ago scientists recognized that every physical or chemical element found in the human body can be found also in the world and universe outside our bodies. Physically, in other words, we are reflections of the universe in which we live. Each chemical element in us is a small part of a much greater quantity of the same element outside us. To be sure, the chemicals in our bodies exist in a unique combination, and we have already seen that something else has been added to them to make us human beings. But there is no chemical or physical element in us that cannot be found also in nature outside us.

There may be a further respect in which you are a mirror. Before you could develop lungs, there had to be air and oxygen surrounding this planet. Your lungs are a *reflection of*, or better yet, a *response to* the oxygen in the atmosphere. If there had never been such oxygen available, the first amphibians would never have developed lungs. The same is true of eyes. The first living forms to develop eyes did so in response to the light in the world around them. Had there been no light, there would have been no eyes. We know that because there are certain forms of fish which have lived all their lives in the waters of caves, where no light ever reaches them; such fish have no eyes! They don't need them, because there isn't any light around to enable them to see anyway. So we know that eyes developed as a response to light in the same way that lungs developed as a response to air.

Many people think it logical to suppose, therefore, that man's spiritual qualities likewise must have developed as a reflection of something spiritual in the universe outside him. In other words, if human beings have souls, the universe must have some kind of soul too. We noted this briefly in Chapter Seven, where we said that the soul of the universe is called God. Be sure to read Dr. Harry Emerson Fosdick's interesting statement about this in your readings for this chapter.

Whether you agree with this particular idea or not, the important part of this chapter so far is to realize that the great power which sustains the moral law doesn't exist only in the world outside yourself; part of it is in you too.

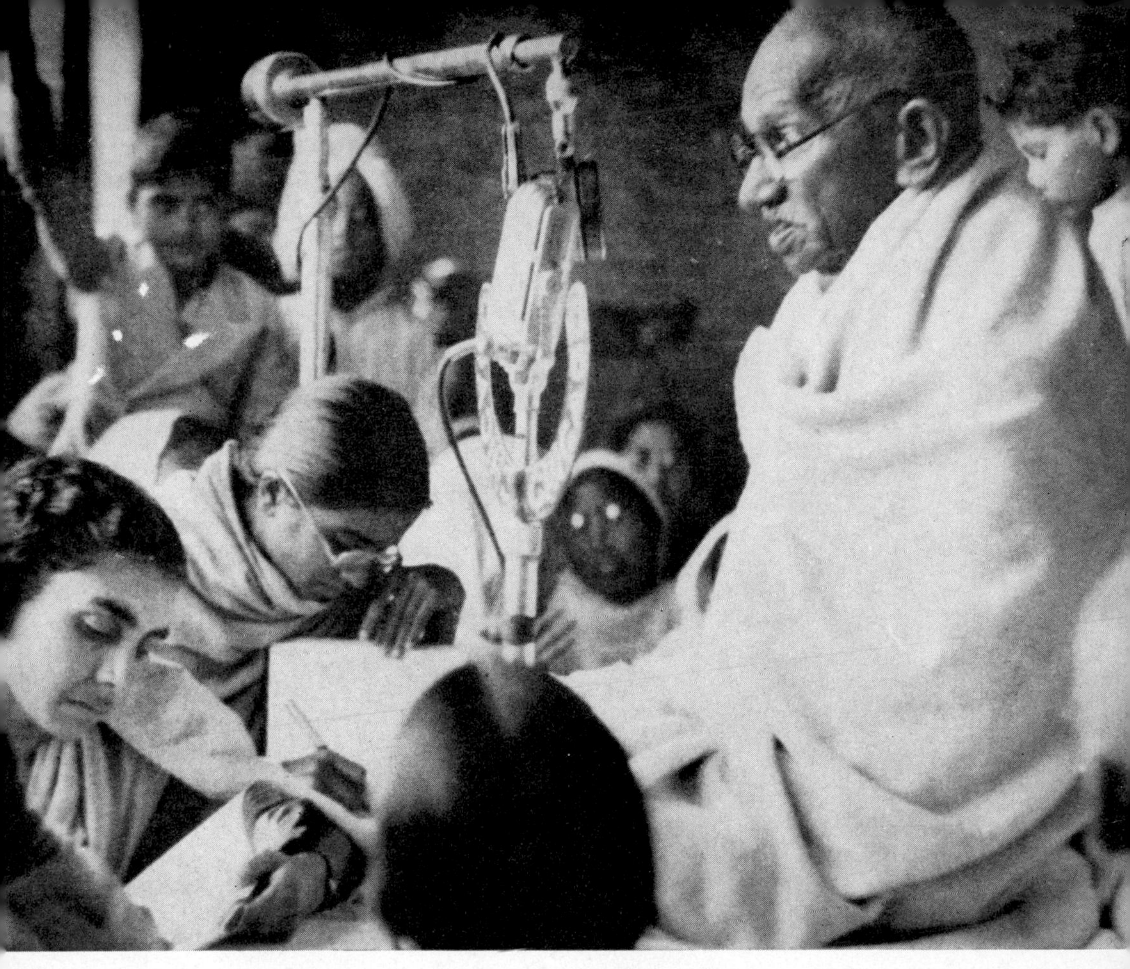

GANDHI SPEAKS TO HIS PEOPLE (See page *63*)

OLD MAN OF THE MOUNTAIN

(See page *108*)

OUR GOAL OF ETHICAL PERFECTION

(See page *134*)

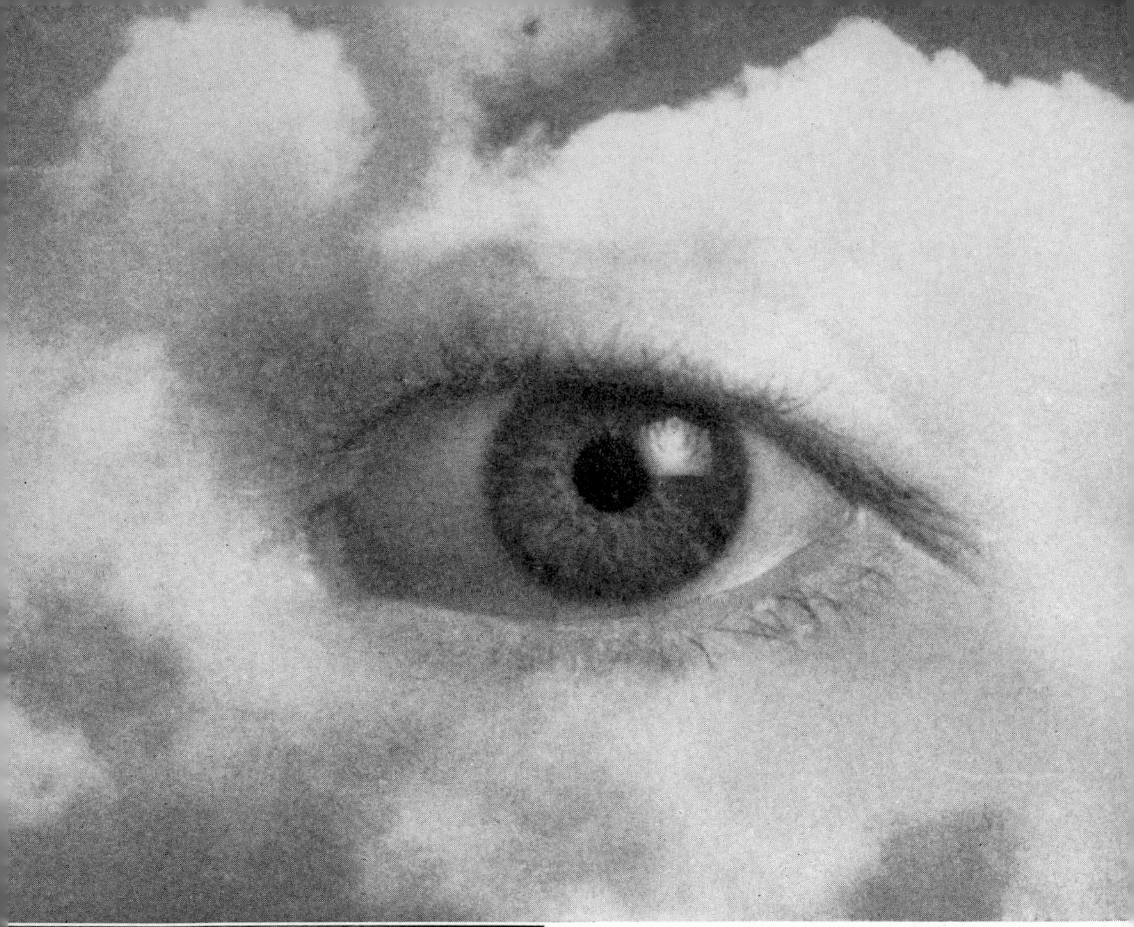

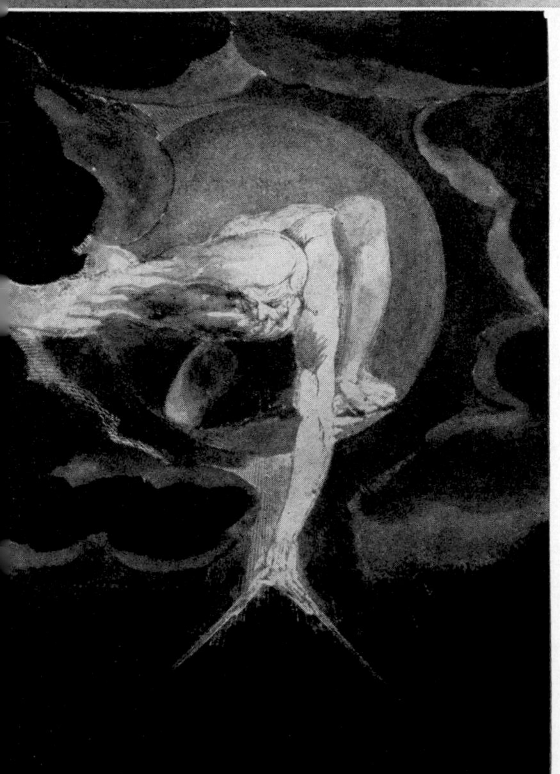

MODERN OR ANCIENT IDEAS OF GOD? (See page *151*)

Goal to Go

It should be very clear by now that the word God has more than one meaning in modern Jewish religion. But we aren't quite finished yet. There is one additional meaning we want to mention before concluding this chapter. The word God can also refer to the moral or ethical goal toward which each of us should constantly strive. Because this may not be immediately easy for you to grasp, we shall try to say it several ways.

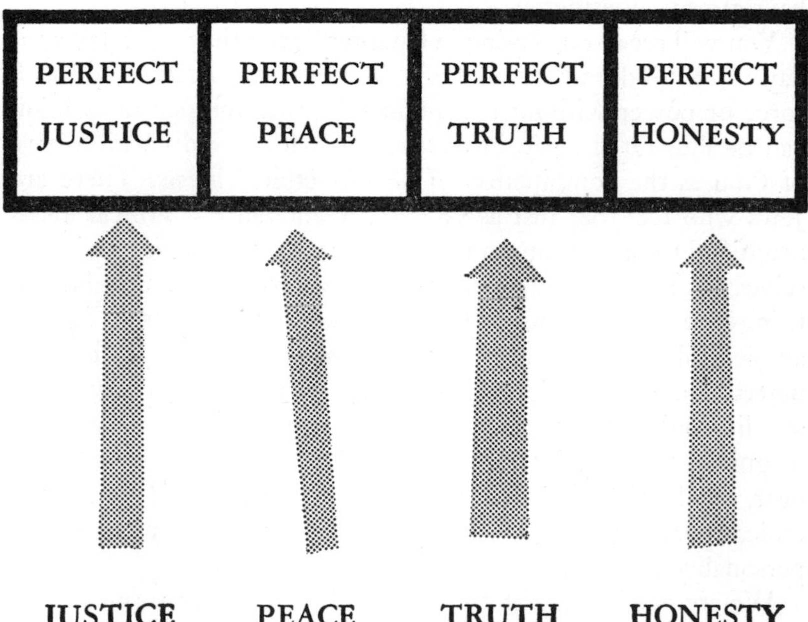

God Is the Sum-Total of All Our Ideals, Magnified to Perfection

First, let's think of all the separate ethical ideals we can, such as peace, humility, honesty, justice, mercy, righteousness, truth, etc., etc. Obviously we could go on listing individual ideals for hours, but these will serve as examples. Now do two additional things: (1) Try to think of each of these ideals magnified to the point of perfection. Try to think of what *perfect peace* would be like as a goal for which to strive—or *perfect truth* or *perfect justice*. Then (2) think of all these separate ideals, each magnified to perfection, put together in one great Master-Ideal which becomes the goal of all our living. The word God can be used in modern Jewish religion to refer to this goal also. God, thought of in this way, becomes a vision of perfection, an ethical pattern for human beings to follow. Remember, however, that this is but one of several modern interpretations, in addition to those we have already considered.

You will recall our saying in Chapter Seven that some Jews today think God has personality while others conceive God as a force or power without personality. This difference of opinion can be illustrated again in connection with our discussion here of God as the combination of all our ethical ideals. There are Jews who feel that just as God represents all our ethical ideals magnified to perfection, so He also contains personality and consciousness magnified to perfection. They would say that human beings are able to think in terms of justice and honesty, for example, only because there is a God who is perfect justice and perfect honesty; and that, similarly, human beings have personality only because there is a God who possesses personality magnified to the point of perfection. Other modern Jews, however, think of God in this respect as the sum total of all our ethical goals and ideals, without finding it necessary to ascribe personality to Him.

We are not the first to think of God partially in terms of our ethical ideals. A member of the writer's Confirmation class of 1942 was thinking of this interpretation of God when he wrote: "God is what man thinks it best for him to be." The writer of Exodus in our Bible may have been thinking along these lines, too, when, speaking of the children of Israel wandering in the wilderness, he wrote: "And the Lord went before them by day in a pillar of cloud, to lead them the way; and by night in a pillar of fire, to give them light; that they might go by day and by night. . . ." God, as the sum-total of all our ideals and aspirations, can be the goal of our lives, and can lead us upward and onward the way the pillar of cloud by day and the pillar of fire by night led our ancestors.

Jewish tradition expresses very clearly our people's belief that there is a portion of God in every human being and that God may be thought of also as a pattern of perfection for us to follow. Thus the famous story in the beginning of Genesis, telling how our ancestors thought God created the world, says that He created man in His own image. We today interpret that to mean that in every person there is some of God, that is to say, some of the power and force found everywhere in the world, by which we can continue our upward progress through evolution. We have already seen that this little bit of God within him is called man's soul. In fact, our Biblical Book of Proverbs says specifically that "the soul of man is the light of the Lord." We believe, furthermore, that each human being can emphasize and encourage the best in himself, thus, in a sense, making himself more and more like God or in God's image. One of our ancient Rabbis said, "The Holy One, blessed be He, the Lord, who is called righteous and upright, has not created man 'in His own image' save in the sense that man be as righteous and upright as He Himself."

Someone has suggested that this notion of God as the ethical goal of our lives may be seen in the very word our ancestors frequently used for God. One of the Hebrew words for God is אֵל (AYL). The identical consonants with a change of vowel make the word אֶל (EL), meaning "to" or "toward." God may be thought of, then, as the goal of ethical perfection *toward which* we should always strive.

Will anyone ever be able to reach this goal? In answering this question we come upon another of the great differences between Judaism and Christianity. Modern Christians believe not only that it is possible for a human being to achieve the ethical perfection which is God, but more than that, that one human being has already actually reached it. To them that person is Jesus. We have already made note of the occasional confusion in Christian prayers between Jesus and God. One reason for this confusion, from a modern point of view, is the Christian belief that Jesus actually reached the goal or vision of perfection we have been discussing, at which moment he thereby ceased being an ordinary human being and became instead, as it were, God.

Our Jewish answer to this question differs. We do not believe that any human being ever has or ever can reach the goal of ethical perfection, because we look upon it as a moving goal. As our ethical evolution progresses, our ideas and ideals of perfection likewise are improved. The closer we get to our goal of perfection, the more able we are to envision an even higher and loftier goal for the future.

In other words, our moving Master-Ideal is much like the horizon. If, standing on a high tower, we looked toward the horizon and arranged for someone, standing where the horizon seemed to be, to mark that spot with a flag, and then started out to walk toward that spot, we would never reach the horizon. We would, to be sure, reach the spot where the horizon had been, but from our new perspective the horizon would still seem to be far off in the forward distance. As we move forward, the horizon moves with us. As we move forward ethically, our ethical horizon or goal also moves with us. So that for modern Jews, God as the combination of all our highest ideals will always be a challenge, urging us to continual improvement. A non-Jewish writer, Barbara Spofford Morgan, wrote very much in the spirit of this Jewish point of view when she commented: ". . . those who set their hearts on what they cannot reach are the ones who carry civilization forward."

SOMETHING FOR YOU TO READ

A. The Prophet Micah's Vision of What the Messiah Would Bring:

But in the end of days it shall come to pass

That the mountain of the Lord's house shall be
  established as the top of the mountains,
And it shall be exalted above the hills;
And peoples shall flow unto it.
And many nations shall go and say;
'Come ye, and let us go up to the mountain
  of the Lord,
And to the house of the God of Jacob;
And He will teach us of His ways,
And we will walk in His paths';

For out of Zion shall go forth the law,
And the word of the Lord from Jerusalem.
And He shall judge between many peoples,
And shall decide concerning mighty nations afar off;
And they shall beat their swords into plowshares,
And their spears into pruning-hooks;
Nation shall not lift up sword against nation,
Neither shall they learn war any more.
But they shall sit every man under his vine and
  under his fig-tree;
And none shall make them afraid; . . .

B. Belief in God, therefore, has to do . . . with human nature, with the way individual men and women act, with their attitudes, their ideas of what is good and what is bad, with their ideals. Belief in God has to do with our attitude toward life itself. Do we find life good? Is life worth while? If we believe that life is worth while, that it is good, that, in spite of sickness and accidents, in spite of poverty and war, in spite of all the sad and difficult conditions in the world, the world is a wonderful place to live in and *can be made a still better place*, then we believe in God. When we believe in God, we cannot be discouraged because we believe that all the misery in the world is due, not to the fact that misery must be there, that it is a necessary part of life, but to the fact that we have not yet discovered how to do away with that misery.—Ira Eisenstein, *What We Mean by Religion*, Behrman House.

C. It is like one who seeks a distant mountain height which he has never climbed, and which nobody has ever quite reached. He doesn't know the exact trail, nor does he know much about what he would find at the end of his hazardous journey. The mists are often baffling and the nights are dark. But through mists and darkness there flames a beacon to guide him, a beacon that never goes out, although sometimes lost to view. The farther he travels, the clearer his objective looms, and the more he learns the true way to achieve it. So with life. We know only the general direction of what we seek. We know that we want to fulfill all the possibilities of our nature, compatible [consistent] with its wholeness. That is the ever-burning beacon that guides our steps. The farther we climb, the more we learn of what such a rich and unified life must mean, what we must do to attain it, and what we must avoid if we are not to lose it.—Jay William Hudson, *Religious Liberals Reply*, The Beacon Press.

D.

When in the west at evening I behold
Lit one by one upon the dusky sky
Torches, like sparks of silver and of gold,
Gazing in wonder, to those lights I cry:
"Tell me, ye stars, ah, tell me, what is God?"
"Order," the stars reply.

When in her festive garb the earth is decked,
Green valley, hill, and field, and river bank,
With many-colored flowery garlands flecked,
Gazing, I ask: "Tell me, ye fragrant bowers,
Ye blazing colors, tell me, what is God?"
"Beauty," reply the flowers.

When the caressing eyes upon me turn
Their softly sparkling ray,
I ask of those pure fires that in them burn:
"Where were ye kindled? Ah, can ye not say,
Bright stars, can ye not tell me, what is God?"
They answer: "God is love."

—Translation from the modern Italian poet, Aleardo Aleardi, taken from R. Rendel, *Anthology of Italian Lyrics*, Frank-Maurice, New York, 1926.

E. . . . Solomon ibn Gabirol, enumerating the "three things which stand together to bring the awareness of Thee ever before me," lists first the heavens and second the earth in its expanse, but as a climactic third "the stirring of my heart when I look inward."—Milton Steinberg, *Basic Judaism*, Harcourt, Brace and Co.

F. Each in His Own Tongue

A fire-mist and a planet,—

A crystal and a cell,—
A jelly fish and a saurian [reptile],
And caves where the cave-men dwell;
Then a sense of law and beauty
And a face turned from the clod,—
Some call it Evolution,
And others call it God.

A haze on the far horizon,
The infinite tender sky,
The rich ripe tint of the cornfields,
And the wild geese sailing high;
And all over upland and lowland
The charm of the golden-rod,—
Some of us call it Autumn,
And others call it God.

Like tides on a crescent sea-beach,
When the moon is new and thin,
Into our hearts high yearnings
Come welling and surging in;
Come from the mystic ocean
Whose rim no foot has trod,—
Some of us call it Longing,
And others call it God. . . .

—William Herbert Carruth. (These three stanzas of the poem are reprinted by special permission of Mrs. William Herbert Carruth.)

G. As one of your readings for this chapter, read again Selection E at the end of Chapter Seven. It belongs here also.

H. . . . man has grown up in this universe, gradually developing his powers and functions as responses to his environment. If he has eyes, so the biologists assure us, it is because the light waves played upon the skin and eyes came out in answer; if he has ears it is because the air waves were there first and ears came out to hear. Man never yet has developed any power save as a reality called it into being. There would be no fins if there were no water, no wings if there were no air, no legs if there were no land. Always the developing organism has been trying to "catch up with its environment." Yet some would tell us that man's noblest power of all has developed in a vacuum. They would say that his capacity to deal with a Spiritual World, to believe in God, and in prayer to experience fellowship with Him, has all grown up with no Reality to call it into being. If so, it stands alone in man's experience, the only function of his life that grew without an originating Fact to call it forth.—Harry Emerson Fosdick, *The Meaning of Faith*, Association Press.

I. (The following interpretation, given by our Rabbis centuries ago, was their way of explaining the relationship between man's soul and God):

As the soul pervades the body, God pervades the world . . .
As the soul sustains the body, God sustains the world . . .
As the soul survives the body, God survives the world . . .
As there is a unitary and single soul in the body, so
there is but a unitary and single God to the world . . .
Wherefore let the soul of the body praise Him who is,
as it were, the soul of the world.

—Quoted by Milton Steinberg, in *Basic Judaism*, Harcourt, Brace and Co.

J. Rabbi Joshua of Sikhnin said: The matter is like a cave which lies by the seashore: the tide rises, and the cave becomes full of water, but the sea is no whit less full. So the sanctuary and the tent of meeting were filled with the radiance (of God) but the world was no less filled with God's glory.—Midrash, quoted in Montefiore and Loewe, *A Rabbinic Anthology*, The Macmillan Co., London.

K. One lesson and only one history may be said to repeat with distinctness: that the world is built somehow on moral foundations; that in the long run it is well with the good: in the long run it is ill with the wicked.—James A. Froude (British historian), quoted in A. Cohen, *The Psalms*, Soncino Press.

L. But the problem of the unjust suffering of the righteous does not become so aggravated a problem in the long course of human history. When we take the life of fifty generations together, we are more likely to see the working out of a divine plan. If not in individual biography, then at least in world history, we see that evil does become national weakness and a corrupted nation does not endure; that inner moral decency does become social strength and that a community can outlast its misfortunes.—Freehof, *Preface to Scripture*, Union of American Hebrew Congregations.

M. A primary function of religion is to help men convert the ideal into the real: that is a basic conviction of religious liberals. They have a huge respect for ideals and the power latent [resting] in them. They believe that if all the ideals in the world with their inherent [inner] power were seen as gathered together into a single unity, that unity might be regarded as one of the aspects of God.—Argow, *What Do Religious Liberals Believe?* The Antioch Press.

N. Thus the Talmud expounds: "What is the meaning of the verse, 'Ye shall walk after the Lord your God' (Deut. 13:4)? It is to follow the attributes [characteristics] of the Holy One blessed be He: As He clothed the naked (Gen. 3:21), so do you clothe the naked; as He visited the sick (Gen. 18:1), so do you visit the sick; as He comforted the mourners (Gen. 25:11), so do you comfort those who mourn; as He buried the dead (Deut. 34:6), so do you bury the dead." The same thought is expressed in the Midrash: "As the All-present [God] is called compassionate and gracious so be you also compassionate and gracious and offering thy gifts freely to all. As the Holy One, blessed be He, is called righteous (Ps. 145:17), be you also righteous; and as He is called loving, be you also loving." —Bokser, *The Wisdom of the Talmud*, Philosophical Library.

O. "We must not claim too much. It is possible that a dishonest man may be happy, and we have all known happy liars. Some people seem to get along pretty well even though they lead immoral lives. Perhaps what we may claim is something of this sort—that although a particular man may sometimes 'get away with' a dishonest way of living, and perhaps not suffer at all, yet this is an utterly unsafe and unsound way of conducting one's life. It is certain that a general rule which prescribes all-round dishonesty and untruthfulness would be disastrous, and that a general rule which prescribes honesty and truthfulness will, if carried out, increase human happiness. After all, it is the same with rules of health. . . . You may possibly get away with bodily uncleanliness, and with unbrushed teeth, without suffering in your health. But to be cleanly is the only sound rule, and this is universally true for all men. . . . Even the man who neglects it with impunity acts wrongly and ought to have obeyed it if he wished for health. And the same is true of the man who disobeys moral rules without suffering."—W. T. Stace, *Religion and the Modern Mind*, J. P. Lippincott Co.

9. *More Answers Bring More Questions*

You might suppose that after all the pages and chapters devoted here directly and indirectly to discussions about God, we would know by now the answer to any question that can be asked about Him. But we are far indeed from complete or perfect knowledge. We said at the very beginning of this book that we were to deal with questions men have been asking for many centuries, and that, while we might be able to come just a little closer to some answers than generations have before us, we would by no means be able to secure sure and certain knowledge. The remarkable (and adventuresome) thing about religion is that the more knowledge we obtain, the more questions we seem to think of. You will never stop thinking, asking, and wondering about God so long as you are alive and intelligent. In this, our final chapter devoted directly to the subject of God, we hope to deal with just a few more questions from among the many hundreds which must have occurred to you recently. First, however, it should be helpful if we pause to summarize the various modern meanings we have already discovered for the idea of God.

There have been at least four of them:

1. God is the force or power we recognize throughout the world of nature, the force which is responsible for the amazing order, harmony, purpose, design and plan, which we discovered everywhere—from the remotest star to our own bodies—and which our minds tell us could not be mere accident or coincidence.

2. God is the force or power which has been patiently working its way upward through the long course of evolution, helping life-forms to develop from the simplest invisible protozoan to the mind, the conscience and the creative genius of man. Actually, of course, evolution is a part of the world of nature. We might, therefore, have included this under number 1. Because evolution is in itself so remarkable a phase of nature, however, it would be wise to make of this a separate point.

3. God is the Master-Ideal, the ethical goal, the pattern of perfection toward which we are evolving and for which we ought to strive throughout our lives. God is the sum total of all our ethical ideals, each magnified to perfection, all joined together as a great super-goal.

4. God is the power or force which strengthens and sustains us in our efforts to reach the goal of perfection, which makes it possible for us to progress toward that goal if we cooperate. The part of this power which is in each of us individually is called our conscience.

We have already seen that one way of summarizing these four

modern meanings of God is to say that He is the soul of the universe, that like our own personalities the universe consists both of physical and non-physical aspects. The non-physical part of a human being, the most important part of him, is his soul. The non-physical part of the universe, also the most important part of that universe, is God.

Remembering that our ancestors centuries ago contributed the thought that God is only spiritual, you can easily understand that it is impossible to represent a modern notion of God through a picture of any kind. The following diagram, however, may help us somewhat to keep in mind not what God is like, but rather the various ways in which we see His effects in the world. You will recognize that in part it is a combination of two diagrams we have used previously.

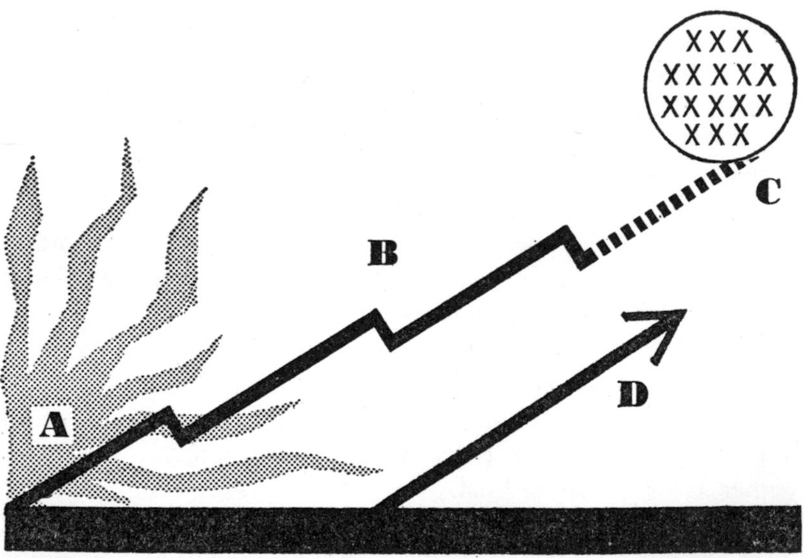

You could by this time probably explain the meaning of these lines pretty well yourself, but we'll help. (A) represents the first moment of creation and the fact that the force called God was in existence then and was responsible for the beginnings of things. The line marked (B) you already recognize as the progress of evolution since the beginning of the universe. The *dotted portion of the line* is for future development. We have used a similar line before to indicate not only biological evolution, but also the course of humanity's upward progress in an ethical sense toward (C), which is the Master-Ideal, the sum total of our ideals (each X there represents one specific ideal). And finally (D) indicates both number 2 and number 4 in our summary just completed: it is the force behind evolution as well as the power helping us to reach upward toward our goal.

It would be a mistake to assume that what we have summarized here constitutes four different things. Actually, they are four ways in which one and the same thing appears to us as phases of human experience. If you have ever spent much time in the vicinity of a great mountain, you know how different it appears from different directions and perspectives. Sometimes it is difficult to believe you are looking at the same mountain when you view it from an unaccustomed angle. What we are doing in this summary is, so to speak, to "walk around" the idea of God, looking at it from different angles and perspectives. That is why it appears to us in these four different ways.

When, in Chapter Six, we described the Jewish contributions to the idea of God, we might have added: our ancestors were the first to realize that the *power behind nature* and the *moral power* of the universe are actually two different ways in which men are able to perceive one and the same power which we call God. Dr. Theodore P. Ferris, a prominent Boston Protestant minister, has written this about the ancient Jews: ". . . to their everlasting credit stands the fact that they were the first to discover that the physical powers from which the universe is derived and the moral forces in life are the same. They realized that God was the source not only of power but of moral law, and so they made that marriage between religion and ethics for which all the world owes them a debt."

We referred several chapters ago to a modern interpretation

of the Sh'ma as meaning that all our ethical ideals are encompassed in one God rather than having separate gods for each. Now we can carry that a step farther and say that whenever we repeat the Sh'ma as part of a Jewish religious service or prayer, what we are actually declaring and what we should keep clearly in mind is that the force or power which we recognize behind nature is the same force which has been responsible for evolution and which we feel as our conscience and which provides for us an ethical goal that gives meaning to our lives. God is not only our goal, but also the means making it possible for us to approach that goal. Theodor Herzl once referred to the word God as "this beloved, old, wonderful abbreviation." For us also, the word God is a wonderful abbreviation or symbol, standing for all the things we have reviewed here. In one of your Reading Selections for this chapter Dr. Freehof expresses the meaning of the Sh'ma very eloquently. And now, with this summary clearly in mind, let us go on to a few remaining questions.

Is God Real?

Ancient people would never have asked such a question as this. Of course God was real. They knew exactly what He resembled and could actually see an image of Him when they worshipped. As we traced the development of the God-idea to modern times, however, and described the modern Jewish meanings of the word God, it may have occurred to you to ask whether God in our modern interpretation is as *real* as God was to earlier peoples.

It will be easy for you to answer this one if you remember our previous discussion on the meaning of the word spiritual. *Spiritual*, you will recall, is the opposite of *tangible* or *visible*, not the opposite of *real*. A table, which is physical, is real. But so is love, which is spiritual. As a matter of fact, love is, if anything, more real than a table; it certainly plays a more important role in our lives, doesn't it? Your love for your parents, and some day for your husband or wife, will be one of the most real experiences in your life, far more so than many things which are tangible. Is your conscience real? Are your thoughts and emotions real? Are school spirit, patriotism, gravity real? As the answer to every one of these questions must be in the affirmative, so too must an affirmative reply be given to the question whether God is real.

Our modern interpretation hasn't made God less real. It has described Him in terms spiritual rather than physical, and for intelligent people at any rate has made Him far more real than before. One or more of your Reading Selections for this chapter will deal with this.

Why Do We Call God "He"?

It must have occurred to many of you to ask this question as we progressed with our discussions. It is easy to understand, of course, why God was referred to with a personal pronoun when primitive men thought of Him as an all-powerful being, much in the shape and nature of a person who could do everything He wanted to do. But why should we, with our modern interpretations, still refer to God as "Him"? Why not call God "It" rather than "He" or "Him"? Would there be anything wrong in that?

People would probably differ in their answers to this question. Many would say it is perfectly proper, if not actually preferable, to call God "It." They might add that there would then be less likelihood of confusing modern with ancient concepts and ideas. There are, however, several reasons why most of us still refer to God through personal pronouns. What are these reasons?

First: custom, tradition, and usage. People have called God "He" for so many centuries that it would sound strange and confusing now suddenly to change. We would have to rewrite much of our prayer book and Bible. It is easier to retain the old wording and reinterpret in our minds what we mean by it.

Second: personal pronouns are very often used in a poetic sense. We have already mentioned that sailors always call their ship "she" and that we often refer to our country as "she." You can probably think of other examples also of the poetic use of personal pronouns when we are not actually thinking of a person.

Third: a careful reading of the second reason will lead logically to the third. You must have noticed in the examples just given that it is especially with reference to things we value very highly that we are inclined to use personal pronouns. A sailor refers to his ship, or a person to his country, as "she" because the ship or the country is precious. We generally attach higher value or worth to things labeled with a personal pronoun than to things called "it." This is particularly so when we refer to God since we are talking then of matters which are so precious a part of our human experience. In speaking of God as our ethical goal, for example, we necessarily think of all the ideals constituting that goal in human terms. Our Rabbis of old, in explaining many things in the Bible which even they couldn't accept literally, said, "The Torah speaks in the language of human beings." That is to say, the writers of the Bible tried to use language which would make their meaning clear to others. For the same reason most people today still prefer to call God "He."

Fourth: another possible answer to this question may be found in the nature of the Hebrew language. Like a number of other languages Hebrew has no neuter gender; every noun must be either masculine or feminine. In other words, Hebrew has no word for "it": a table is referred to as "he"; the human eye is "she." It is interesting to speculate that this too may have something to do with the fact that our ancestors who, of course, expressed their early religious thinking in Hebrew, referred to God as "He."

This brings us to a most important problem, one which we aren't going to try to solve for you. Instead, we'll challenge you to do your own thinking. Both the prayer book and the Bible contain numerous terms referring to God which obviously originated at a time when people's notions of God differed very considerably from our own. It is important that we clarify our thinking concerning such traditional ways of addressing God as Ovinu Malkenu, אָבִינוּ מַלְכֵּנוּ, "Our Father, our King," and Melech Ho-Olom, מֶלֶךְ הָעוֹלָם, "King of the Universe," and Ovinu Sheba-shomayim, אָבִינוּ שֶׁבַּשָּׁמַיִם, "Our Father who is in

Heaven." (Incidentally, notice that this is the origin of the phrase with which the Christian Lord's prayer begins—"Our Father who art in Heaven." Many of the other phrases and ideas in that prayer can also be found in earlier Jewish liturgy.)

> Your workbook for this chapter will give you an opportunity to decide which of these phrases you think should be kept and which abandoned. Be sure to give good reasons for your decisions. Which do you think express a modern view of God? Which can be so interpreted that they are not inconsistent with a modern view? What interpretation is necessary? Which are so misleading from a modern point of view that it would be better to drop them altogether? Why?

While thinking about these phrases used in addressing God, it might be interesting to notice the statement of a Chasidic rabbi. He said: "As yet, God is not actually king over the world, and I have a part in the blame that this is not so." What do you suppose this rabbi meant? How would you say the same thing in your own words?

Does God Still Speak to People?

The Bible is full of incidents in which God is described as actually speaking to human beings. We have already noticed the example of God speaking to Moses from the burning bush. According to the Bible God also spoke directly to Moses on Mt. Sinai, to Abraham on Mt. Moriah, and to countless other individuals. An interesting story in which God speaks to a very young boy may be found in 1 Samuel 3:1–11; a question based on this story will be included in your workbook.

> Does God still speak to people, as He apparently did in Bible times? What would you say if a classmate told you that God talked to him last night? Did God ever speak to you? Do you think the Bible writers believed literally that God had spoken to

people? How would you today interpret their stories?

Did Man Create God?

Genesis tells us, of course, that God created the first man in His own image. We have already discussed the significance of that statement. There are people, however, who have suggested that perhaps it would be at least equally true to say that man created God in *his* image. By that they mean in part that God is the product of man's mind and thoughts. That brings to mind a number of important and interesting questions:

> Does God exist only in men's minds, or outside man and independent of him also? Was there any God before the first human being evolved? If all human life were to be destroyed from the earth and the universe, would there be any God left? If only plant and animal life remained on earth, would God still exist? Would any animals be aware of Him?

There are two stories from Jewish tradition which pertain to these questions and which might be helpful to you in working out your answers. According to one ancient legend God created several worlds before He made this one. Each time He had finished creating a world He looked at it carefully, decided it wasn't worth preserving, and destroyed it, only to commence the experiment over again. It was only when this world had been created that, in the words of the Bible, "God saw that it was good," so He allowed it to continue and develop. What would this legend seem to show about the answer the Rabbis of old would have given to the questions asked above?

Another old Jewish story which belongs here tells us that before Adam was created neither the plants, the animals, nor even God Himself had a name. It was only after the first man was created that he then gave to each creature on earth and to God a name. Of what significance is this in answering the questions we are considering here?

It may help you in this connection to remember the words of "Adon Olom," a Hebrew hymn which we often sing in the synagogue. Here are two verses in English translation:

The Lord of all, who reigned supreme
Ere first creation's form was framed;
When all was finished by His will
His name Almighty was proclaimed.

When this, our world, shall be no more,
In majesty He still shall reign,
Who was, who is, who will for aye
In endless glory still remain.

What two thoughts are expressed here which help answer our question in this section? Is there any idea of God in these verses which would be unacceptable to you as a modern Jew? What is your answer to the question whether man created God?

Ancient or Modern?

In 1941 the town of Cambridge, Mass., along with much of the Atlantic seacoast, suffered from an exceptionally severe snowstorm. The mayor of Cambridge refused to appropriate the sum of money required to purchase a snow-plow, saying by way of reason, "The Almighty sends snow, and if we are patient enough, He will remove it."

Is "Almighty" a good way to refer to God? Why? Do you approve or disapprove the mayor's statement? Why? Does it indicate an ancient or a modern concept of God? Is it true that God sent the snow which fell on Cambridge? Does God remove it? Could He remove it at any time He wanted? Explain your answers in the proper place in your workbook.

There is a similar example from modern Jewish life. During all the years of Zionist effort to rebuild Palestine, a group of very strict Orthodox Jews who belong to an organization called the *Agudas Yisroel* refused to have anything to do with the Zionist movement. It wasn't that they didn't want to see Palestine rebuilt; on the contrary, no group of Jews wanted it more fervently. But members of the Agudah said God had destroyed the Jewish State nearly 1,900 years earlier for a reason, that He had promised to send the Messiah to rebuild it, and when He would be ready to fulfill that promise He would do so. For human beings to "interfere" with God's plans by trying to rebuild Palestine themselves, they said, would be a sin.

> In what respects is this similar to the case of the Cambridge mayor? In what respects different? What is your reaction to the reasoning of the Agudah members? Is their notion of God modern or ancient? Why?

How would the author of Selection E at the end of this chapter answer these questions? What would she think of the Cambridge mayor and the Agudah?

A little child was observed one day swinging dangerously on a school-yard swing without holding the ropes. When her teacher cautioned her, she said, "Oh, don't worry: God will take care of me; He won't let me fall!"

> If you were the teacher, how would you have answered this child? Would you have agreed with her? Would you have told her to hold on because God would not take care of her? Was her concept of God ancient or modern? What would an ancient person have meant by saying, "God is my support"? What might a modern religious person mean by the same words?

Three statements from Jewish tradition may help us think through this part of our problem. In one place the Talmud says: "Man, to be Godlike, must be partner with God in the act of creation."

> What do you think this means? How can man's creations be compared to God's? Could a human being create a new universe or a planet? Can you give a specific example of human conduct or behavior which might illustrate the meaning of becoming a "partner with God in the act of creation"?

A second statement from Talmudic times is a comment based on the verse in Exodus in which God is described as saying to Moses: "Behold, I will stand before thee there upon the rock of Horeb." The Rabbis interpreted God's meaning to be: "Wherever thou findest the footprints of men, there I stand before thee."

> What does this comment mean? Would the same thing be true of the footprints of animals? Why? How do these last two quotations help us solve the problem of the Cambridge mayor and the Agudah?

A third Talmudic saying goes: "A man does not hurt his finger unless it is decreed from above."

> What do you think this means? Does it help us make up our minds about the cases described in this section? Does it agree or disagree with the first of the three Talmudic quotations given here?

The diagram in this chapter and the picture on page 3, Group II, photo section, represent modern concepts of God. On page 4, Group II, photo section, are two additional pictures which might be interpreted as representing concepts of God. In your workbook you will be given an opportunity to explain whether you think these two are modern or ancient interpretations.

Are We Free?

The questions raised in this section obviously deal with man's role in cooperating with God. We have referred to this relationship before but it deserves another word here. In our earlier chapters when we reached the conclusion that this seems to be a universe of law and order, in which a given cause always leads under similar circumstances to the same effect, some of you may have felt that everything in human life is determined in advance by causes outside us, leaving us no freedom or choice.

Such a conclusion would be contrary to the teachings both of science and of Judaism. Modern science tells us that within the larger laws of cause and effect there is much individual freedom. If, for example, a blue solution of some kind is poured into a glass of water, it is impossible to predict the direction that will be taken by each molecule of blue. If we know the amount of water in the glass as well as the amount of blue solution and its exact shade, we can predict the blend of color that will result, but we cannot tell in advance the direction in which individual molecules will move. We might almost say that individual molecules have "freedom" within the larger framework of predictable cause and effect, though unlike human beings, molecules cannot make a conscious choice.

In similar vein Judaism teaches that as individuals we have great freedom and choice within the laws of nature established and maintained by God. To be sure, we cannot escape or defy these laws. But we can choose countless different kinds of behavior while observing them.

One great thinker has compared the freedom within law of human life to playing bridge or, for that matter, most other games of cards. We are dealt a certain number of cards with which we must play, whether we like them or not. The "hand" we pick up corresponds to the laws of cause and effect in accordance with which we must live our lives. But we have freedom to play our "hand" in any way we like. One person may play his cards skilfully, while another will play the identical cards poorly. In like manner, though all of us are bound by the laws of nature, within those laws we have freedom to live our lives skilfully or poorly, which means to say, freedom to cooperate or not to cooperate with God.

Here is another comparison which may help you to understand this: fire is always governed by the same laws of nature. Without exception, whenever the circumstances leading to a fire are present there will be a fire. But sometimes fire burns to our advantage, as in the furnace on a cold day, while at other times it burns very much to our disadvantage, as when an entire forest is destroyed by it. Because this is a universe of law and order, we cannot change the circumstances which cause fire. But because we have a large degree of freedom within the framework of law and order we can, by the skill and care we exercise, usually determine whether fire is to burn to our benefit or our harm.

There is another fact to be remembered when we discuss the freedom each of us possesses within the framework of nature's law and order. Before evolution had reached the level of human development, there was little or no such freedom. A protozoan or a plant has no free choice; its life and movement are entirely determined by the laws of cause and effect which operate on it from outside itself. A human being, however, is in a different category. In discussing earlier how mankind differs from all other creatures in evolution, we noted that two such differences were: (1) man's knowledge of how he reached his present stage of development through evolution; and (2) his ability in some degree to affect the future course of evolution. These differences are important to remember again here. While all forms of life are subject to nature's laws, the higher one proceeds in evolution, the greater is the freedom each individual has to make important decisions and choices of his own within the framework of law and order.

Rabbi Akiba may have had this very thought in mind when he said, "Everything is foreseen, yet free will is given." The two parts of this statement are not as contradictory as they may at first appear. "Everything is foreseen" refers to those laws of nature which we human beings cannot change and by which we are restricted. "Yet free will is given" refers to the wide area of choice we have to cooperate with God and His laws if we wish.

Narrow Escape

Whenever a natural catastrophe like an earthquake occurs or a tragic wreck takes place we read about some individual who, by a stroke of last-minute luck, barely missed death. Many years ago scores of people were killed in a ghastly hospital fire at the Cleveland Clinic. For days afterward the newspapers recounted stories of patients who had had appointments in the hospital at the exact hour of the explosion but who had, for one reason or another, canceled their appointments for that day, in some cases only an hour or so before the tragedy.

A fairly recent example of this kind took place during February of 1950 when thirty-two people were killed in a terrible wreck on the Long Island Railroad at Rockville Centre, New York. The wreck occurred on a Friday night at about 10:30. Several members of the writer's congregation had been on that very train, returning late from business in New York, every night that week except the night of the fatal accident. Because it was Friday, they had taken an earlier train that night in order to reach home in time for Shabos dinner and synagogue services. Had the wreck occurred any other night that week, one or more of them might easily have been injured or even killed.

> How can we explain such things? Are they coincidences, or part of the plan and order we have observed in the universe? Did God arrange for the accident to occur on Friday night in order to protect good Jews? Was it a lesson to teach Jews to attend synagogue services on Friday nights? Is there any difference between the way in which a person with an ancient concept of God would explain this and the way a man with a modern concept might explain it?

One of the many hair-raising stories that came out of the Long Island wreck was that of a man who had taken that train home from work six nights a week for ten years, always occupying the same seat in the first car. On the night of the wreck he had just taken his usual seat while the train was still in the station, when a friend entered the car and sat across the aisle. To sit with his friend he got up, crossed the aisle, and for the first time in ten years did not sit in his accustomed place. In the wreck he was injured, but the man who had taken his usual seat after he left it was killed!

> Well, how would you account for that? What did God have to do with the man's changing seats? Was his life saved because he was a good person? Our discussion of these last two stories should help us still further to understand the modern Jewish meaning of the word God.

You Write the Conclusion

We could go on like this for the rest of our course, asking questions as important and fascinating as those included in this chapter. No doubt you have noticed that we didn't try to answer most of them for you. It will be both more interesting and more valuable if you do your own thinking about these questions. In doing so, keep in mind especially our modern conclusions about the meaning of the word God. You will be expected to answer some of them in your workbook; all of them will be discussed in class. It is necessary, therefore, for you to think about all of them—even those you do not select to answer in writing. Otherwise you will not be able to participate in our discussion.

Do you remember the chapters in which we surveyed our universe without once using the word God? We're going to conclude this chapter now by asking you to do something even more difficult than that. Your final assignment here will be to write a two-page essay defining an atheist, without using the word God, Lord, or any synonym for them!

Everyone knows that an atheist is a person who doesn't believe in God. But how can you describe one without using the word God? It can be done! But you'll have to do some careful planning, and you'll have to understand and remember just about everything we've said in the last few chapters. Incidentally, you'll find this not only an unusual assignment, but if the experience of other classes is any index, a most interesting one, too. When you finish it, you should have a very clear modern understanding of God, and you will be ready then to go on to the next chapter, which commences our consideration of the meaning of *religion*. Reading Selection F will help you with this assignment.

SOMETHING FOR YOU TO READ

A. Any effort to visualize [picture] God reveals a surprising childishness. We can no more conceive Him than we can conceive an electron. Yet many people do not believe in God simply because they cannot visualize Him. They forget that this incapacity is not, in itself, a proof of non-existence, considering that they firmly believe in the electron. We are in the habit of juggling nowadays with entities known to us only through their effects. These are the particles, electrons, protons, neutrons, etc. Individually, they are rigorously inconceivable [strictly beyond picturing] and physicists who specialize in this branch of science "forbid" any attempt at visualization. This does not disturb anybody, and their existence is not doubted for an instant because the physicists . . . affirm that without these particles our material objects, the forces we employ—in other words, our whole inorganic [not alive] universe becomes incoherent [senseless] and unintelligible.—Lecomte du Nouy, *Human Destiny*, Longmans, Green and Co.

B. (In the following poem, by George Eliot, the great violin maker, Antonio Stradivari, is speaking. This excerpt appears on page 173 of Dr. Samuel S. Cohon's book: *Judaism—A Way of Life*):

I say, not God Himself can make man's best
Without best men to help Him.
. . . 'tis God gives skill,
But not without man's hands: He could not make
Antonio Stradivari's violins
Without Antonio.

C. Modern theology is not willing to eliminate the concept of God, but it tries to reinterpret it. When a modern theologian speaks of God, he does not mean the Father in Heaven, a supernatural Personality, enthroned somewhere beyond the stars and controlling the destinies of men, but he means a spiritual Power working within the framework of history or in the minds of men. This Power may be defined as an . . . ideal, as a goal or value, towards which the whole evolutionary process is moving through the activity of man. . . . Nobody will deny that this conception of God and the world is a deeply religious conception and worthy of our profoundest reverence, devotion and sacrifice.—Immanuel Lewy, in *The Reconstructionist,* February 10, 1950.

D. In the early days of the struggle against actual polytheism [worship of many gods] this sentence (the Sh'ma) must have meant primarily a denial of idolatry. But through the ages its psychological effect was to summarize and climax the idea that, whether you are moved by the miracle of nature or by the grandeur of history, whether you think in terms of space or of time, you think of the wonders of the natural world or of the upward struggle of man, through whatever avenue of wonder and understanding God enters your heart, "The Lord our God is One." All human concepts of God are but fragments of the Infinite unity.—Solomon B. Freehof, *Preface to Scripture,* Union of American Hebrew Congregations.

E. When you said there are some things even God can't do alone, you were saying one of the most important things about God, at least so it seems to me. He never transgresses [sins against] human personality, He doesn't "make" us do a thing. He doesn't even compel us to be good. If He did, He would be only a driving arbitrary force in a world of automatons. There would be no choices for human beings to make, no struggle to know which things are good to do and which work harm. There would be no passionate devotion to finding out the secrets of nature, no sharpening of man's wits against the universe, no growth. It takes a really great God to leave man free to make his own mistakes.—Marguerite Harmon, *When Children Ask,* Harper and Bros.

F. Atheism at bottom means the inability of a man to utter an all-embracing "yea" to existence. It is the denial of meaning in life. It is the distrust of the universe. The atheist's real creed might be reduced to these sentences: "I honestly believe that the world is an accidental creation of exploding suns, a place of terror and of death. I honestly believe that man is an animal who happens to be endowed with more cunning than the rest of the animal kingdom. . . ."

This creed stands in absolute opposition to the outlook of religion, which, in essence, maintains that the universe is friendly, that man is trustworthy, and that God exists. . . .—Joshua L. Liebman, *Peace of Mind*, Simon & Schuster.

10. *What Is Religion?*

DOES it strike you as strange that we have written nine chapters of a book on religion without once trying to define just what we mean by religion? If you thought it strange in the beginning, our reason should be fairly clear by this time. Obviously, the most important concept we must deal with in discussing religion is that of God. All religions are based on a belief in gods or God. It was wiser first, therefore, to decide what modern Jews mean by the word *God* before attempting to define the meaning of the word *religion*. With the modern Jewish meanings of God now clearly established in our minds, it should be comparatively easy for us to decide upon definitions for the word *religion* and the other terms we shall deal with in the remainder of this course.

Just as we found many different notions about God, so we must expect varying ideas on the meaning of religion. There will be differences between Jews and the members of other religious groups. There will even be some differences among Jews themselves, especially between those whose ideas about religion are still pretty much what the thoughts of our ancestors were and those who have been developing new ideas based on the old. Our aim here is not to find a definition of religion which will necessarily suit everyone, but rather one which will be adequate from the modern Jewish point of view we have been developing throughout this book.

Let's begin by looking briefly at a number of people and experiences, in order to see what others think religion is. We shall try to extract from each whatever truth there may be which we can later include in our own definition. Many of our examples will be either in the form of newspaper clippings or digests of news items which have appeared in recent years. With some of them you may already be partially familiar.

1. Case number one is that of a forty-five-year-old mother named Anna Sullivan whose story was published in many papers the early part of 1949. For ten years she had kept her son, Gerald, locked in a room. He had never seen the outside world, met people, or even worn shoes! His hair had never been cut. She fed him through a small window in the door of the tiny room which served virtually as his prison. Now the interesting part of this story, from our point of view, is the statement in one paper that his mother "was known among her neighbors for her church work and charities." Apparently she was a regular attendant at church services and worked actively for her church.

> Would you call her a religious person? Do you think anyone would? Would she have considered herself a religious person? What, if anything, can we learn from her story about a definition of the word religion?

2. Here is a second example. There is a church in New York which holds a most unusual ceremony annually during the coldest part of the year, some time in January. A gold cross is first

blessed by their priest. Then members of the sect march with him to the river. If necessary, a hole is chopped through the ice; in any event, of course, the water isn't far from freezing. The cross is then thrown into the icy waters and several swimmers dive in after it. As soon as one of them retrieves the cross, he returns it to the priest who then proceeds to bless the successful swimmer. One year the ceremony had an unexpected climax when two swimmers brought the cross up together and proceeded to indulge in a public fist-fight, each claiming he had won the blessing.

> According to our modern Jewish ideas, would this properly be called a religious ceremony? Why? Do the members of the church involved consider it a religious ceremony? If two groups differ on a definition like this how can one decide which is the true interpretation? Does the description above remind you of any Jewish ritual or ceremony which takes place at the waterfront? What obvious differences are there between the Jewish and the Greek ceremonies? Would you call the Jewish ceremony religious? Why?

3. One more case now, before we try to reach some conclusions. This is a clipping, taken from the April 15, 1949, edition of the *New York Herald-Tribune:*

CROWDS FLOCK TO SEE GIRL'S KISS MAKE STATUE OF ST. ANNE "WEEP"

SYRACUSE, April 14.—Reports that the kisses of an eleven-year-old girl brought tears from the eyes of a broken statuette of St. Anne, mother of the Virgin Mary, caused hundreds of persons to congregate today in front of the home of the child, Shirley Anne Martin, at 511 Hawley Avenue. . . .

The figure of St. Anne was one of two statuettes which Mrs. Laura Allen, of 111 Lombard Avenue, gave to Shirley and her family. They were about three feet in height. The statuette of St. Anne fell and was broken into several pieces some two weeks ago. Shirley's mother, Mrs. Arthur E. Martin, then threw the remaining fragments into a trash can.

KISSES BROKEN FRAGMENT

Shirley subsequently found the cowled head, about three inches long, in the driveway. She picked it up, cuddled it and kissed it, then stared at it with amazed eyes and ran into the house.

"Mom," she said, "the statue cried. I kissed it and it cried."

Mrs. Martin was busy and paid little attention until Shirley's insistence brought her to the child's side. Tears, she said, were rolling down the face of St. Anne. . . .

Within a few days hundreds were visiting the second-story apartment daily and the police began to take official notice. Today, when visitors to the house were barred, Shirley made occasional appearances at the windows or on the front steps. . . .

Her mother sent her to her maternal grandparents, Mr. and Mrs. James Secreti. . . . Mrs. Secreti, a firm believer in the supernatural nature of the phenomenon, says that several days ago she collected a vial of St. Anne's "tears" and found that they eased her neuralgia when they were rubbed on her skin.

How can we explain this strange incident? Do you believe that tears actually flowed from the statue's eyes? If they did, would you call this a religious experience? If they did not, would you call it one? Have you ever had a similar experience? Ever heard of one? Why would so many people want to visit Shirley and see her? How can we explain the fact that Shirley's grandmother cured herself of neuralgia by rubbing the "tears" on herself? From our modern Jewish point of view, would this be a religious experience? Would all Christians consider it a religious experience?

4. Though it isn't an incident like the preceding, perhaps the following statement will also help us reach a definition of religion. A student in one of the writer's previous Confirmation classes, when asked for the definition of Orthodox, Conservative and Reform Jews respectively, answered somewhat as follows: "Orthodox Jews," he said, "are very religious Jews. Conservative Jews are less religious than Orthodox, but more religious than Reform. Reform or Liberal Jews are the least religious of all."

Would you agree with this statement? With his use of the word religious? Can you think of any other word which would better describe his actual meaning than the word religious?

The probability is there may be differences even among the members of our class as we discuss these cases and examples. Some of us may consider a particular incident to be a good example of religion, while others will strongly disagree. Despite any disagreements, however, most of us will probably feel that the above descriptions contain more *superstition* than *religion*. This isn't too surprising, since what we today call religion originally grew out of what now appears to be superstition. Nor is this the only example; the same thing is true in the realm of science.

One of our most valuable and interesting branches of modern science is astronomy, the study of the planets and stars of our universe. Before there was a science of astronomy, however, there was a superstition called astrology. As a matter of fact, there are people even today who believe in the nonsense of astrology, according to which a person's character and future may be foretold by the position of the stars when he was born. You may have noticed that horoscopes, which claim to predict a person's future through astrology, are published daily in some newspapers and can be bought in many stores. But intelligent people recognize this to be only superstition. In this connection it is interesting to note that as long ago as the twelfth century, when most people accepted astrology as valid, Maimonides proclaimed it to be a superstition.

Now the fact that the science of astronomy developed out of the superstition of astrology doesn't detract from astronomy or its value, any more than the origin of religion in superstition diminishes the value of religion today. It is highly important, however, that we keep in mind the distinction between religion and superstition, especially since there are large numbers of people today, Jews and Christians alike, who confuse the two. Superstition may be defined as a belief which runs counter to known facts; no really modern religion can accept a belief which demonstrated or proved fact shows to be impossible.

There are other examples, besides that of astronomy and astrology, showing how a science has grown out of a superstition.

In Section I of your workbook you will be given an opportunity to give one more such example of your own.

Still Searching

Well, we've discovered the difference between religion and superstition, but we still don't have a definition of religion, do we? Furthermore, we don't intend yet to give you one, until after you've done a great deal more thinking on your own. To help you do that, we're going to give you now a number of cases which differ from those we considered above. The following will be descriptions of well-known individuals in American history. In each case we shall present a brief outline of the person's career, and your task as you read is to make up your mind whether or not you think that individual is or was truly religious. Perhaps deciding what a religious person is will help us define religion.

1. Example number one is a man named Daniel Drew, a wealthy man who earned much of his money through financial fights with other wealthy men like Vanderbilt, in the course of which his tactics weren't always completely honest. The foundation of his original fortune was laid during his years in the cattle business. The people among whom he spent his early life said that often he gathered up cattle from his neighbors on credit, drove them to New York where he sold them, but failed to pay the individuals from whom he had secured them. Another of his favorite tricks was to keep his cattle thirsty during the long journey to market, allowing them to drink all the water they wanted just before time to sell them. The water they then consumed in enormous quantity because of their terrible thirst would greatly add to their apparent weight. The purchaser would thus be cheated because he was actually paying for a certain amount of weight in water rather than meat.

One biographer of Daniel Drew tells us that he thought the honest people of the world were a "pack of fools." After he had established his tremendous fortune he donated a quarter of a million dollars to build the Drew Seminary in New Jersey for the training of ministers. It later developed that he had actually given only a note, not cash, and all or part of the sum he had promised was never paid.

Besides establishing the Seminary, Drew donated sums of money for the building of chapels and attended frequent prayer services himself. Particularly in hours of trouble or worry he would pray at great length, sometimes in church, sometimes at home.

> Would you call Daniel Drew a religious man? Why? Suppose he had paid his pledge to the Seminary—would that have made a difference in your answer? Why? Can a man be religious if his conduct is unethical? Having once indulged in unethical conduct to amass his fortune, could such a man ever in the future be considered religious? Think about these questions and decide what your tentative answers would be before going on with the text.

The great leaders of Jewish religious thought would have said that a man like Daniel Drew was not religious, because he was not ethical. There is, as we shall see shortly, a difference between ethics and religion, but according to Judaism it is impossible to be religious without being ethical. Many statements and stories could be cited from Jewish tradition to show how deeply our ancestors felt this. The prophet Isaiah, for example, said, ". . . the Lord of hosts is exalted through justice and God the Holy One is sanctified through righteousness." The first two Reading Selections at the end of this chapter are additional Biblical selections showing how closely our ancestors believed religion and ethics to be related. One of the post-Biblical rabbis showed how important he considered ethical conduct to be when he imagined God, as it were, saying of the children of Israel, "Would that they would forget Me, and keep My commandments!" How would you express his meaning in your own words?

Similar to this is the statement of the Talmud: "He who only studies Torah without applying its precepts to conduct is as if he were without God." Rabbi Akiba once said, "He who pleases people, pleases God, but he who does not please people fails to please God also." How would you apply these two opinions to the case of Daniel Drew?

Many stories from Jewish literature likewise illustrate this truth. A medieval Jewish story, for example, concerns itself with a Torah Scroll in which a mistake was discovered. A pious scribe was brought in to correct the mistake, but after he had finished, the mistake appeared again. As often as he would correct it, it seemed to reappear. Finally, upon due investigation, it was discovered that the money with which that scroll had originally been purchased was "rake-off" money from a gambler. Not even a Torah was acceptable to the Jewish people if it had been purchased by money obtained unethically!

In similar vein is the Chasidic story of a famous scholar, Rabbi David of Lelov, who was hurrying to the synagogue one Yom Kippur eve to pray Kol Nidrei. On the way he heard an infant crying. He entered a nearby house, where he found a frightened infant whose parents had left it alone while they went to pray. Rabbi David remained with the infant, soothing and rocking it until it stopped crying. When the parents returned from their prayers, they found a great rabbi who had prayed Kol Nidrei alone on the most sacred night of the year in order to comfort a little baby!

A similar story tells of another famous rabbi, Israel Salanter, who, also on his way to Kol Nidrei services, saw an animal that was lost. While the whole congregation waited for him to lead them in prayer, he carefully brought the lost animal home. When his congregation came looking for him, they found him leading it safely into its master's stall.

> What would the writers of such stories as these say about the relationship between religion and conduct? What would they say about Daniel Drew? How would they define religion? Would they say that praying in the synagogue is not an important part of religion?

Are Religion and Ethics the Same?

2. Another case:—a man named Clarence Darrow. You may already have heard of him. He was one of this nation's outstanding lawyers a generation ago. Darrow insisted in public that he was an atheist, that he believed in neither God nor religion. He even used to travel around the country debating against clergymen, trying to prove that there is no God and that religion is nonsense. After he had earned enough money to provide for his needs, he delighted in taking on the legal defense of clients whom he believed to be unjustly accused and who could not afford first-rate legal talent. Many was the labor union organizer or minority political leader whose case was taken by Clarence Darrow for little or no fee.

> From this brief recital of biographical facts, would you or would you not call Clarence Darrow religious? Why? Would you call him ethical? Why? Can a man be ethical without being religious? (As in the case of Drew, think about these questions now, before proceeding with the chapter.)

There is a Midrash which may indirectly help us decide whether or not Clarence Darrow may be called religious. It tells us that when Abraham and Isaac, together with their two servants, approached Mount Moriah, on which Isaac was to be sacrificed, Abraham and Isaac looked up and recognized that God was on the mountain. They turned to their servants and asked if they saw anything there. When the servants replied in the negative, Abraham said to them, "Abide ye here with the donkey, and I and the lad will go yonder and we will worship. . . ."

> How would you express in your own words what this Midrash meant to teach about religion? Does it help in trying to decide whether Darrow was religious?

No one would deny that occasionally we find men and women who lead ethical lives without being religious. This brings up an interesting and important question. If it is possible to be ethical without being religious, why then do we need religion? There are a number of possible answers; we shall attempt to give only one. An intelligent person needs some good *reason* for being ethical. A little child obeys his parents merely because they order certain types of conduct, but as a child grows older, he begins to ask for reasons; he wants to know *why* it is necessary for him to behave one way rather than another.

How much truer this is of intelligent adults! If this is a universe of accident, in which things just happen willy-nilly, without reason or purpose, if we have no assurance that our high ethical ideals can be achieved and that ethical conduct is part of the plan or scheme of things, then why should people sacrifice for the sake of others things they want very much for themselves? If material, physical things are the most important goals in human existence, why shouldn't people get all they can for themselves without thinking of others? On the other hand, if this is a universe in which the power of God rules, if our ethical conduct enables us to advance the cause of human evolution, if indeed we were born for that very purpose, then a person has good reason to forego some of the conveniences and comforts he might want for himself in favor of ethical conduct which will help others. Which of your readings at the end of this chapter agrees with this point of view?

Someone has compared the relationship between ethical conduct and religion to working out a jig-saw puzzle. An intelligent person will work at such a puzzle only if he is confident that he has all the pieces and that, with proper patience and persistence, it is possible to fit them into a picture. If he suspects that there are numerous pieces missing or that the parts of several puzzles have been mixed so that no picture can be made despite his patience, he will quickly lose interest and quit. So it is with ethics and religion. In order to live ethically, most of us need the conviction that life has some purpose and that ethical conduct is part of that purpose. We need to feel that we have an opportunity to advance the development of evolution by choosing right.

> Later in this chapter you will be told about two men, Albert Schweitzer and Leo Baeck. From the facts given about their lives, do you think they could have made such sacrifices purely through ethics, without religion?

True, now and then a man like Clarence Darrow appears who seems able to live an ethical life without any religious belief. But such a man is an exception. Most of us cannot divorce our conduct from what we believe about the universe and the purpose of human life. So we need to have religion before we can be fully ethical.

Religion, therefore, is *ethics plus*. Until we decide just what the *plus* is, we won't have our definition of religion. It will help us to say that while ethics merely tells us what is right and what is wrong, religion does the following in addition:

a. By giving us a valid *reason* for behaving ethically, it *stimulates* and *motivates* us to strive for ethical improvement.

b. Because of our faith in God, it gives us the *assurance* and *confidence* that in the end our ethical ideals will prevail.

3. Another brief biography which may help us in our quest for a definition of religion is that of Albert Schweitzer, who visited the United States in the summer of 1949. Schweitzer is a man of three distinguished careers. A musician, he is known as one of the finest organists in the world and an expert in the music of Bach. As a Christian minister he has written one of the finest studies in the world on Jesus. But he is also a physician and has spent about forty years of his life doing missionary work in French Equatorial Africa. He and his wife operate a hospital and mission for the natives there, curing them of their diseases and teaching them Christianity.

Albert Schweitzer could easily be a man of both fortune and fame anywhere in the civilized world. Instead, he prefers to serve the black men of Africa. When he needs additional money for his mission he returns to the continent of Europe, where he gives organ recitals to raise money. He then goes back to the jungles for another three or four years to serve the natives whom he loves.

> Compare Albert Schweitzer now to Daniel Drew and Clarence Darrow. Is Schweitzer ethical? Why? Is he religious? Why? Do the facts given here about him help us toward a definition of religion?

After you have thought about these questions, we should be ready to reach our definition. It is not necessary for all of us to agree exactly or to express our definition in precisely the same words. We ought to recognize, however, that two things are necessary for religion: belief and action. Someone has defined religion as believing in God and carrying out that belief in daily conduct. Do you agree with that definition? Is there anything you would want to add to it? Can you express it in a better way?

The Oxford dictionary gives this definition of religion: "Recognition on the part of man of some higher unseen power as having control of his destiny, and as being entitled to obedience, reverence, and worship." Is this definition acceptable to you? What do you like in it? What do you dislike? Why? Is it helpful in arriving at your own definition?

However you decide to express your own definition, always keep in mind that in religion *belief* is important only if it leads to *action*. We Jews especially have always conceived religion as a *way of life*. Our beliefs and faith have been the prelude to that way of life. We have lived a certain way because only such conduct would be consistent with what we firmly believe about the universe in which we live and our own role in that universe as human beings.

The close connection in Jewish tradition between *belief* and *action* in religion is illustrated by one of the most famous of all our Bible passages: "Thou shalt love thy neighbour as thyself." This directive for the highest type of ethical conduct is immediately followed by: "I am the Lord." In other words, as far as Judaism is concerned, the reason for ethical behavior is that there is a God in whom we believe.

What a man believes about God and religion is wholly unimportant if, as a result of that belief, he doesn't live a better and more ethical life than the way he would live if he had no faith. All these things should be kept clearly in mind as you prepare to write in your workbook your own personal definition of religion.

Were the Following Religious?

After you have decided upon your definition of religion and have written it in the workbook, your final task for this chapter will be to read each of the following brief biographies and decide whether the individual being described was or was not a religious person. Answer the following questions about each: (1) Was he ethical? Why? (2) Was he religious? Why?

A. You have undoubtedly heard about *Louis Dembitz Brandeis,* one of the outstanding American Jews of the latter nineteenth and early twentieth centuries. Justice Brandeis began his career as a brilliant attorney in the city of Boston. He fought many legal battles against great monopolies which fleeced the public. He worked actively in support of workers and labor unions. He was the first Jew ever to be appointed to the Supreme Court of the United States. For many years he was an active leader of the American Zionist movement, and it is no exaggeration to say he played a major role in bringing the Balfour Declaration into existence and in establishing the foundations of the State of Israel. A colony in Israel is named after Mr. Brandeis. So far as we know he never belonged to any synagogue, nor did he attend Jewish religious services. He is reputed to have kept his office open and later to have officiated in court even on Yom Kippur.

B. *John D. Rockefeller, Sr.* was probably at one time the richest man in the United States. Most of his fortune came from the Standard Oil Company which he founded. He began as a small oil operator in the city of Cleveland, gradually buying out his competitors in order to establish one gigantic oil company. His customary method was to lower his prices temporarily in order to drive a given competitor out of business. When the competitor could no longer afford to hold out, Rockefeller would buy his concern, after which his prices would go up again. Dozens of business men were driven to the wall in the founding of Standard Oil. Rockefeller's policies toward his workers were no less severe. He fought tooth and nail against the establishment of labor unions in his plants. In at least one instance his company police fired on a large group of workers who were trying to organize a union, killing men, women and children.

One of Mr. Rockefeller's biographers has written of him: "At times it was difficult to understand the guiding principle which fostered extensive missionary work in China at a moment when the workers of his Colorado Fuel and Iron Company were being shot down or burnt alive in industrial war." What another biographer said about him will be found in a Reading Selection for this chapter.

With his millions, however, he supported and built a considerable number of churches. He also supported Christian missions abroad and established the Rockefeller Foundation, which has contributed funds to a large number of medical, scientific, and charitable institutions.

C. *Stephen Samuel Wise*, who died in 1949, was one of America's outstanding rabbis. (Don't just assume that because he was a rabbi he must have been religious according to our modern definition. Read this case and the next as if the individuals being described were not rabbis. It is possible, after all, for some people who are not professional religious leaders to be more truly religious than some clergymen.) He established the Free Synagogue in New York, dedicated to the proposition that members should pay only what they can afford and that there must be no assigned or reserved seats. The latter provision was to prevent special seating privileges to those who happened to be wealthier. He also insisted on a free pulpit, from which he constantly preached against selfishness in business, in favor of working men and their unions, against war, etc. He battled all his life on behalf of justice for the underdog and for a safe Jewish homeland in Palestine.

D. *Dr. Leo Baeck* was the most prominent Liberal rabbi of Germany when Hitler came to power. He was already advanced in years at that time. On a number of occasions friends urged him to leave Germany at a time when he might well have escaped. He consistently refused, insisting that so long as his people remained there, they needed his instruction and guidance. Finally Dr. Baeck was himself imprisoned in a concentration camp. For about four years he was a prisoner, forced to perform such menial tasks as hauling rubbish and garbage for the Nazis. In the camps where he was kept, he managed somehow to conduct both religious services and classes for the children even though they were prohibited under penalty of death. Without schoolrooms, pulpit, books, light, or any other equipment, he preached sermons and taught religion. It was only after the war had ended that Dr. Baeck was released. He now teaches at the Hebrew Union College-Jewish Institute of Religion.

When you have given your opinion of each of these cases in the workbook and have read the selections below, you will have finished this chapter.

SOMETHING FOR YOU TO READ

A. The following is Psalm 15:

Lord, who shall sojourn in Thy tabernacle?
Who shall dwell upon Thy holy mountain?
He that walketh uprightly, and worketh righteousness,
And speaketh truth in his heart,
That hath no slander upon his tongue,
Nor doeth evil to his fellow,
Nor taketh up a reproach against his neighbour;
In whose eyes a vile person is despised,
But he honoureth them that fear the Lord;
He that sweareth to his own hurt, and changeth not;
He that putteth not out his money on interest,
Nor taketh a bribe against the innocent.
He that doeth these things shall never be moved.

B. (In the following Bible passages, the second Isaiah was criticizing his people for the wrong kind of fast on Yom Kippur):

Is such the fast that I have chosen?
The day for a man to afflict his soul?
Is it to bow down his head as a bulrush,
And to spread sackcloth and ashes under him?
Wilt thou call this a fast,
And an acceptable day to the Lord?

Is not this the fast that I have chosen?
To loose the fetters of wickedness,
To undo the bands of the yoke,
And to let the oppressed go free,
And that ye break every yoke?
Is it not to deal thy bread to the hungry,
And that thou bring the poor that are cast out to thy house?
When thou seest the naked, that thou cover him,
And that thou hide not thyself from thine own flesh?

C. Religion is not so much knowledge of God as godly living. What distinguishes a religion from a system of science or philosophy is its concern with man's behavior. Theories of reality are vital to it only to the degree to which they help transform the lives of men and to affect their conduct. . . .

. . . Unless religion affects human life and conduct, it is of small worth.—Samuel S. Cohon, *Judaism—A Way of Life*, Union of American Hebrew Congregations.

D. . . . man cannot engage in ethical activity in a world which has no meaning.—George Seaver, *Albert Schweitzer*, Harper and Bros.

E. A man shall do good works, not until then shall he beg the Torah of God.

A man shall do righteous and worthy works, not until then shall he beg wisdom of God.

A man shall walk the way of humility, not until then shall he beg understanding of God.—Rabbinic Literature, quoted in Glatzer, *In Time and Eternity*, Schocken Books, Inc.

F. When man appears before the Throne of Judgment, the first question he is asked is not—"Have you believed in God?" or, "Have you prayed or performed ritual acts?" but "Have you dealt honorably, faithfully in all your dealings with your fellow man?"—Talmud, quoted in Newman, *The Talmudic Anthology*, Behrman House.

G. Sometimes the question is asked, "But isn't liberal religion just a system of ethics and not a religious position at all?" Definitely no! A system of ethics is simply a group of rules men ought to follow in order to lead the good life. There is no particular motivation or attempt made to induce them to follow those rules. Ethics tends to be a take-it-or-leave-it proposition. Whereas religion not only presents rules or principles of conduct; it also tries to motivate and inspire men to live by them.—Argow, *What Do Religious Liberals Believe?* The Beacon Press.

H. It is important that men should not murder, and it is important that men should not steal, but it is far more important that they should have central convictions which give them courage to refuse to murder and steal, even when a tyrant may require it. This is why religion is always more primary, both in logic and in human experience, than ethics can ever be. To know what is right is important, but to have the power and courage to do it is far more important. —Trueblood, *Foundations for Reconstruction*, Harper and Bros.

I. Rockefeller found nothing inconsistent between his religious beliefs and his business practices. He regarded his wealth as a reward for his virtue. The entire philosophy of his life—a philosophy which he had acquired in the home environment of his childhood—could be summed up in a few words: "Serve the Lord and exploit thy neighbors.". . .

He never for a moment suspected that what he was doing was not good in the eyes of the Lord. . . .

He was unable to distinguish between right and wrong. Justice was as vague a quality to him as light is to a man physically blind. He lacked the moral vision to see himself in relation to other people. The world, as he imagined it, consisted of one man—himself—surrounded by millions of worms. He used them as bait or stepped upon them with equal indifference. Their wrigglings served merely as a source of amusement to him. . . .

The Rockefeller Institute for Medical Research . . . has resulted in the saving of many lives. But what of the many lives stunted and crushed in Rockefeller's relentless reaping of the harvest of his wealth?—Henry and Dana Lee Thomas, *Fifty Great Americans*, Doubleday and Co.

J. The quest for right living, the question of what is to be done right now, right here, is the authentic core of Jewish religion.—Reprinted from *Man Is Not Alone*, copyright by Dr. Abraham J. Heschel, with the permission of the publisher, Farrar, Straus and Young, Inc.

11. *Religion and Science*

Now that we have an acceptable modern definition of the word religion, we can go on to consider the very interesting relationships between religion and a number of other things. After all, religion isn't something isolated from other experiences in life; it doesn't exist in a separate compartment of its own. We said in the previous chapter that especially for Jews religion has always been looked upon as a *way of life*. That being the case, our purpose in this chapter will be to discover the relationship between that *way of life* and other important human experiences. Our first relationship will be that between religion and science.

Do you remember, back in an early chapter, when someone asked whether we were studying religion or science? We learned then that there is a very close relationship between the two. You may have heard somewhere that there is a conflict between religion and science. Perhaps in your history or social studies at school you have read how the leaders of religion have on occasion resisted the advance of science. It was the church, for example, which fought Galileo when he first taught that the earth revolves around the sun rather than the sun around the earth. Likewise, many churches and religious denominations at first fought against the teachings of evolution; some few, as a matter of fact, still do. There are still church organizations which believe that to teach evolution is to cast doubt on the truth of the Bible story of Creation and to degrade human beings by considering them as animals. So apparently there has indeed been some conflict in the past. What we want to consider here is whether there still need be—whether or not religion and science, each properly understood from a modern point of view, are antagonistic toward each other.

Has there been a conflict between religion and science as far as Albert Schweitzer is concerned? The information about him in our previous chapter should enable you to answer this. Are there any other renowned men of science who were also religious men? Surely one index to the relationship between religion and science may be found in the feelings of prominent scientists.

One man whose life story will help us greatly in our effort to answer these questions is George Washington Carver. We wish we had time and room here to give you his entire biography. The few facts we are about to review will convince you, we hope, that one of the most fascinating experiences you could possibly enjoy would be to secure his biography and read more about him. George Washington Carver was one of America's greatest heroes. This despite the fact that he never wore a uniform or piloted a plane or carried a gun. He was a great hero of science. The son of Negro slaves in the South, he overcame unbelievable handicaps in his search for a scientific education, and despite poverty and discrimination, advanced to the point where he became an outstanding chemist and college instructor in science.

Greatly worried over the fact that the South was entirely dependent upon its cotton crop—and the price of cotton was so uncertain—he set about to discover possible unsuspected uses for the peanut, another crop wide-spread in the South. Up to that time, the peanut was considered almost a waste product of the soil. Dr. Carver, to begin with, found the peanut to be one of the most nutritious foods in the world; it contains very nearly every food element required to sustain human life. Then through patient research and experimentation, he discovered more than a hundred commercial uses for peanuts and peanut oil. As a result, the agricultural economy of the South was practically revolutionized.

The peanut became a major crop in many southern states, chiefly because of the scientific genius of a Negro chemist who wasn't even recognized as a human being by many of those whom he most greatly benefited. To the end of his life, when Dr. Carver lectured at a convention of distinguished white scientists anywhere in the South in order to share with them the results of his work, he was forced to use rear entrances and freight elevators, and could not eat publicly with those whom he was instructing. All because his skin happened to be a little darker than theirs!

Another person might have become angered or embittered through such experiences. But Dr. Carver retained a sweetness of character which was quite as remarkable as his scientific genius. He was also a very deeply religious person, which brings us to the point of discussing him in this chapter. He wrote a number of statements which can help us greatly in our present search to discover whether or not there must be a conflict between religion and science. For example: "I discover nothing in my laboratory. If I come here of myself, I am lost . . . I am God's servant, His agent, for here God and I are alone. I am just the instrument through which He speaks, and I would be able to do more if I were to stay in closer touch with Him. With my prayers I mix my labors, and sometimes God is pleased to bless the results."

That, you will admit, is quite a remarkable statement, especially coming as it does from so eminent a scientist.

But there were many equally impressive sentiments voiced by Dr. Carver. On one occasion he said, "Without God to draw aside the curtain I would be helpless." Another time he said, "What I have done, I have done in communion with God. He has revealed all these marvelous things to me. I deserve no credit for them whatever. . . . My laboratory has been called God's workshop by Dr. Glenn Clark and so it is." You will find another extraordinary quotation from Dr. Carver in your readings at the conclusion of this chapter. And if you would like to read more about this truly wonderful man, we recommend a book called, *George Washington Carver: An American Biography*, by Rackham Holt, Doubleday and Co., 1950. You will also find in this chapter's Reading Selections the words of another world-famous scientist whose opinions agree with Dr. Carver's.

> Has there been any conflict between religion and science for this great man? Does he sound as if his concept of God is an ancient or a modern one? What evidence do you find for your answer in his statements? What do you suppose Dr. Carver meant in calling himself "God's servant"? Of what possible use could his prayers be in the laboratory? What did he mean by God drawing aside the curtain? By calling his laboratory "God's workshop"?

Enemies or Allies?

We shall learn a great deal about the relationship between religion and science through a careful consideration of these questions about George Washington Carver. And we shall see just why, for modern science and modern religion, there is no conflict. There are two respects in which religion and science, far from being opposed to each other, are entirely necessary to each other.

1. God, you will recall, is the power or force behind nature

and responsible for the wonderfully thrilling story of evolution. But nature and evolution are precisely the fields in which science does its work, are they not? It is science which has given us our knowledge of how harmonious nature really is. It is science which disclosed to us the whole story of evolution. The scientist, more than any other type of person, should appreciate that this universe isn't the kind of thing which could have developed just by accident, that there must be a purpose of some kind behind our lives, and therefore a power or force which we can recognize. The more science teaches us, the more awesome and impressive does the universe become, and the more convinced we should be of God.

2. We also decided that God is the force or power within each of us which impels us toward our ethical goal and which drives us upward (*if* we cooperate!) to advance the progress of evolution still higher. The scientist's search for knowledge is obviously one of the ways in which such progress takes place. Therefore, it is precisely the force of God, operating within the scientist, which drives him to greater and greater discovery. Just as it is God working within the writer, the musician, and the artist which stimulates them to do their best creative work. This is exactly what Dr. Carver was trying to say.

It is also what Jewish tradition has taught for many centuries. No doubt you remember the story of how Moses remained on the top of Mt. Sinai forty days and nights in order to receive the Ten Commandments. Our ancestors, of course, interpreted quite literally the Bible account which tells us that he talked there with God and finally was given the tablets of stone containing the Decalogue. Our own modern interpretation would be somewhat different. We would say that Moses went to the top of the mountain in order to get away from all the noise and confusion of daily life—just as an artist or writer today needs to be alone to accomplish his creative work—to meditate, to commune with the best in himself, to establish contact with God, and then to bring his people the Ten Commandments. This is exactly what the scientist does in his laboratory.

There is a statement in the Talmud which says: "Man is a co-worker with God in the work of creation." This too is what Dr. Carver said in his own way. And this is one of the great differences we noted some time back between man and all the other forms of life which preceded him in evolution. Only human beings have developed to the point of intelligence and understanding where they know what is going on in evolution and can themselves aid and hasten their own upward development. "Man is a co-worker with God in the work of creation."

All this should help us understand why eminent scientists like Albert Schweitzer and George Washington Carver have also been deeply religious individuals. There have been many other examples too. Lecomte du Nouy, a great French scientist, wrote: "Science . . . leads to the necessity of the idea of God." Robert Millikan and Sir James Jeans are two additional scientists of fame who have written interesting statements about religion. *Dr. Millikan:* "Modern science of the real sort is learning to walk humbly with its God. And in learning that lesson it is contributing something to religion." *Sir James Jeans:* "We discover that the universe shows evidence of a designing or controlling power that has something in common with our own individual minds. . . ." You may recall this last statement from an earlier chapter.

Albert Einstein, perhaps the greatest scientist of our generation, has also had some interesting things to say about religion. Two of his views will be found among your Reading Selections for this chapter. One brief statement we give you here, however; you will be asked to explain it in your workbook. He said, "Science without religion is lame, and religion without science is blind." Be prepared, especially in the light of the preceding chapter and this one, to explain exactly what Dr. Einstein meant by each half of this statement.

We do not mean to give the impression here that all scientists are necessarily religious people. You will no doubt in time meet some college teachers of science who are indifferent to religion or even opposed to it. Our purpose in giving you quotations like those you have just read is to demonstrate that for some of the greatest scientists of our century there is no conflict between religion and science; they complement and supplement each other. Each is needed by the other; neither alone is enough. We can understand this mutual need one for the other if we think in terms of so simple a thing as a bicycle. What interest does science have in the bicycle? *What sort of question would science ask about it?*

> Of what material is this bicycle made? How much did it cost to produce it? How much does it weigh? How fast can it go? Can I find a way to produce it cheaper or make it go faster?

What kind of question would religion ask about the same bicycle?

> For what is this bicycle being used? Will its owner use it to steal something and run away, or to bring medicine to a sick person in an emergency? What can we do to provide a fine bicycle like this for every child, not just for the children of the rich?

It is easy to see that no conflict exists between these two sets of questions and of interests. To the contrary! The better the bicycle produced by science, the more likely are the interests of religion to be served. And the more questions of the second type religion asks, the more incentive will science have to produce a better cycle.

The example of the "bike" of course, is a very simple one. Perhaps a better illustration would be atomic energy. In your workbook you will be given an opportunity to indicate what the interests of science and religion respectively are in atomic energy. Someone once said that science is concerned with "what is" while religion is interested in "what ought to be." Do you agree that this is an accurate statement? Does the increase in our scientific knowledge make religion *more* necessary or *less* necessary? Or doesn't it make any difference? Why?

If our conclusion here is true, that there is no conflict between religion and science, then how can we explain the examples of conflict given at the beginning of this chapter? The answer is to be found in terms of the difference we noted in Chapter Ten between religion and superstition. There *is* a conflict between science and superstition, even when that superstition calls itself religion. There is no conflict between science and *modern* religion.

In the Beginning—What?

We don't want to leave the subject of religion and science without dealing at least briefly with one of the most interesting cases of the relationship between them, namely, the story of Creation as it is found in our Bible. We have already referred to this story in passing. Now it will be necessary for you to read it through in your Bible so that we may intelligently discuss it. Do that now, before continuing: turn to Genesis 1:1–2:3 in your Bible, and read the story through thoughtfully. We'll wait for you to do that. . . .

Finished? Then you surely must have noticed plenty of room for disagreement and conflict. Chief among the disagreements is the Bible statement that it took God six days to create the world and everything in it. But we already know that it required more than a billion years of slow evolution to "create" man as we know him now. How can we reconcile six days and a billion years? Doesn't it seem obvious that either science or religion must be right about Creation, not both? Well, there are several ways for us to approach this interesting story in Genesis.

1. One way is to look upon it as a *poetic account* of how our early ancestors thought the world and life began. Without our knowledge and experience in science, this is the way things seemed to them. The story is interesting to us now as history and as poetry, but we no longer believe it literally.

2. Another way to accept the story of Genesis is figuratively, that is to say, making the actual words of the story serve as symbols rather than accepting them literally. Many people have sug-

gested that each "day" in the story doesn't mean a day of twenty-four hours at all; that each "day" stands for a period or era of many centuries. They would say, then, that the Bible story is to be interpreted as a description of long periods or epochs of development, each represented or symbolized by a day.

Those who interpret the story this way would probably also add that in the main, the writer of Genesis, Chapter One, even without any direct knowledge of evolution, managed remarkably well, perhaps only by intuition, to list the forms of life in pretty much the order of their actual appearance. Notice, for example:

a. The first thing that happens is that light appears. God's very first words are Y'hi Or! יְהִי אוֹר, "Let there be light!" The very latest theory of science is that our earth may have originated in a tremendous explosion of some kind, with a blinding flash of light which filled the entire universe.

b. In the beginning the whole earth is covered with water; only later and gradually do the waters recede, exposing dry land. We have already seen in our review of evolution that the modern scientist says the same thing.

c. The first forms of life mentioned in the Bible story are sea monsters. After them come birds. In general, this follows very closely the pattern of evolution told in the rocks.

d. Only after the sea-creatures came animals which could live on dry land, and only as the final step in the creation of land animals did man appear. Here, too, the order is amazingly close to that given us by modern science.

We must not stretch the point too far, of course. It would be a mistake to suppose that the writer or writers of the Genesis story actually knew about evolution. But it is all the more remarkable that without knowing about it, they nevertheless came so close to scientific fact.

3. Though there is much to recommend each of these interpretations, there is a better way yet to look upon the Bible story of Creation, which is to recognize that the Bible isn't a science

book or a source of scientific knowledge at all. We turn to the Bible for an altogether different kind of knowledge from that of science. Actually we might speak in this respect of two kinds of "truth." We shall call them here *truth* and *Truth*. The first kind of truth refers to the actual details of any story in the Bible. When we ask whether a given story is *true*, we mean, did God really create the world in six days, or did the Red Sea really split for the children of Israel to pass through, or was there actually a great flood in the days of Noah?

When we ask, however, whether a story in the Bible is *True*, we mean, is there some great, lasting moral or ethical *Truth* which the writer of this story was trying to teach us? Are the details of the story as given merely symbols for something far more important which the author meant to convey to us? Can we find in this account some great principle we ought to remember, which can help us understand life and live it better? A story which is told primarily to teach a moral or ethical truth is called a *parable*. Let us examine the Biblical story of Creation more closely now, to see if it could properly be called a parable. Is it—

true or TRUE?

What can we learn from this story that may be more important than the actual details? We'll do the work for you on this one, after which you'll be asked to do the same thing on one or two other stories from the Bible. If you'll reread the story of Creation in Genesis, you'll find the following were some of the *Truths* we can find there:

a. Human beings are the highest order of creation. We are the only form of life created in the image of God, that is to say, the only form which has developed a soul. This means we also have a much greater responsibility than animals have, in that we alone are co-workers with God.

b. Life and the world in which we live it are good. Some religions are pessimistic, believing that human beings are essentially evil. Judaism is a religion of optimism. After each day in the story of Creation, the writer pictures God saying "It is good." Our faith proclaims that life is good and people can be good if they try. The pleasures of the world are here for us to enjoy, not to prohibit or deny.

c. God is the force or power behind everything. No part of the world exists without God. The spirit or intelligence known as God is responsible for everything we are and know.

d. Rest is as important for human life as work. After six days of labor, every human being is entitled to a day of rest. This includes not only the man who works for himself, but also his servants and employees, and even the stranger who happens to be with him.

These four ideas are only part of the moral message or lesson which the writer of this story meant to express. In your Reading Selections for this chapter you will find others. One of your workbook tasks will be to state at least seven of these in your own words.

Does this make the difference between *truth* and *Truth* a little clearer for you? And does it help you understand the kind of thing for which we look when we read a Bible story? If it does, then you will understand still better that there is no conflict between religion and science.

Now we want you yourself to find the *Truth* in two additional Bible stories with which you are probably already familiar. One is the story of Noah (which will be found in the following verses: Gen. 6:9–14 and 17–22; Gen. 7:1–7 and 17–24; Gen. 8: entire chapter). The other is the story of the Tower of Babel (to be found in Gen. 11:1–9). In your workbook you will be asked to choose one of these stories, read it carefully, and then list the *Truths* you think the writer was trying to teach us.

Do You Believe in Miracles?

There are many stories of miracles in the Bible. The Burning Bush and the Red Sea stories, to which we have already referred, are two examples. Are we to believe these stories about miracles when we read them in the Bible? If we do, then surely there will be a conflict between religion and science. For science tells us that the universe operates by laws, to which there can be no exceptions. And a miracle is an exception to one of the laws of nature. So apparently we shall have to choose; either science or the miracle, not both. Which shall it be? Again, there are two ways to interpret the miracles reported in the Bible:

1. Often there is a way of explaining what actually must have happened, without attributing it to a miracle. We must constantly keep in mind that our ancestors centuries ago were simple folk as far as science was concerned. They knew so much less than we do about the natural causes of things that whenever something wonderful or spectacular happened which they couldn't explain, they concluded that it must have been a miracle. If one of them had lived in our times, for example, and had seen the small, weak army of Israel defeat the very much larger and stronger armies of six Arab nations, the only way they could have explained it would have been through some miracle sent by God. (Remember, their idea of God wasn't exactly the same as ours.) We today explain the victory of Israel in terms of God, too, but not as a miracle. We say that it was God as a vision of ethical perfection and God as a driving force within the men and women of Israel which enabled them to survive and to establish their state.

To illustrate still further: there have been several natural explanations proposed of what might have happened when our ancestors under the leadership of Moses came to the Red Sea, with the Egyptian army pursuing them. There may have been a sand-bar known to Moses, while the Egyptians were drowned because they knew nothing about it. The tide may have come in between the time when the Jews crossed and the time the Egyptians reached the sea. There may have been a very strong desert wind blowing the water near the shore back while Moses led his people through; the wind could have subsided when Pharaoh followed, drowning all the Egyptians. We do not mean to say definitely which of these things actually happened, or indeed that we are sure any of them happened. There is a strong probability, however, that one of these things or something very much like them may have occurred. In the eyes of our ancestors, their escape from the jaws of certain death was too wonderful to be explained by any natural event of which they knew. Therefore, they told it in terms of a miracle. And as it was passed by word of mouth from generation to generation, the miracle no doubt grew greater in the telling.

The same thing was probably true of the flood story. One theory is that originally the whole Mediterranean Sea was dry land, a huge valley below sea-level, with only a mountain range near what is now Gibraltar to keep out the waters of the Atlantic Ocean. According to this theory, at some time or other in antiquity something happened—perhaps a tremendous earthquake—which resulted in the ocean waters breaking through at Gibraltar and flooding the entire Mediterranean area. No one can prove that it actually occurred this way. But it is easy to see that if it did, the mind of ancient man could explain such a catastrophe only in terms of a miracle. Incidentally, the fact that many other Mediterranean peoples besides our own have, in their literature, legends about an enormous flood, makes it more plausible to suppose that a great flood may actually have taken place.

So the first way to approach the miracle stories of the Bible is to remember that there may have been an actual event which our ancestors could understand only in that way.

2. A second way to interpret our Bible stories of miracles is in terms of the two kinds of truth with which we dealt a moment ago. Often these miracle stories too were really parables. Part of your assignment for this chapter, which you may already have done, was to discover the *Truths* which the writer of the story about the flood wanted to convey to us. So in addition to looking for a natural explanation for these stories, we today, if we are wise, search for the real meaning beneath the surface, the important lesson we are supposed to learn. It is interesting to note, by the way, that in this respect our Bible story about the

flood differs from the stories told by such other ancient peoples as the Babylonians. When they wrote their story about a great flood, there was no ethical principle they were trying to teach; when our own ancestors told about Noah, the ethical lesson was the main purpose of the story.

Do we today believe in miracles? Not as exceptions to the laws of God, no. We believe in the "miracle" of the orderly universe in which we live. We believe in the "miraculous" beauty of the autumn colors on the mountainside. We believe in the "miracle" of the human body, more complicated and wonderful by far than the most ingenious piece of machinery ever invented by man. In short, to us today the way God works according to the laws of the universe is far more wonderful than the exceptions to the law in which our fathers once believed. In the words of Rabbi Robert Gordis: "The modern religious spirit finds God revealed far more impressively in the majestic harmony and order of the universe than in the miracles which earlier generations delighted to chronicle."

This completes our survey of the relationship between religion and science, two of the most important areas of modern life. Our next concern, commencing in Chapter Twelve, will be the connection between religion and business.

SOMETHING FOR YOU TO READ

A. (The following is an additional interesting statement made by George Washington Carver):

I asked the Great Creator what the universe was made for. . . .

"Ask for something more in keeping with that little mind of yours," He replied. . . .

"What was man made for?"

"Little man, you still want to know too much. Cut down the extent of your request and improve the intent."

Then I told the Creator I wanted to know all about the peanut. He replied that my mind was too small to know *all* about the peanut, but He said He would give me a handful of peanuts. And God said,

"Behold, I have given you every herb bearing seed, which is upon the face of the earth . . . to you it shall be for meat. . . ."

I carried the peanuts into my laboratory and the Creator told me to take them apart and resolve them into their elements. With such knowledge as I had of chemistry and physics I set to work to take them apart. I separated the water, the fats, the oils, the gums, the resins, sugars, starches, pectoses, pentosans, amino acids. There! I had the parts of the peanuts all spread out before me.

I looked at Him and He looked at me. "Now you know what the peanut is."

"Why did You make the peanut?"

The Creator said, "I have given you three laws, namely, compatibility, temperature, and pressure. . . . All you have to do is take these constituents and put them together, observing these laws, and I will show you why I made the peanut."

I therefore went on to try different combinations of the parts under different conditions of temperature and pressure, and the result was what you see.—Rackham Holt, *George Washington Carver*, Doubleday and Co.

B. (The following three selections are additional comments on religion and science made by Dr. Albert Einstein, reprinted here by his personal permission):

I believe in God, the God of Spinoza, who reveals himself in the orderly harmony of the Universe. . . . I believe that intelligence is manifested [shown] throughout all nature. . . . The basis of all scientific work is the conviction that the world is an ordered and comprehensible [understandable] entity [thing, being] and not a thing of chance.

C. My religion consists of a humble admiration of the illimitable [unlimited] superior spirit who reveals himself in the slight details we are able to perceive with our frail and feeble minds. That deeply emotional conviction of the presence of a superior reasoning power, which is revealed in the incomprehensible [beyond understanding] universe, forms my idea of God.

D. . . . anyone who has seriously studied science is filled with the conviction that a spirit tremendously superior to the human spirit manifests itself in the law-abidingness of the world, before whom we with our simple powers must humbly stand back. So, the study of science leads to religious feeling. . . .

E. At first it seems daring, if not heretical, for us to say that God is . . . limited. We ask in amazement, "How can God be limited? If

He is not all-powerful—able to do anything that He wills—then surely He cannot be God!" I deny this conclusion. If I did not believe that God is *limited* by the very nature of the world He created, then I would have to surrender my faith.—Joshua Loth Liebman, *Peace of Mind*, Simon and Schuster.

F. . . . there does seem to be significance in the fact of the order, design and pattern of our universe. Forgotten centuries ago, primitive man saw the rise and fall of the tide, the regular phases of the moon, the renewal of life each spring, and in his own childlike fashion he paid homage to what he sensed was a reliable order and functioning behind all natural phenomena. Today the scientist in his laboratory feels a sense of awe, not too much removed in spirit from that of his primitive ancestor, when he gazes into a microscope and sees the astonishing perfection of microcosmic forms, or when he consults his astronomical data and realizes that there are galaxies beyond counting out there in interstellar [between the stars] space. Modern science has opened up a universe so vast, so brilliantly engineered and operating according to such astonishing mathematical formulae that the scientist today is . . . inclined to bow his head in wonder before a mystery that he cannot explain or even understand. Some of our most outstanding modern scientists, men like Sir James Jeans, Sir Arthur Eddington and Albert Einstein, have come to a point in their thinking beyond which they have not been able to go without recourse [reference] to the God idea. . . . The fact that men who understand the physical nature of our universe better than any others see in its amazing design, construction and operation a faint reflection of something they call God is an impressive and persuasive fact for most liberals. They believe, therefore, that the . . . design of our universe, its . . . cause and effect, its operation according to dependable law all may be regarded as evidence of what they choose to call God.—Argow, *What Do Religious Liberals Believe?* The Beacon Press.

G. For these stories (in the Bible) contain mysteries of Torah, and were written down for us not for their own sake, that is, not as the story of visible events, but for the principles behind them, that is, their inner secret.—Ephraim Zalman Margaliot (19th century), quoted in Agnon, *Days of Awe,* Schocken Books, Inc.

H. If the law consisted of nothing but ordinary words and recitals . . . why should it be called the law of truth, the perfect law, the faithful testimony of God? Why should the wise man deem it more precious than gold and pearls? But it is not so. Every word hides a very high meaning; every recital contains more than the events it seems to contain. And that higher and more holy law is the true law.—The Zohar (medieval Jewish book), quoted in Millgram: *An Anthology of Medieval Hebrew Literature*, Associated Talmud Torahs of Philadelphia.

I. What the story of Genesis means to us is not that the Creation took place in accordance with a certain specific method there described and that the animals were created in a certain order; . . . The divinely inspired idea is that God is the Source and Creator of all life, that man is created in His spiritual image and is therefore bound to strive to become more Godlike, that all men are descended from one source of life and must therefore work toward brotherhood. This is the divine and the eternal message of Genesis. . . .

. . . The Bible begins with the creation of man as one person. The rabbis in the Talmud say that God could have created many individuals at one time, a whole species simultaneously, but He created man alone in order to indicate that each individual in each generation is a unique person, created in the image of God.

Life then is precious; we dare not destroy it. Life is unique; we dare not suppress it in anyone else. Each one has the potentiality of growth, of using and developing the God-spirit in him. For ourselves in our place in the world, for our fellow men in their places in the sunlight, the modern world needs to renew allegiance to the Bible teaching of the uniqueness of man endowed by his Creator with inalienable rights and the possibility of noble living. . . .

. . . The Mishnah says that although God could have created an entire species of man, He purposely created one man and one woman so that no group or race could claim to be better than another, being all descendants of the same ancestors. The brotherhood of man . . . is an essential principle of the entire Bible.—Freehof, *Preface to Scripture*, Union of American Hebrew Congregations.

J. Our masters taught:

Man was created on the eve of the Sabbath—and for what reason?
So that in case his heart grew proud, one might say to him:
Even the gnat was in creation before you were there!

—Rabbinic Literature, quoted in Glatzer, *In Time and Eternity*, Schocken Books, Inc.

K. (The following is the answer given one day by Pierre Curie, the scientist, when a student who walked into his laboratory thought he was praying because he saw him bent over the table but did not see the microscope through which Curie was looking):

"I was (praying), son. All science, research and study is a prayer; a prayer that God will reveal his eternal secrets to us. For God does have secrets which he reveals only when man searches reverently for them. God did not make all his revelations in the past. He is continually revealing himself, his plans and his truths to those who will search for them. Throughout the ages God's revelations are made to man through prophets, scientists, preachers, priests, poets and musicians. There is beauty in God's universe and he reveals that part of his nature through poets. There is melody, rhythm, and order in his universe, and he reveals that to musicians. There is kindness, sacrifice and love in his universe and he reveals that to little children, great lovers, and kindly and kingly men and women. Yes, my son, I was praying. You were right. Research is always a prayer if it is done reverently."—Stidger, *Sermon Stories of Faith and Hope*, Abingdon Cokesbury, 1948.

L. As one goes deeper into such things, the fact of orderliness everywhere becomes increasingly apparent. I am not saying that a scientist cannot be an atheist, but it is my personal opinion that no atheist can be a very good scientist. An atheist believes that what we have today has evolved by chance. No real scientist can accept this.

Most men of science are aware that there are really two universes, the physical universe concerning which we know a great deal and the spiritual universe concerning which we know little or nothing. To deny the existence of that second universe is, it seems to me, foolish.—Dr. Robert A. Millikan, *New York Herald-Tribune*, Feb. 22, 1952.

M. (The following quotation is from the Mishnah):

Only one single man was created in the world, to teach that, if any man has caused a single soul to perish, Scripture imputes it to him [blames him] as though he had caused a whole world to perish; and if any man saves alive a single soul, Scripture imputes it to him [credits him] as though he had saved a whole world. Again, but a single man was created for the sake of peace among mankind, that none should say to his fellow, "My father was greater than your father.". . . Again, but a single man was created to proclaim the greatness of God, for man stamps many coins with one die, and they are all alike to one another; but God has stamped every man with the die of the first man, yet not one of them is like his fellow. Therefore every one must say, "For my sake was the world created."

ALBERT SCHWEITZER (See page *169*)

GEORGE WASHINGTON CARVER (*right*) (See page 178)

STEPHEN SAMUEL WISE (See page *200*)

WE CAN WORSHIP HERE . . .
Temple Israel, Boston (See page 247)

. . . OR HERE
Cathedral of the Pines (See page 249)

N. (The following parable was written by Rabbi David Nieto, born in 1654. In it he seeks to explain his attitude toward miracles):

A skilled architect once built a great and beautiful city, with market-places and streets. He erected stately residences for the aristocracy, and a royal palace which, for structure and beauty, had no equal. All who saw it said that there was not a skilled architect like unto him. One day the king said to the architect: "I would like you to tear down a room in my palace because, on a certain day, I want to give a banquet and I do not want this room to be in the way of my guests. And, after the banquet, rebuild the room as it was at first."

The architect did as he was commanded. When the room was reconstructed, the young men marveled at the skill of the architect. But the elders, who knew that the architect had built the whole city, and the houses, and the terraces, said to the young men: "How can you marvel at the fact that he demolished and then reconstructed a single room? Surely, this is nothing for him, seeing that he had originally built the whole city!"—Translated by Rabbi Jakob J. Petuchowski, *Commentary Magazine*, July 1954.

12. Dear Rabbi

Jan. 12, 1949

Dear Rabbi:

I am writing this letter to resign from the congregation, and feel you are entitled to an explanation.

Frankly, my reason for resigning is that I do not approve the kind of sermon you often preach. I was educated to believe that a rabbi ought to preach on subjects which are religious and spiritual. When you preach regularly about labor unions, profits and wages, voting rights for Negroes, and other such subjects, I do not feel that I am in a synagogue.

The only honest thing for me to do is to resign.

Very sincerely yours,

A Member

The above is an imaginary letter, but any rabbi can tell you it could be a real one. There are very few congregations in which individual members do not from time to time express similar points of view.

> What is your reaction to such an opinion? Do you agree or disagree? Does religion have anything to do with business? Is the subject of labor unions a proper one for clergymen to preach on? Is it a religious subject? A spiritual one? Why?

Religion and Business

In one of his early books the author, John Gunther, made a statement which will help us make up our minds about the relationship between religion and business. He wrote: "For six days a week the Englishman worships at the Bank of England, and on the seventh day at the Church of England."

> What do you suppose Mr. Gunther meant? How can one worship at a bank? Could the same charge be made against Americans? Would it be all right if the Englishman worshipped three and a half days at each place?

As a further aid in making up our minds, suppose we look once again in the Bible. Did the great religious teachers and prophets of ancient Jewish life think there was a relationship between religion and business? Did they try to tell the businessmen of their day how to conduct their affairs? In answering these questions, of course, we must keep in mind that in those days businessmen were largely farmers, not industrialists and manufacturers such as we have today. In Section I of your workbook you will find a list of Bible passages. Your task will be to rephrase in your own words what the religious leaders of those days tried in each passage to tell the businessmen of their time—what directions they gave for business to follow, what types of conduct they prohibited, etc.

Long before you have finished all these references it will be clear to you that Judaism has always tried to apply its teachings to business, as it has to politics and to every other phase of life, public and private. Religion, to be worth anything at all, cannot be limited either to one day or to any special building or place. It must apply to every minute and every aspect of man's life. Accordingly, our religious leaders always instructed businessmen how to conduct themselves. This is what Rabbi Pinchas of Koretz meant when he said, "Who ever says that the words of the Torah are one thing and the words of the world another must be regarded as a man who denies God."

The fourth of the Ten Commandments is one such instance. Later in our course we shall consider all these Commandments. For the time being, just notice, if you will, that the Fourth Commandment (Exod. 20:8-11) told businessmen and employers they couldn't work their employees seven days a week, that the worker is entitled to a reasonable amount of leisure and of rest. The Talmud contains directives on wages, prices, commissions, the relationship between employers and employees, and many other subjects having to do with business. One Talmudic statement reads: "The shopkeeper must wipe his measure twice a week, his weights once a week, and his scales after every weighing." So it is quite clear that the writer of our imaginary letter didn't know very much about the meaning of religion or the spirit of Judaism.

What should the message of religion be to businessmen today? To help you think this question through, we're going to give you six brief descriptions of business situations. In each case, your task in the workbook will be to tell briefly what religion should teach or say in that specific situation.

1. Company X has been making the largest net profit in its history. Its plants have been operating at capacity, orders have been coming in faster than they can be filled, and profits are zooming. The union representing the workers of Company X has asked for a raise. The company has refused to grant it, saying that it cannot assume business will continue that way forever

and it therefore cannot pay additional wages. The union has gone on strike.

2. The union at Company Y is also about to go on strike. The story here, however, is different. For a number of years the company has been barely able to hold its own. The only thing which has kept it in business, as a matter of fact, is the invention of a new machine which does the work formerly accomplished by two workers. The union insists that two men must be employed to operate each machine, though one can do the work easily. The company replies that it cannot remain in business if it is forced to do this.

3. Manufacturer Q. has been running his plant in New Jersey for many years. After a long period of resisting the organization of his workers into a labor union, he had to give in because of public opinion and the law. He is unhappy about the outcome, however, and has decided to move his plant to a southern state, where there is no union and he can pay much lower wages. He has always been able to make a reasonable profit in New Jersey, but figures he can make much more by moving.

4. Mr. L. has been manufacturing toys for many years. Of late, however, business has been bad, and he has decided to switch over to the manufacture of children's furniture. He intends to use the same factory and machinery, to employ the same people and pay them the same wages.

5. Two unions have been fighting over the employees of C., Incorporated. Each claims the right to represent the workers. The owners of the firm are quite willing to have a union in the plant, but say it must be one or the other. Because one union claims to represent a majority of the workers, the other has called all its members out on strike.

6. The owner of W. Co. has bitterly opposed labor unions all the years of his business career. He has frequently said he would go out of business before he would allow any union to come into his plant to tell him what wages to pay and how many hours to work. In order to prevent the union from succeeding, he has hired spies to join the union and to bring him secret information

about its plans. When the union attempted a parade in town recently, he spoke to his friend, the police chief, who saw to it that the parade was broken up. Either he or his friends own most of the real estate in the community, and he himself is on the Board of Education. He has been able, therefore, to prevent the union from using either a school building or any other public hall for meetings.

> In order now to compare the role of religion in business centuries ago to its present position, turn to Section II of the workbook for this chapter. There you will find space to give your opinion concerning each of the six cases described above. In which, if any, does religion have a right to "interfere"? Which, if any, are no legitimate concern of religion? In either case, explain your reasons. Where you think religion does have a right to enter the situation, just what should its message be? In any dispute between a wealthy man and a poor man, whose side should religion take? How does Leviticus 19:15 help us answer this last question?

It would be dishonest to pretend that all religious leaders agree without exception that religion has a role to play in modern industry and business. Ignazio Silone, a well-known Italian writer, tells that years ago when he and some of his boyhood friends went to their village priest to complain about economic injustice in their little town, the priest replied, "I'm here to teach you Christian doctrine and not to talk nonsense. What happens outside the church is no concern of mine."

Every Moral Question

Very few religious leaders in America today, however, would say that what happens outside the church or synagogue is no concern of theirs. Most of them would agree with the late Dr. Stephen S. Wise. When some people criticized him for preaching the kind of sermon referred to at the beginning of this chapter, he answered, "I felt it my duty to take into the pulpit for consideration every problem of public life that involved a moral question."

Don't make the mistake of assuming, because of the two specific illustrations used above, that it is only Jews who are concerned about applying the ideals of religion to modern economic life. While our rabbinical organizations have admittedly been outstanding in this field, such organizations as the National Council of Churches (Protestant) and the National Catholic Welfare Conference have also been active in this work. One of your readings for this chapter will give you the attitude of many Protestants in the Congregational churches.

Most modern rabbis follow Dr. Wise in taking very seriously their responsibility to apply the teachings of Judaism to the problems of modern business and industrial life. Both the Central Conference of American Rabbis (Reform or Liberal) and the Rabbinical Assembly of America (Conservative) have official commissions whose task it is to hold institutes and issue pronouncements with this in mind. More recently the Central Conference, representing all the Liberal rabbis of this country, and the Union of American Hebrew Congregations, representing the laymen in American Liberal congregations, have combined to form a Joint Commission on Social Action, which studies the areas of economic life today where religion has something to teach. At the Rabbinical Assembly's 1950 convention, one of the principal speakers was Walter Reuther, foremost American labor union leader.

Some of your Reading Selections at the end of this chapter are taken from statements issued either by the Commission on Justice and Peace (CCAR) or the Joint Commission referred to above. It would be interesting to have several of the pamphlets published by these groups assigned to members of our class for reports. This will give us a clearer idea of how Judaism in our day seeks to influence the conduct of businessmen. Your teacher or rabbi will help you secure copies of pamphlets listed below; they may be obtained through the Union of American Hebrew Congregations. Perhaps you would like to volunteer for a report on one of them. You'll find it interesting.

Judaism and Civil Rights, CCAR, 1948
Judaism, Management and Labor, CCAR, 1948
The Jewish Tradition of Human Equality, Joint Commission on Social Action, 1949
Charter of the Joint Commission on Social Action, 1949

There are also statements and pronouncements issued each year since 1949 by the Central Conference of American Rabbis' Commission. Your rabbi can obtain for you copies of the most recent ones.

Before leaving our discussion on the relationship between religion and business we ought to think also about religion and politics.

> What should the relationship between them be? On what kind of political problem would religious leaders and organizations have a right to speak? On what kind would they not have such a right? Try to give specific examples of each.

Religion and Ceremonies

What is the relationship between religion, as we have defined it from a modern Jewish point of view, and the various holiday customs and observances you have studied since the beginning of your Jewish education?

> Does the observance of such customs as lighting Shabos candles help make a person religious? Does it have anything to do with being religious? Can a person who observes no such ceremonies be more religious than one who observes many of them? Have these customs outlived their usefulness?

It will help us answer these questions if we forget about religion for a moment, and consider the role of custom and ceremony in other areas of life. Take patriotism, for example. When you remove your hat or salute as the American flag passes in parade, does that make you a more patriotic American? In itself, obviously not. A traitor can salute just as convincingly as a good American; no one watching them can tell the difference. Two men can stand side by side while saluting, one of them concentrating seriously on the meaning of what he is doing, while the other is just going through a series of meaningless motions but thinking of something else.

Yet all of us would agree that saluting the flag does have something to do with patriotism. The flag is a symbol of American history and of the values and ideals for which America ought to stand. Saluting the flag should make us think of those who died in the American Revolution in order that a new nation, founded on the principles of liberty, might be established. It should consciously remind us of what the flag meant in Lincoln's time as a symbol of freedom from slavery, of the self-sacrifice and devotion of those who raised the flag in World War II on Mt. Suribachi, etc. If, in honoring our flag, we also rededicate ourselves to the best in America and Americanism, then truly we become more patriotic.

In other words, our flag is a dramatic symbol of what it means to be an American. One can, to be sure, be a good American without saluting the flag. One can also be a very poor American even though he does salute the flag. But, everything else being equal, the act of honoring our national emblem serves to strengthen our devotion to the things for which this nation stands.

Now then, the same thing is true of many other ceremonies and symbols in our daily lives. We don't need birthday cakes or parties, but somehow they add drama and color to our lives. Two people could get married without a religious ceremony or a wedding ring, but these things dramatize the meaning of marriage and of love. You don't have to wear your school colors at a big game, but the demonstration of loyalty and support which the colors give your team may make the difference between victory and defeat.

It is in such terms as these that most modern Jews think of their religious ceremonies. They, too, are dramatic symbols of the ideals in which Jews believe and the goals we strive to reach. As such, they remind us of the things Jews believe in, and they stimulate us to express our beliefs in daily conduct. In that sense, properly understood and intelligently carried out, they certainly can make us more religious.

How does a modern Jew decide which ceremonies to observe and which to reject? Though we may differ widely on specific customs, there would be considerable agreement among us on the following principles:

1. We keep those ceremonies which have esthetic value, that is to say, those which are beautiful and pleasing to the eye and ear, adding warmth to our lives. For example, when we have a dinner party at home, even if it doesn't happen to be Shabos or a holiday, we often serve wine, use our very best dishes, and light candles on the table. Why? Simply because wine and candles add an element of beauty and enjoyment to a festive meal. In the same way, then, the Kiddush wine and candles at our Shabos dinner, in addition to their other values and advantages, are esthetically pleasant, increasing our enjoyment of the meal.

2. We follow those customs which remind us of some important event or series of events in Jewish history. A good example would be the Seder ceremony, which of course reminds us of the Exodus from Egypt under the leadership of Moses, one of the most important developments in all the centuries of our Jewish past. In addition to meeting the first requirement described above, the Seder dramatizes for us the beginnings of our people as a free nation. This is closely related to the next principle which follows immediately.

3. Especially important are those customs and ceremonies which symbolize the great ideals of our Jewish religion. The Seder is an excellent example of this too. While reminding us of the Exodus from Egypt, it thereby dramatizes for us our Jewish ideal of freedom. One who observes the Seder intelligently thinks not only of the liberation of Jews in ancient times, but also of

freedom and equal rights for Negroes, for workers, for Mexicans, and for all minorities in American life today. By so thinking, he becomes rededicated to the struggle for freedom in our generation.

4. Besides these three, there is another value in the observance of religious ceremonies. They serve as a bond, uniting Jews in many different countries and places. Again, an example from American life will be helpful. If, instead of observing one day each year as our national holiday of Thanksgiving, we simply followed the practice of having each American family choose one day of its own on which to celebrate Thanksgiving, we would lose the close feeling of unity which comes from every family knowing that every other family is observing Thanksgiving on the same day. Our fighting men overseas in the last war understood this; it meant much to them, while eating their Thanksgiving dinner thousands of miles away from home, to know that on the very same day their families were also celebrating. In the same way, a Jew who celebrates the Seder, knowing that almost at that very moment Jews all over the world are doing likewise, feels closer to them, more united within the same people and religion.

The very best kind of custom or ceremony, of course, is one which meets all four of these requirements. Others are worth observing even though they meet only three, or even two of them. There is room for difference of opinion among us on specific customs, so long as we understand these principles and follow enough Jewish customs to give our lives a distinctive Jewish "flavor" and remind us of our Jewish ideals. We ought to keep in mind also that if Judaism is to continue growing, we must develop new customs and ceremonies in each century, too. As we discard some because they no longer meet the requirements discussed above, we keep on adding others, which grow out of new Jewish experience.

To make sure you understand the relationship between religion and ceremony, in your workbook give an original example illustrating each of the above principles.

What Does "Sin" Mean?

Our ancestors would have had no difficulty at all in answering this question. To them any serious disobedience of a law which they believed to have been commanded by God would be termed a sin. This would include lighting a light or turning one off on Shabos, eating forbidden foods, transgressing one of the Ten Commandments, or violating any other law found in either the Bible or the Talmud.

We must expect our modern definition of sin to differ from theirs, just as our interpretations of God and religion are changed from ancient times. How would you define the meaning of sin today? Which of the following kinds of conduct would you call sins, and which not? Be prepared to explain your answer in each case:

1. Eating foods that are forbidden in the Torah.
2. "Crashing" a traffic light.
3. Paying workers an inadequate wage in order to increase business or industrial profits.
4. Not doing an honest day's work for which one is being properly paid.
5. Using the wrong fork at dinner.
6. Being rude to one's elders.

Can a type of conduct be morally wrong without actually being a sin? Explain your answer.

Possible Definitions of "Sin"

Various people have suggested a number of modern definitions for the word *sin*. We give you some of them here to stimulate your own thinking on the subject. After considering them carefully, decide which comes closest to your own ideas, then see if you can write a better definition yourself. There will be proper space for all this in your workbook.

1. Failing to use all our potential ability to its utmost.
2. Living our lives so that we contribute nothing to the fur-

ther development of evolution beyond the point it had reached when we were born.

3. Failing to come closer to the goal of ethical perfection we have mentioned many times in our discussions about God.

4. Permitting others to do evil, without trying to stop them.

Jewish literature and tradition contain a number of interesting statements on the subject of sin. We give you below several of them which are related directly or indirectly to the tentative definitions of sin just suggested. In each case try to identify the definition that comes closest to a given statement.

a. According to the teaching of Jewish mystics sin is separation from God. Every act which separates man from God is a sin.

b. The Talmud says: "Whosoever is in a position to prevent sins from being committed by the members of his household, but refrains from doing so, becomes liable [guilty] for their sins."

c. One of the medieval rabbis used to say to his son, "Honor the Lord with that which he has bestowed upon you."

d. According to the Zohar, a medieval Jewish mystical book we have mentioned in an earlier chapter: ". . . just as a man is punished for uttering an evil word, so is he punished for not uttering a good word when he had the opportunity. . . ."

We aren't going to give you a definite conclusion here about sin because we want you to do your own careful thinking. We do want you to know, however, about one very important difference between the Jewish and Christian concepts of sin. Most Christians believe that because of the sin which Adam and Eve are supposed to have committed in the Garden of Eden, every person to this day is born guilty of inherited sin. This is called the doctrine of Original Sin. One of the primary purposes of the Christian rite of baptism is to cleanse a baby from the sin with which it was born.

Judaism does not agree that human beings are born sinful. Our religion teaches that every person is born with the capacity to do good and to become more Godlike. When we sin, it is because we have failed to cooperate with God, not because we were born sinful. The Hebrew word for sin is choto, חָטֹא, which also means to "miss the mark" when one aims at a target. To which of our tentative definitions of sin just given would this seem to come closest? Of which tentative definition are you reminded by Reading Selection K? By Selection L?

The subject of atonement is, of course, closely related to sin. On this, too, Judaism has its own point of view, which insists that confession of sin is only the first step in seeking forgiveness. We must also (a) repair any damage we may have done to another human being by our sin; (b) avoid repeating the same sin; and (c) do constructive good deeds instead. Only a combination of all these steps makes for true atonement. This is the message of the most sacred of all Jewish days, Yom Kippur, יוֹם כִּפּוּר (the Day of Atonement). It has been expressed by the Zohar as follows: "There is a higher and a lower form of penitence. If a man repents of his evil deeds and ceases to do them again, his is a lower form. If he repents of his evil deeds and then strives to perform good deeds, his penitence is the higher type."

Religion and the "Chosen People"

Before leaving the subject of religion we ought to think briefly about one of the most misunderstood of all Jewish doctrines. No doubt you have heard us called the "chosen people." Usually when our enemies refer to us this way, they do so rather sneeringly, thinking we consider ourselves superior to all other peoples. Surprisingly enough, there are many Jews also who completely misinterpret this Jewish belief. So much so that one important group in modern Jewish life has even urged that we drop the idea of considering ourselves a chosen people. In order for us to decide whether or not we agree with them, first let's try to understand just what this doctrine means.

There are a number of prayers which mention the idea of Jews as chosen people. The first Torah blessing, for example, contains the phrase asher bo-char bo-nu mi-kol ho-a-mim, **אֲשֶׁר בָּחַר בָּנוּ מִכָּל הָעַמִּים**, "who has chosen us from among all peoples." The holiday Kiddush repeats the same thought as follows: ". . . for Thou hast chosen us and sanctified us from among all the nations." Another traditional prayer reads, in translation: "Thou hast chosen us, O God, from among all peoples, and hast given us Thy love and Thy grace; Thou hast distinguished us above all nations, for Thou hast sanctified us by Thy commandments, and brought us near to Thy service, and hast called us by Thy great and holy name."

Does this sound as though we Jews are an egotistical people? Some of our enemies have even charged there is no real difference between this belief and the national egotism and pride of the Nazis, who said they were a superior race. What do you think?

If you go back now and read again each of the references to prayers above, you will see that it is only in one respect that we Jews have considered ourselves chosen. We were chosen to study and follow the Torah. We were chosen for special service to God. How and why we were chosen is made clear in the statement from Exodus: "Ye shall be unto Me a kingdom of priests, and a holy nation."

A story told by the rabbis centuries ago illustrates our meaning even more clearly. They said that before the Torah was given to Israel it was offered to other ancient peoples. One people, when given a chance to accept the Torah, asked what was in it. They were told: "The Torah contains 'Thou shalt not steal.'" They turned it down, because this was too difficult a law to follow. Another people refused the Torah when they heard it would bind them to prohibit murder. And so on and on, until every ancient people had refused the Torah because they didn't want to abide by its teachings.

Finally, said the rabbis, when the Torah was offered to our Jewish ancestors, they heard what it contains and they said: Na-a-seh v'nish-ma, **נַעֲשֶׂה וְנִשְׁמַע**, "we will do, and we will hearken." We will observe the laws of this Torah and we will study them! This is the sense in which we have for centuries considered ourselves chosen. Not for privilege are we a special people, but for responsibility. We are chosen not to receive special benefits *from* God, but rather to render special service *to* God. That makes all the difference in the world.

Do you remember our earlier discussion about the special contribution we Jews have made throughout history to the ideas of religion? We mentioned then that the ancient Greeks contributed to civilization particularly in the realm of art, the Romans in the field of law, etc. In a sense, each of these other peoples can be called a chosen people, too—in the area of its own special talent or contribution to civilization. The American people is a chosen people in the sense that it has contributed more than any other to the dream of political freedom. The Jewish people has considered itself chosen in the field of ethics and religion. Our fathers were the first, as we have seen, to advance the religious thinking of mankind from childish ideas to mature, intelligent thought. We have an obligation today to continue such bold religious thinking, and—even more important—to give the world an example by living up to our highest religious ideals. Dr. Stephen S. Wise once said, "The Jewish people is a God-chosen people because it is a God-choosing people."

> In the light of this explanation, do you agree or disagree with the Reconstructionists, who would have us drop this belief? What harm has been done by the Jewish idea of a chosen people? What good has been accomplished by it? Which seems to be the greater, the harm or the good? What, then, would be your personal recommendation? Should we retain or reject this doctrine? Why?

This brings us to the close of our discussion on religion and its relationship to other areas of life. Having arrived at a modern understanding of the words *God* and *religion*, our next concern will be with the word *prayer*.

SOMETHING FOR YOU TO READ

A. The Bible, in contrast to other ancient literature, ascribes dignity to toil. "When thou eatest of the labor of thy hand," declared the Psalmist, "happy shalt thou be, and it shall be well with thee." "Great is work, for it honors him who performs it," said the Sages.

Both prophets and rabbis inveighed [criticized] against the exploiters of labor. This was the law of Deuteronomy: "Thou shalt not oppress a hired servant that is poor and needy; whether he be of thy brethren or of thy strangers that are in thy land within thy gates." Biblical and Talmudic law recognize no caste system. All men are regarded as free and equal. Employer and worker should respect one another. . . .

Too often in their search for greater profits, giant corporations disregard the rights of employees and consumers alike. The accumulation of vast profits beyond the needs for capital expenditure are socially indefensible. The consumer should benefit by lower prices, the worker by higher wages or some form of profit sharing. Such policies are particularly called for to meet the threat of inflation and to avoid a wave of bitter strikes to secure adjustments that will meet the increased cost of living.

In a democratic society the right of the workers to band together in associations that will defend their interests and secure their rights has become axiomatic [taken for granted]. The role of the unions in enhancing the dignity of labor and improving its economic status has been a source of blessing to the nation at large. . . .

We voice the belief that there is no basic contradiction between what is ethically right and what is economically good. Policies which result in the benefit of society as a whole are both materially good and ethically right for the individual employer and those who work for him. Only by promoting the general welfare, may we exalt the Lord through justice and sanctify the Holy One through righteousness.—Judaism, Management and Labor, Commission on Justice and Peace, CCAR, 1948.

B. Upon American Jews there devolves a double obligation ever to be in the forefront among those who demand that no man's political, social, economic or educational rights shall be abridged by reason of his color, creed or national origin. It isn't sufficient merely to point with justifiable pride to the glorious prophetic teachings. . . . We must endeavor to practice them conscientiously in our every day relations with our fellow human beings.—Judaism and Civil Rights, Commission on Justice and Peace, CCAR, 1948.

C. In the Talmud, a familiar story is interpreted as follows: Why did God begin the creation of man with only one couple? Why not with several couples?

The answer is: To teach us that all human beings are descended from one common ancestor, so that no man may ever be able to say "My family is better than thine," or "My tribe is better than thine." The remarkable insight of the Talmudic interpretation has since been vindicated by the findings of science and of human experience. . . .

Most of the peoples of the world are "colored" peoples. We can exercise no moral leadership in the cause of international amity [friendship] if they suspect our sincerity. We cannot advance the reign of law among the nations as long as our own laws are enforced with injustice based on racial grounds. . . .

The Federal Government should proceed at once to realize our democracy in its complete form by enacting into law the proposals of the President's Committee on Civil Rights. It should eliminate all forms of segregation in our armed forces and should give no aid or subsidy to any state using such funds in a program of discrimination or segregation. It should forbid race discrimination or segregation in the production of goods and services which go into Interstate Commerce. It should use its constitutional powers to prohibit the poll tax and to make lynching a Federal offense.—The Jewish Tradition of Human Equality, Joint Commission on Social Action, 1949.

D. The God whom we serve is a God of righteousness who would have us be holy as He is holy. The Torah which we cherish is a guide for spiritual living concerned with every aspect of human experience. The prophets of Israel, dedicated to God and the welfare of their fellow men, bid us pursue justice, seek peace, and attain brotherhood with every one of God's creatures, whatever their race, creed or class. In loyalty to our priceless heritage, in the furtherance of our historic ideal of righteousness, we, the Union of American Hebrew Congregations and the Central Conference of American Rabbis, jointly create a Commission for Social Action. . . .

The Social Action Commission shall relate the ethical and spiritual principles of Judaism as expressed in the teachings of the Torah, of the prophets, of the sages and rabbis of Israel to the problem of the world we know today, in order that our society may be established on the principles of divine justice and love and of human brotherhood.

The Commission shall prepare studies with the aid of authorities and specialists on challenging social issues and suggest specific solutions whenever possible, taking appropriate action when deemed advisable.

A. It shall uphold the inalienable divine rights of men as interpreted in our Torah and in the American Bill of Rights and Constitution.

B. It shall work to eliminate discrimination based on race, religion, or national origin to the end that all men may enjoy equality of opportunity.

C. It shall study the causes of war and advocate measures which will advance the establishment of a lasting peace based on the principles of justice and world unity.

D. It shall examine the relations between management and labor where ethical issues are involved. It shall suggest solutions in keeping with Judaism's teachings of righteousness. . . .—Revised Charter, Joint Commission for Social Action, CCAR and UAHC, 1949.

E. Self-dedication to God means to carry religion into the home, the market-place, the factory, the shop, the city hall, the courthouse, the studio, the classroom, and the laboratory. . . . While religion is . . . distinguishable from other human interests it must never be isolated from them. They must be stamped and permeated with its spirit and purpose. . . .—Samuel S. Cohon, *Judaism—A Way of Life,* Union of American Hebrew Congregations.

F. (The following quotation from the Midrash, included by Prof. Cohon in his book, *Judaism—A Way of Life*, shows the traditional Jewish attitude toward customs and ceremonies):

. . . The Midrash calls attention to the sequence of the verbs in Numbers 15:39—"Ye shall *look* upon it (the fringe), and *remember* all the commands of the Lord, and *do* them!"—and remarks that "seeing leads to remembering, and remembering to doing."

G. "Ye shall be Mine own treasure from among all peoples" was understood to mean: you shall distinguish yourselves by your devotion to God and engage in the study of Torah rather than in other matters.—Samuel S. Cohon, *Judaism—A Way of Life.*

H. We are asked, "By what right does the church concern herself with the problems of industrialism?" And we answer in the most uncompromising manner: By right of the plain fact that the whole range of life belongs to God. Nothing human is alien to Him, nor can it be to us.

Gone is the day when churchmen would permit themselves to be shoved unceremoniously or bowed politely out of any area where human values, human relationships, and human lives are at stake. The church is involved all along the line in every major problem of industry, since the church is composed of the men and women in management, labor and the consumer groups. Whatever affects them—any of them—affects the church, and the church has the right and duty to take serious cognizance [thought, notice] of the situation.—From a sermon by Dr. Harold A. Bosley, quoted by permission of the National Council of Churches.

I. Religion must save the worker from becoming merely an attendant to a machine and the employer from becoming a mere cash register with no awareness of the emotions, the desires and the aspirations of employees and consumers.—Editorial, *The Reconstructionist,* March 10, 1950.

J. If Jews were to disappear, the Torah would disappear and God Himself lose the most effective witness of His presence.—Midrash, quoted in Newman, *The Talmudic Anthology,* Behrman House.

K. . . . the Gaon of Vilna (18th century) was really diligent in Torah study, and if he lost a minute of his study, he would write in his notebook that on such and such a day he had lost so many minutes of Torah study. On the eve of Yom Kippur he would take his notebook and reckon up the minutes he had lost during the course of the whole year, and would cry and make confession for his iniquity in wasting time that he should have devoted to the Torah. It was further said of the Gaon of Vilna that the minutes he lost during the course of a single year never added up to more than three hours.—From the writings of a modern rabbi, quoted in Agnon, *Days of Awe,* Schocken Books, Inc.

L. Good is that which contributes to the course of ascending evolution and leads us away from the animal toward freedom.

Evil is that which opposes evolution, and escapes it by regressing [going backward] toward the ancestral bondage, toward the beast.

In other words, and from a strictly human point of view, good is the respect of human personality; evil is the disregard of this personality.—Pierre Lecomte du Nouy, *Human Destiny*, Longmans, Green and Co.

M. The doctrine of the chosen people offers the Jews no privileges denied to others; on the contrary, it imposes on them a mission, loyalty to which must bring them suffering, humiliation, agonies of pain and death; . . . the doctrine implies no superiority inherent in the Jewish people, apart from the superiority that is attached to one who is charged with the duty to carry an important message. It is the message and not the messenger that is superior.—Milton R. Konvitz, quoted in Finkelstein, *The Jews,* Harper and Bros.

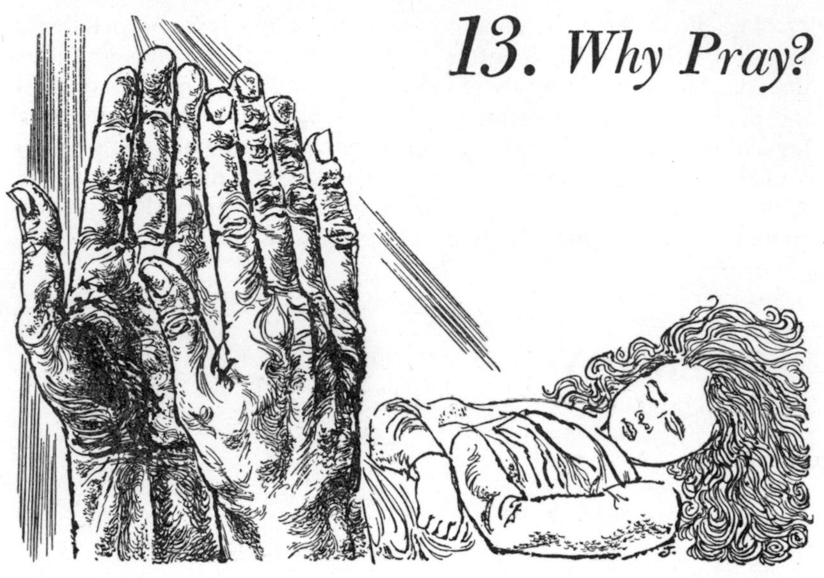

13. *Why Pray?*

LIKE the terms *God* and *religion,* to which we have devoted our attention thus far, the word *prayer,* too, needs considerable rethinking for modern Jews. Much that our ancestors believed about prayer we shall find still useful and valid for ourselves; some of what they believed we can no longer accept. It is easy to see why people prayed when they thought of God as a supreme being seated somewhere on a throne, pleased when His obedient subjects addressed Him with their supplications. If they had been good and their prayers were quite proper, what they requested would be granted.

But why should we pray today, if we think of God as the creative power or force behind the world of nature and in ourselves? Can our prayers influence that force in any way? Do they accomplish anything? Can we change the course of events in the world through prayer? Does praying make us more religious? In this chapter we shall try to answer these and many other important questions about prayer.

We shall follow the same procedure used at the beginning of our discussion on religion. Instead of telling you what someone else thinks about prayer, we're going to list a number of cases and examples for you to think about. It will be your responsibility as you read each to decide whether it is a good illustration of prayer, whether we can learn anything from it in our search for an acceptable, modern definition of prayer.

1. We begin with two newspaper clippings on the subject of prayers for weather—good or bad. Here they are:

BRITONS PRAY FOR SUNSHINE

Millions of Britons, their cupboards almost bare because of the long war years of shortages, invoked prayer yesterday to save what is left of this year's crops. What had appeared would be a bumper harvest, perhaps never more sorely needed in the Isles, had been 60 per cent ruined by the worst August weather in half a century.

Unless a few days of sun come quickly to the drenched and rain-beaten fields, England faces a disaster to her oat, corn, wheat and barley crops.

Even as city folk trudged in flooded streets to St. Paul's Cathedral in London, however, and farmers drove to their churches through hub-deep muck, and rain lashed the great stained-glass windows of Canterbury Cathedral, the forecast was for rain or showers through tonight.

—from *P.M.* (New York), Sept. 9, 1946

TOWN PRAYS FOR RAIN, GETS IT IN FEW HOURS

WACO, TEX., Feb. 13 (AP)—A thunderstorm shortly after midnight today dumped half an inch of rain on Waco just a few hours after an interdenominational prayer meeting for rain.

Individuals had visited the First Baptist Church chapel all day yesterday to pray for rain for this drought-stricken area of Central Texas. At 7:30 P.M. seventy persons gathered in the chapel for an interdenominational prayer meeting for rain. Not a cloud was in the sky then, but one woman brought her raincoat. A few hours after the prayer meeting adjourned, the lightning, thunder and rain hit.

To these clippings we should add, though not in the form of a newspaper clipping, that during the seasons of the year when rain or dew is most necessary for the agricultural welfare of Palestine, the traditional Jewish service of worship also includes a special prayer for rain or dew.

> How about such prayers for weather, wet or dry? Would you call them valid or legitimate prayer? Should a modern Jew pray for weather? Does it do any good? Is it all right to pray for good weather when you have planned a picnic? For rain when the crops need it? According to the ancient idea of the relationship between God and nature, would such prayers accomplish anything? According to the modern idea? Suppose at the same moment in the same town two people pray for the next day's weather: one man prays for sunny weather the next day because his son is sick and needs warm sunshine; the other prays for rain because his crops are burning. Whose prayers in that case would be answered? The one who prayed most eloquently? The one who lived most righteously? Could prayers for weather do any good under any circumstances? In addition to rain, what are some of the things one might pray for during a drought? (Reading Selection F will help you here.) How can we explain the fact that in Waco the people's prayers apparently brought rain? To what conclusions do all these questions lead us in the matter of prayers affecting the weather?

2. Our next example is intended particularly for those of you who are baseball fans. In September of 1946 the Brooklyn Dodgers and St. Louis Cardinals were in a neck-and-neck race for the National League championship. Not more than a half-game separated the two teams for weeks. At the most hectic point in the race, a Brooklyn minister announced he would hold a prayer service for the Dodgers on the steps of the Brooklyn Borough Hall. Hundreds of people who read about the service actually attended and prayed for a Dodger victory.

> Do you approve this idea of prayer? Why? Is it more or less worthy than prayers for the weather? Why? Could such a prayer service actually do any good for the Dodger cause? If not, why? If yes, in what way?

3. In October, 1947, the Southwest Pentecostal Holiness College, a religious institution in Oklahoma City, found itself facing a desperate financial emergency. The sum of $2,000 was needed immediately to repay a loan which was overdue. The Rev. R. O. Corvin, in charge of the school, called a prayer meeting. No sooner had the students begun to pray when they were interrupted by a long-distance telephone call. A friend of their church was calling from another city to say that he was mailing a check for $2,000, which they would receive the next day. The prayer service continued, but now it was one of thanksgiving.

> Do you think there was any connection between the prayers and the long-distance phone call? Would the money have been contributed if the service had not been called? Would the purpose for which the money was needed make any difference in determining whether the prayer would be answered? Do you think the fact that those who were praying were religious students had anything to do with the result? Are there any other ways in which prayer could help in a case of this kind?

4. In July of 1949 a newspaper item reported the capture in New Jersey of a man who admitted having robbed fifty-five Catholic churches of more than $15,000 over a period of a year and a half. When questioned regarding his motives, the man said that nine years before, when his mother had been critically ill, he had prayed for her recovery. Despite his prayers, she died. The series of robberies, he said, constituted his revenge because his prayers had been unanswered.

> Whose fault was it that this man's prayers were apparently in vain? Toward whom should he have

> directed his anger? If he had been a more ethical person or had prayed more eloquently, might that have made a difference? Was his conduct justifiable? Would it have been all right if, instead of robbing churches, he had simply washed his hands of religion and determined never to pray again? Did he have a right to pray for his mother's recovery?

5. During World War II many stories were told about prayers being answered. Later in this chapter we shall have more to say about prayers in military combat. Our present purpose is just to remind you of the story told by the famous aviator, Captain Eddie Rickenbacker, and the companions with whom he drifted for days in a lifeboat when their plane had been forced down in the Pacific. Parched with sun-baked thirst and driven almost insane by hunger, they prayed each day for food. One day in the midst of their prayers, sea gulls descended on their shoulders; by killing the birds and eating them uncooked, they obtained enough moisture and energy to go on living. Some days later their prayers for rescue were answered too; they were sighted by a search party in another plane and brought back safely to land.

> Were the sea gulls sent in answer to their prayers? Without prayers would they have come anyway? Was the final rescue an answer to their prayers? Would they have been rescued anyway? Is there any other way in which prayer might have helped the men? What other things might they have prayed for?

Is Prayer a Medicine?

6. Obviously, the man who robbed churches because his prayers for his mother weren't answered is far from the only person ever to pray for health. There is probably no other type of prayer voiced so frequently. Let's look for a moment at some prayers for health, again, in the form of newspaper reports. Several years

ago the *New York Times* reported the death of an eleven-year-old Kansas City boy whose mother refused to call a physician when he fell ill with infantile paralysis, because she believed sickness could be cured by prayer. The following is taken from the newspaper account: "Mrs. Bowers said that her child was better off because he was 'with God.' She had relied upon prayer to restore his health after a physician had diagnosed his illness and predicted that he would die within three days if he did not receive immediate medical attention. Mrs. Bowers refused and he died in seven days. . . . Her faith remained unshaken, Mrs. Bowers said, pointing out that a doctor had said Philip probably would live only three days and that he did live more than a week. She declared, 'That proves the Lord is the better doctor.' "

This incident reminds us of a group in our own midst which has similar beliefs, namely, the Christian Scientists. They believe that sickness is the result not of germs or other physical factors, but of faulty mental attitudes and beliefs. If a person who seems to be sick will only have enough faith in Jesus, and will pray properly to get the thought of illness out of his mind, he will be cured. While some Christian Scientists will call a doctor when they are seriously sick, the most faithful of them do not believe in doctors at all.

> What is your opinion regarding this concept of prayer? Can prayer help a person who is ill? Is it a substitute for medical attention? What is the attitude of Judaism toward the central belief of Christian Science? (See Reading Selection I.)

BLIND BABY, LAME GIRL, 5, ON PILGRIMAGE TO LOURDES

PITTSBURGH, July 11 (AP)—Two little girls, one born without sight and the other born without ankle bones, today departed on a 4,000-mile air journey to the shrine of St. Bernadette in Lourdes, France.

Their parents were hoping hard for some "miracle" at the shrine that would enable their children to live normally.

Somewhat different, but still on the subject of prayers for health is the newspaper clipping on page 221.

EAGER FOR TRIP

Ten-months-old Karen Woods of nearby Gibsonia, Pa., has a film growth over the retina of her eyes which doctors say cannot be cured by operations.

"If God is willing, Karen will see," declared her twenty-three-year-old father, Robert Woods. "We hope we won't be disappointed with the trip. . . ."

Five-year-old Mary Ann McMahon, who flew here with her parents from San Francisco last night, eagerly looked forward to the second lap of her journey. . . .

Mary Ann, born without ankle bones, has undergone two operations but cannot walk without the heavy plaster supports.

The children were in a party of thirty persons making the air pilgrimage to the Catholic shrine under the leadership of Father Francis M. Hoffman.

—from *New York Star*, July 12, 1948

The shrine at Lourdes is probably the most famous of many in Europe. There are several on this continent also, notably the shrine of Brother Andrew in Montreal. If you were to visit any of these shrines you would see tremendous collections of crutches, canes, bandages, braces and casts, left there by people who had been crippled or ill for years, but upon visiting the healing-shrine and praying there for recovery, were able to discard their aids and walk away cured. Sometimes prayer alone seems to accomplish this result; sometimes the patient is sprinkled with holy water also. Not all those who visit such shrines by any means are cured. But enough are cured each year to attract many thousands of ill and afflicted persons to try.

How can we explain the relationship between prayer and these cures? Can germs and bacteria be affected by prayer? Could a broken bone be influenced by prayer to mend faster? Could the people who were cured at these shrines have accomplished the same results with the same faith and prayers at home? Does a person's faith in the healing power of such a shrine have anything to do with the outcome of his visit?

Later in this chapter we shall consider a different kind of prayer for health. For the time being, we are interested only in the belief of people like Christian Scientists and of those who go to various healing shrines for cures.

Temporary Conclusions

There are a number of other examples and illustrations to be discussed before we are ready to attempt our modern definition of prayer. It will be helpful, however, if first we pause to summarize our thinking thus far. Here are five questions to keep in mind as you review the clippings and cases you have already read in this chapter:

a. Should a person pray for *anything* he wants? Is there any type of prayer which should not be used by a modern religionist?

b. Should we pray for exceptions to the laws of nature? Can such prayers accomplish anything?

c. From the cases already described, give one example of a poor concept of prayer, explaining why you don't approve it.

d. From the illustrations above, which do you think comes closest to an acceptable modern notion of prayer? Why? How could it be improved?

e. What have you learned thus far about prayer? How can you summarize your conclusions from the cases thus far considered?

Before continuing with the rest of this chapter, go over pages 216 to 222 again in the light of these five questions, think about them carefully, then do the work of Section I of your workbook. Only when that has been done will you be ready to continue.

More Examples

It should help us reach a satisfactory modern definition of *prayer* if we consider now several types of experience which may be, in some respects, types of prayer. In thinking about each of the following, ask yourself whether (a) it is a form of prayer, or (b) just quite similar to prayer, or (c) has nothing at all to do with prayer.

1. Mr. A. loves to read the biographies of great men and women. Nothing inspires him quite so much as reading about a truly great person who served his fellow men, then meditating and reflecting on how he can follow the example in his own life. Whenever he finishes such an experience, he feels considerably enriched and improved himself.

2. Mrs. L. feels about the theater much the way Mr. A. does about reading biographies. Particularly when she has seen a good play presenting an ethical problem, she often says it has been "a religious experience." Furthermore, she feels stimulated and challenged to do something about the problem presented by the play.

When she saw the motion picture, "Grapes of Wrath," which deals with the poverty of migrant farm workers in the West, she was so stirred that she organized a local chapter in her community of an organization working for justice on their behalf. When she saw the play, "Home of the Brave," dealing with anti-Semitism in the army, it made her think a great deal about the injustices of anti-Semitism in civilian life, too. As a result, she did much work to fight prejudice. Experiences like these always make her think seriously and inspire her to do everything in her power to combat the evil conditions she has seen dramatically presented on stage or screen.

3. One more somewhat similar example: What biographies are to Mr. A., what the theater is to Mrs. L., good music is to Miss D. She never misses an opportunity to attend a symphony concert. Sometimes listening to the music just makes her feel uplifted. At other times, when the theme of the music is on a serious ethical problem, or when the composer was a person who surmounted great handicaps to create his music, she feels strengthened herself to live a more self-sacrificing life for the good of others. She feels this way particularly when listening to the music of Beethoven.

Since these three cases are obviously similar, consider them together now, before proceeding. What relationship, if any, do you see between these experiences and prayer? Would any of them be prayer? What difference would the two types of reaction Miss D. feels toward music make in answering these questions for her case?

Peace and Health

Have the examples and the discussion thus far in this chapter helped you in your effort to find a satisfactory modern definition of prayer? Do you feel you have learned anything about prayer from them? We hope so, but in any event, let's continue in our quest for information and questions which will help us. Now instead of considering experiences which may or may not be similar to prayer, suppose we talk for a few moments about two different kinds of prayer itself.

Let us imagine that all the synagogues and churches in the world were to set aside one week-end as Peace Sabbath. In each synagogue on Friday night or Saturday morning, and in each church on Sunday, a special service would be held to pray for world peace. The prayers and readings would be especially selected for this theme and in every case the sermon would be on the subject of peace.

Perhaps this isn't quite so imaginary after all. In the spring of 1949, Trygve Lie, Secretary General of the United Nations, proposed that each session of the U.N. General Assembly be opened with a moment of silent prayer, and that the new headquarters of the U.N. should include a prayer chamber.

Can prayers help bring peace to the world? If a Peace Sabbath were held, would the world be any closer to peace on Monday morning than it had been the previous Friday? What specific, concrete good might be accomplished by such services? What effect might they have on the hundreds of thousands of people who would participate in

> them? Of what might they be reminded? What sort of action might these services inspire in them? Of what value, if any, might a prayer chamber be in the headquarters of the United Nations?

The second type of prayer experience we want to discuss briefly here is a type already referred to in the beginning of this chapter, namely, praying for health or for recovery from illness. There are a great many people of various faiths who, while they do not believe in Christian Science or in visiting healing shrines, nevertheless feel that prayer does have something to do with health. Suppose someone very near and dear to us were lying dangerously ill, and all of us gathered at that person's home to pray for his recovery.

> Could such prayer do any good? Would it aid his recovery? If he knew we had gathered to pray for him, what difference might that make? What if he were unconscious and did not know? What effect might such prayers have on us? Could they stimulate us to any kind of action on his behalf? Could they make us feel better? Would it in any way help the sick person if he were himself to pray for his own recovery (see Reading Selections A, C and L)? Could prayer influence his attitude toward his own illness? Does his attitude have anything to do with his recovery?

Here is a true story which may help us answer some of these questions: One evening some years ago a physician who almost never attends synagogue services telephoned his rabbi. (He did belong to a congregation but seldom, if ever, attended.) His conversation ran something like this: "Rabbi," he said, "I don't like to bother you, but my brother has been seriously ill in the hospital for a couple of weeks now. We have given him every kind of examination, put him through every sort of medical test, called in some of the biggest specialists in New York, and frankly, we're completely stumped. We don't know how to treat him because no one has the remotest idea what's really wrong with him.

He continues to lose weight, takes no nourishment, is unconscious or half-conscious most of the time, but his symptoms just don't indicate any known disease. We don't want to leave any stone unturned, Rabbi. Since we've tried everything in science that we know and have been unsuccessful, as a last resort we're willing to try prayer. Will you please say a prayer for my brother tonight?"

> If you had been the rabbi, what would your answer have been? Could the rabbi's prayers have helped that patient? Would they have been of any more value than prayers by the physician himself? Could prayers in general help the patient in any way? Could prayer help the doctors who were treating him?

In addition to thinking about all these questions, Reading Selection E at the end of Chapter Three and Selection A at the end of this chapter will be helpful to you here. So will the information in Chapter Three itself.

> What would an ancient man have meant if he had used the phrase "God watches over us"? What might a modern person mean by the same phrase? One of our Hebrew prayers refers to God as rofey cho-lim, רוֹפֵא חוֹלִים, "healer of the sick." What would the ancient and the modern interpretations respectively be of this term?

Listed below are some of the things a sick person might ask for or say in prayer. Be prepared, in your workbook for this chapter, to list them in what you believe to be their proper order as legitimate goals for prayer. If any of them are, in your judgment, not worthy at all, be prepared to explain why you think so.

1. O God, please take away my pain immediately.
2. What have I done wrong, that I should be sick now?
3. Grant me patience and strength to endure this pain.
4. O God, this pain is too much; take my life away.
5. May my illness and pain make me more sympathetic toward others who suffer.

6. O God, strengthen the hand of the doctor who is doing his best to cure me.

7. O Lord, how can I believe in You if You do not cure me when I pray so much?

Reading Selection L for this chapter is a prayer for health written by the late Rabbi Milton Steinberg. What does it reveal of the relationship between prayer and health? Could a Christian Scientist use this prayer?

What Is Prayer?

We should be ready now, after thinking about all the questions and examples given in this chapter, to reach our definition of prayer. The paragraphs which follow will suggest to you a number of definitions which various individuals have given. Some of them will contain ideas you may want to include in your own definition; others will not. It is for you to decide in each case. Your final and most important task in this chapter will be to write your own modern definition of prayer. You may want to accept one of the following suggestions or combine several of them to make your own statement. Better yet, take what you like from all of them, add whatever else you feel should be included, and then write an original definition of your own. With that in mind, here are the tentative definitions of prayer which have been suggested by various people in the past.

1. *Prayer is a magnified wish.* It must be magnified in two ways. The thing a person wishes for must be magnified in importance, and the degree of his wishing must be magnified in strength. A wish for an ice cream cone, no matter how strong, could never be called prayer because its object isn't important enough. But if I wish for something unselfish, something very important in the lives of others as well as myself, that wish can be called a prayer.

2. *Prayer is "tuning in" on God.* Just as radio waves are all around me at all times and in every place, so God as the power or force responsible for life is around me all the time. I do not

always hear the radio waves around me. I must have a radio set; I must turn it on and tune it in; then the sound waves which were there all the time are converted into a form which I can hear. When I tune in my radio, what actually happens is that I match the frequency of my set to the frequency of the incoming radio waves. In other words, I do not change the radio waves at all; I do something to my own radio equipment which makes it possible for me to hear the waves that were there all the time. In the same way, I am not always conscious of God being around and near me. Prayer is the process whereby I "tune in," so to speak, on God. I match my "frequency" to His. I make myself aware of the fact that God is there, and establish direct relationship and communication between God and myself.

3. *Prayer is taking inventory of myself.* The purpose of prayer is to remind me of the ethical goal of perfection I should constantly be striving to reach, and to challenge me toward greater effort to reach that goal. Each time I pray, I must ask myself what I have done since last praying to approach the goal of perfection. The Hebrew word from which prayer is derived can also mean *to think*, *to judge*, or *to hope*. Prayer is therefore a process of thinking about my highest ideals, judging what I have done to reach them, and hoping that I may live by them in the future.

4. Prayer is any form of reading, thinking, or meditating which reminds me of God as the ethical goal of my life and as the power which can help me toward that goal; and which inspires me to cooperate in my conduct with that power in order to come closer to the goal.

5. Dr. Barnett R. Brickner, an eminent American rabbi, has given this as his definition of prayer: "For me prayer has become meditation upon the best we know, communion with the noblest that we understand, and reaching out of what we are to what we yearn to be."

Think carefully about these suggestions, then write your own definition of prayer in Section VII of your workbook. Be sure to explain your meaning fully. After this is done, we shall spend some time in class discussing all the definitions given, and we may be able to select one which can serve as our class definition. There are many additional questions about prayer which we shall consider in the next chapter. First, however, it is vitally important that we have a clear understanding of what prayer means to a modern Jew.

SOMETHING FOR YOU TO READ

A. God . . . is the plan of this world. Our bodies have been built up in evolution as part of that plan. They show us that plan, never slumbering, watching over us when we sleep, exerting in our bodies an intelligence which we try to imitate and to reinforce by our medical and our surgical work. God does not do all our work for us. He leaves undone enough to challenge our intensest energy. He also helps those who help themselves and some who do not, but He is never neutral in our life struggle. He offers us a model of healing work and does most of the healing himself.

His plan also includes enemies to our welfare, bacteria, wild beasts, earthquake, famine, torrid heat and freezing cold. He intends that we shall have plenty of enemies to fight. But in our fight against disease we have a . . . powerful force always at work on our side. —Cabot and Dicks, *The Art of Ministering to the Sick*. Copyright, 1936 by The Macmillan Co. and used with their permission.

B. (The following passage from a message issued a number of years ago by the Central Conference of American Rabbis illustrates one of the functions of prayer. See if you can explain it in your own words):

In the Ryks Museum in Amsterdam the Dutch people treasure the masterpiece of Rembrandt called, incorrectly, the Night Watch. Rembrandt painted this picture three centuries ago. It was placed in the great hall of the Tavern in which the Arms Guild met, and in time came to be covered with smoke and soot. The colors grew so dark and somber that those who gazed upon the canvas thought it portrayed the guard marching out at night to meet the enemy. Then someone cleansed the canvas and restored it to its original colors. Now we see it is not a picture of the night but a picture of the day, filled with glorious hues and flooded with sunlight and glowing with noontide warmth and beauty—a picture reborn, the pride of Holland and one of the chief glories of the world of art.

We have allowed too many of our great ideals and visions to be covered with the smoke and grime of this Iron Age. We mistake them for pictures of darkness and despair when in reality they are brilliant with light and glorious with richness and power.—Judaism and the Social Crisis, Commission on Social Justice, CCAR, 1934.

C. I remember learning gradually, when I could not sleep at night because of pain or discomfort, to pray not for myself but for all those who, all over the world, were unable to sleep. This helps me to avoid tension and self-pity. I try to imagine the myriad kinds of suffering, physical and mental, that are keeping men and women from sleep. I try to let my prayer reach out to all of them. My own suffering dwindles in importance. When the mind turns away from self, relaxation comes and one holds pity rather than self-pity at the center of one's thought. One gets to thinking of oneself as a private in a vast human army fighting a cosmic battle against pain.—Dr. Richard C. Cabot, in Cabot and Dicks, *The Art of Ministering to the Sick*. Copyright, 1936 by The Macmillan Co. and used with their permission.

D. The object of prayer is not to get what we want, but what God wants; not to change God, but our own ignorant and sinful hearts. It is like the pull of a rope from a small boat upon a great ship at anchor; it is not the ship that moves but the little boat.—Sherwood Eddy, *I Have Seen God Do It*, Harper and Bros.

E. (In his book, *Basic Judaism*, Rabbi Milton Steinberg quotes the following comment in which an eighteenth century Jewish scholar, Joel, son of Abraham Shemariah, tells the procedure he often followed in the midst of a religious service):

. . . I have often made it my practice . . . to look over those present one by one, to ask myself whether in truth I loved everyone, whether indeed my acceptance of the command to love my fellow was genuine. With God's help I often found such to be the case. Whenever I noticed one who had done me some wrong I made it my rule to forgive him at that very instant, undertaking to love him nevertheless. But if my heart refused to allow me to love him, then I would force myself to say great goodnesses concerning him until I had removed rancor from my heart.—Steinberg, *Basic Judaism*, Harcourt, Brace and Co.

F. Now, we must remember that prayer, like belief in God, has undergone serious changes since long ago. For example, when belief in God had to do with changing nature (such as bringing rain or raising crops), prayer dealt with rain and crops. Today we can no longer pray for rain, but we should pray for the wisdom to use that rain properly, the courage to face the difficult times when rain is scarce, the knowledge necessary to give us a substitute for rain if rain does not come. Will such prayers come true? Such prayers have a very good chance of coming true because the very praying has a strange effect upon us: it gives us the determination to go ahead and accomplish those things for which we pray. Our natures are such that we can generate our own power, that is, we can, by sincere prayer for courage, gain courage; we can, by sincere prayer for understanding, be inspired to seek understanding. When we explore our hearts, looking for goodness, praying and hoping that that goodness will come, *we bring it out*. This is what we mean by prayers coming true: the *godliness* in ourselves answers the prayer. . . .

Bear in mind that the purpose of prayer is to keep us always aware of our ideals and to give us the enthusiasm to work for our ideals. —Ira Eisenstein, *What We Mean by Religion*, Behrman House.

G. It is instructive to note the contrasting relations of man to deity [God] in primitive and in advanced religions. Whereas the primitive religions seek to win over or to coerce the gods by means of magic, to do man's will, the advanced religions strive to direct man to do the will of God and to imitate Him.—Samuel S. Cohon, *Judaism—A Way of Life*, Union of American Hebrew Congregations.

H. Thus prayer enlarges our vision of God and of the world and opens to us new goals of endeavor. It makes our shadowy ideals shine forth like radiant stars upon our horizon, and shows us the role that we are to play in life. We learn to judge ourselves in the light of these ideals. . . .

Thus, too, prayer gets us out of ourselves, of our self-centeredness and self-love, and unites us with high purposes that make for the well-being of our fellow men. We are stimulated to appreciate the lives and efforts of others. We think of our kindred, our friends, our compatriots, our co-believers, our nation and humanity. . . .—Samuel S. Cohon, *Judaism—A Way of Life*, Union of American Hebrew Congregations.

I. The attitude of Judaism toward medicine is strikingly expressed in the following story: "R. Ishmael and R. Akiba were walking through the streets of Jerusalem, and a certain man accompanied them. They were met by a sick person, who appealed to them: My masters, advise me wherewith to be cured. As they prescribed for him, their companion asked: And who smote him? To which they replied: God. Then why do you interfere in something which is not your affair? He smote and you cure! Are you not transgressing His will? In reply, the Rabbis asked him: What is your occupation? A farmer, he answered, as you see from the sickle in my hands. And who created the soil? they asked. God, was his reply. And you interfere in something that is not your affair? they demanded. He created it and you cut its fruit! If I did not go out to plow, hoe, fertilize, and weed the soil, it would not yield anything. The Rabbis said: Most foolish man, from your work do you not understand the saying of the Scripture, *man's days are as grass?* Even as the plant, if not weeded, fertilized and plowed, does not grow, and if it begins to grow and is not properly watered and cared for, cannot thrive and withers, so is the body of man. The fertilizer is the medicine and the husbandman is the physician." They in nowise conflict with God's . . . care of man. The Rabbis further maintain that a city without a bath-house, physician and bloodletter is not fit for a scholar to live in. . . .

. . . In time of sickness it becomes a religious duty to consult a physician. The neglect of calling for medical aid constitutes an act of presumption on the part of the sufferer, for he seems to presume such righteousness as to merit the direct miraculous help of God. . . .—Samuel S. Cohon, *Judaism—A Way of Life*, Union of American Hebrew Congregations.

J. The analogy [comparison] may seem a little undignified, but there is reason for suggesting that prayer may be described as a kind of spiritual pep talk. Everybody knows what can happen to a football team when, at a critical moment in the game, the coach talks to his players and somehow inspires them with the spirit and determination to go out and win the game. Whether or not the analogy is appropriate, it is profoundly true that one of the end results of prayer is a fresh sense of dedication and enthusiasm, a renewed kind of inspiration. Every man talks to himself, and the things he says to himself in the tiny chapel of private prayer can be wonder-working in their possibilities. More than one person has discovered that when he becomes surfeited [filled] with the irritating little problems that sometimes bother us all, the most effective antidote [cure] is a walk in the evening, for two or three hours perhaps, and preferably somewhere out in the woods or fields. Invariably he comes back as cleansed and refreshed as though he had taken a bath.

Now the act of prayer can have much the same cathartic [cleansing] effect. It washes away the trite and unworthy, it leaves the shining core of our ideal unsullied [pure] and inspires us to greater effort on the morrow. When a man prays you see him at his best, all his faculties [abilities] marshaled in the quest for goodness and truth, his whole being turned toward the light.—Argow, *What Do Religious Liberals Believe?* The Beacon Press.

K. *"What Is Worship?"*

It is a thirsty land crying out for rain.

It is a candle in the act of being kindled.

It is a drop in quest of the ocean.

It is a man listening through a tornado for the Still Small Voice.

It is a voice in the night calling for help.

It is a sheep lost in the wilderness pleading for rescue by the Good Shepherd. . . .

It is a soul standing in awe before the mystery of the Universe.

It is a poet enthralled by the beauty of a sunrise.

It is a workman pausing a moment to listen to a strain of music.

It is a hungry heart seeking for love. . . .

It is my little self engulfed in the Universal Self.

It is a man climbing the altar stairs to God.

He who neglects Worship neglects that which separates man from the birds, the animals, the insects, the fishes.

The unworshipful man is an anthropoid [ape] with a highly developed brain.

He may be a paragon of morality, but so are bees and ants.

He may be keenly intelligent, but so are wolves and foxes.

He may provide for his family, but so do hyenas and orang-outangs [apes].

He may be successful in affairs, but so are beavers and muskrats.

He may be artistic, but so are birds and butterflies.

Worship is the chief concern of highly developed human beings.

A human being must be graded according to his capacity for worship.

Worship for men is what song is for a thrush, or physical beauty for a tiger, or speed for a race horse.

Worship lifts men to the next level of experience and justifies their existence as men.

Worship is Man expressing his entire personality.

To neglect Worship is to accept low rating as a man.

To neglect Worship is to fail in life's highest function. . . .

Intelligent Worship is the most remarkable achievement of which a human being is capable.

The primary functions of a Church are to supply incentive for Worship and to furnish the atmosphere for Worship.

If one cannot worship in Church, the Church may be at fault or the Man may be at fault.

If the Church is at fault, it will eventually perish unless it remedies the condition.

If the Man is at fault, he will dry up and become a spiritual mummy unless he changes himself.—Dr. Dwight Bradley, in *The Congregationalist*, October, 1928.

L. *Prayer for Health*

O Lord our God, Thou art the fountainhead of life, the health and vigor of bodies and minds. From Thy wisdom derives the physician's skill to bind up our wounds and to restore our well-being.

Wherefore, like our fathers before us, we hail Thee as the great Physician of all mankind.

Give us wisdom to preserve the endowment [fund] of health which Thou hast bestowed on us. May we never forget that our bodies and their powers are Thy gift entrusted to us for Thy service.

Help us, O Life of all that live, so to comport [behave] ourselves that we may be fitting vessels for Thy presence.

But if disease or pain be our allotted portion, then we pray Thee, grant us the courage to bear our burdens.

May we, though limited in strength, still find the resources to serve Thee and our fellow men.

May we be untouched by bitterness and despair. May our pain open our hearts to the anguish and distress of others, so that, tested in the crucible of our own trials, we may emerge cleansed and purified in purpose.

We pray Thee, O our God, for the life health of all our fellow men.

Mankind is one brotherhood under Thy paternity, and all men are bound together in one humanity.

May we perceive then that the ailments of others are our disease and their health our strength.

May we so order the skills and wisdoms of science, and so tend the welfare of one another that all humanity may become resplendent [bright] with vigor and joy.

May we see in Thee the common Source and common Physician of all who are created in Thine image. Amen.—*The Reconstructionist Prayerbook*, used by permission of the Reconstructionist Foundation.

14. *More about Prayer*

ARRIVING at an acceptable modern definition of prayer—as we did in our last chapter—will help us answer some of the very important questions about prayer which remain in our minds. While we shall by no means be able to include all of them, we do want to consider at least the most urgent. You will easily recognize that on our answers to such questions as these will depend whether or not modern Jews will be able to continue the regular practice of prayer. For example:

Are Prayers Answered?

Don't make the mistake of supposing that we moderns are the first to doubt at times whether or not our prayers are answered. As long ago as Bible times the prophet Habakkuk complained:

How long, O Lord, shall I cry,
And Thou wilt not hear?

For the most part, however, our ancestors were confident that God heard and answered their prayers. One of the psalmists expressed their view in saying, "God is nigh to all who call upon Him, to all who call upon Him in truth." The crucial words there, of course, are *in truth*. If a person's prayer were not answered, the psalmist would have explained no doubt that he hadn't called upon God *in truth*, that is, either he hadn't prayed properly or his past conduct didn't warrant an answer to his prayer. Another expression of the ancient Jewish confidence that God answers prayer may be found in this sentence from the Talmud: "However high God is above His world, let a man but enter a Synagogue and pray in a whisper, and the Holy One, blessed be He, hearkens to his prayer."

How about our opinion today? With our modern ideas of prayer, do we still believe that God hears and answers when we worship? Well, that depends on at least three things:

1. What do we mean by "answering our prayers"?
2. Do we pray for things that are impossible?
3. How sincerely do we pray?

After we have spent a moment or two considering each of these three questions, we should be better able to decide whether or not prayers are answered.

What Do We Mean?

What do *you* mean when you speak or think of prayers being answered? Do you have in mind what William James, a great thinker, meant when he said some people use God as a "cosmic bellhop"? (The word "cosmic" refers to anything which exists not just in human life or on this earth, but throughout the entire universe.) He meant that many people, when they pray, are like folks who call the bellhop in a hotel. They expect him to respond at once and to bring whatever they need or want at the moment.

When he does, they tip him as a reward. In the same way, there are men and women even in these modern times who think prayer is intended as a means of asking God for whatever they want. To them, answering prayer means God is to grant their request; if He does, they "reward" Him by continuing to worship Him or by giving contributions to religious institutions.

We hope the spirit of this course has impressed your mind sufficiently by now so that you recognize immediately this is an ancient and immature notion of prayer. If this is what you mean, then we must say in all honesty that God does not answer our prayers. But this is not the proper modern interpretation of prayer; nor, indeed, was it the proper Jewish interpretation even as long ago as Bible days.

We could cite a number of examples. For one thing, Exodus 14:5–16 tells us that when the children of Israel were pursued by the Egyptians to the shore of the Red Sea, where they found themselves apparently trapped between the sea and the enemy, Moses turned to God for help. At that point God said to him (and these are the very words of the Bible): "Wherefore criest thou unto Me? Speak unto the children of Israel, that they go forward!"

One of our ancient Rabbis added a most significant comment to this story. He pictured God, as it were, interrupting Moses in the midst of his prayer and saying, "My children are in trouble; the sea shuts them off on one side, the enemy pursues them on the other, and you stand and make long prayers. There is a time to lengthen prayer, and a time to shorten it." These remarkable comments show that our ancestors did not use God as a "cosmic bellhop." They didn't pray, then just sit back, waiting for God to answer. They realized that prayer was supposed to do something to them which would enable them at least in part to move toward answering their own requests!

Other ancient comments lead us to the same conclusion. The Rabbis said, for example, that the Red Sea didn't part, permitting the Jews to pass through safely, until after they had actually walked into the water up to their noses! In other words, even after praying, they had to act courageously and daringly themselves before their prayers could be answered. With the same thought in mind, the Talmud tells us that the Roman governor of Palestine once said to Rabbi Akiba, "If your God loves the poor, why does He not supply their needs?" To which the famous Rabbi replied, "So that we may supply them ourselves."

Some of these ideas may have sounded somewhat strange to you at the beginning of our course. By this time, however, we have said enough about the partnership between man and God, and about man's obligation to cooperate with God, so that it shouldn't surprise you at all to learn that we have something to do ourselves with answering our own prayers. We have emphasized again and again that man must do his part, must work together with the power or force he sees in the world and in himself, if he is to make progress in the direction of his master-ideal of ethical perfection. As moderns we do not believe it either fair or possible for man to "pass the buck" to God.

Many modern Christians feel the same way about prayer. One professor in a Christian seminary used to tell his classes this about prayer, "The trouble with most Christians is that they get down on their knees, pray hard, then sit back comfortably in their chairs, twirl their thumbs and say, 'All right, God. I'm ready. Go ahead!' "

Would it be accurate, then, to say that we answer our own prayers? Not quite. There is a very important difference. It is "we" together with the God-power within us and the God-power outside us, who actually answer. Neither we nor God can answer our prayers alone. We might compare the answering of prayers to the lighting of an electric light bulb. The electricity itself can't turn the light on nor can we without the electricity. Electricity is a force with which you and I as human beings must cooperate and which we must use if we want the bulb turned on. Similarly, then, God is a force with which we have to cooperate if we want our prayers to be answered (see Reading Selection C). So much for the first factor determining our modern attitude toward the answering of prayer.

Praying for What?

Now we are ready for the second question: *Do we pray for things that are impossible?* Such as: praying that a bullet headed straight for me in combat should be turned aside and miss me. Such as: two men praying—at the same time and in the same place —one for rain, the other for sunshine, both expecting their prayers to be answered. As a matter of fact, even one person praying for the kind of weather he wants would be a case of praying for the impossible. When this question was asked in Chapter Thirteen, you probably came to the conclusion that we should not pray for anything requiring an exception to the laws of nature.

If this were the kind of universe in which such exceptions could occur regularly, in which a person through prayer could change the laws of nature, then it would be a thoroughly undependable universe, one in which it would be impossible to see a force or power like God. It is precisely because such exceptions do *not* occur that we believe in God. So we ought not pray for the weather, or for anything else which means setting aside the normal laws of nature. To be sure, there are some things a man *can* pray for when the weather is unfavorable for his purposes, but sunshine or rain is not one of them. A glance back to Reading Selection F at the end of the last chapter will give you a hint of what we mean.

Once again, it is interesting to see how Judaism, in the course of its constant development and growth, reached this "modern" conclusion many centuries ago. One of the Chasidic Rabbis, named the Bratslaver, said, "Do not ask God to change the laws of nature for you." The Talmud itself says that a man whose wife is pregnant should not pray: "May it be Thy will that the child carried by my wife prove to be a boy (or a girl)." Such a prayer would be foolish, because actually the sex of the child is already determined while it is in its mother's womb.

In a similar reference the Talmud tells us that a man who hears a fire alarm in his city should not pray: "May it be Thy will that the conflagration be not in my home." There are two reasons why such a prayer is not permitted. In the first place, it means praying that the calamity should harm someone else; and in the second place, by the time the man hears the alarm, the fire has already started and it is silly to pray that its location be changed. Elsewhere Talmudic literature includes this comment: "To pray for the impossible is disgraceful. It is as if one brought into a shed a hundred measures of corn, and prayed: 'May it be Thy will that they become two hundred.' "

Our conclusion, then, must be: a prayer for something impossible will certainly not be answered. A prayer for something which is possible may indeed be answered.

With All Our Hearts?

The third and last question we asked with reference to the answering of prayer was: *How sincerely do we pray?* It isn't the eloquence of our language that counts most; it's the sincerity and unselfishness with which we pray, and whether or not we live up to the ideals for which we pray. A person who is insincere or dishonest has no right to expect answers to his prayers. Which is another way of saying: since one of the important purposes of prayer is to encourage us to cooperate with the little bit of God within us, a person who has no intention of so cooperating has no chance at all of having his prayer answered. Again we call the Talmud for our witness: "A person's prayer is not heard unless he places his heart in his hands." Or again: "Only that man's prayer is answered who lifts his hands with his heart in them."

There is a wonderful Chasidic story which expresses the importance of sincerity in prayer. One Kol Nidrei evening Rabbi Israel Ba-al Shem Tov, founder of Chasidism, was chanting Kol Nidrei in the synagogue. He kept repeating it again and again, much to the surprise of the congregants, who wondered why he did not continue the service.

Meanwhile, a village Jew had entered the synagogue with his little son, who was a mute. Listening to the chanting of the

Rabbi, the boy became filled with a strong desire to pray. But he could neither read nor understand, and his lips could not speak the words of the prayer book. Suddenly, before his father could even notice, he took out a wooden reed he had made and blew on it. As the congregants stood listening breathlessly to the Rabbi's chant, without warning they heard the shrill whistle of the boy's reed. Immediately they wanted to throw the boy and his father out of the synagogue.

But the Ba-al Shem Tov stopped them, and said to them joyously, "I kept repeating the Kol Nidrei because our sins of the past year stood like a wall between God and Israel, preventing my prayers from reaching Him. But when this mute little boy whistled through his reed, the wall was suddenly removed. The desire to pray burned in his heart, and God desires but the heart of man."

Are prayers answered? If they are spoken sincerely by one who understands that he must himself *help* provide the answer, and if they do not ask for the impossible, our modern answer is, "Yes!" The Talmud gives us another very interesting statement concerning the type of prayer we may expect to have answered. It says, "Whoever prays in behalf of his fellow men, his prayer is answered first."

Perhaps this is as good a place as any to ask briefly about a somewhat different kind of prayer. Thus far we have dealt with the desirable effect of prayer in bringing a person closer to God and stimulating his cooperation with God in providing the answer.

> But how about a prayer of thanksgiving? Can such a prayer be modern? Does it make any sense to utter a prayer which doesn't ask for anything? Can a thanksgiving prayer bring one closer in any way to God? Can it influence one's conduct?

Reading Selection I will give you part of the answer to this question about prayers of thanksgiving, but you will have to add to it your own careful thinking.

Another question: should prayer give us what is commonly called "peace of mind"? Is it a proper function of prayer to relieve us from our burdens and worries? After reading the following description, be prepared to discuss the role of prayer in Jane X.'s life:

Jane was taught to pray as a very little child. The habit of daily prayer never left her. As she grew older, married, and had a family of her own, she found that prayer always brought her great comfort and peace of mind. Whenever one of her children was ill, praying made her feel better. When she saw any human beings suffering or in need, a prayer asking God to help the unfortunate made her feel much better.

> Was prayer functioning properly in Jane's life? Should it have given her peace of mind, as described above? Why? Is there anything wrong with the peace of mind she received from prayer?

Reading Selection B for this chapter describes a somewhat similar experience.

> Compare the peace of mind Dr. Westwood receives from prayer to that of Jane X. Do you see any possible danger in this kind of reaction? Is there anything else you would want to know before passing judgment on the validity of Dr. Westwood's "prayers"? Is there more than one kind of peace of mind which prayer might give us?

"By the Bomb's Bursting Light"

Before we leave altogether the idea that there are some things for which we have no right to pray, we want to keep the promise we made some pages back to say more on the subject of prayer during military combat. Someone said, during World War II, that "there are no atheists in foxholes." That was a foolish thing to say: there were some atheists in fox holes, as there are everywhere else. What the person who said that meant was that many people who didn't ordinarily pray did when they were in combat.

The writer of this book was a chaplain in the United States Marine Corps during World War II. He remembers very well that the night before D Day off Iwo Jima, there was quite a line-up of Jewish boys outside the ship chaplain's office, asking for Bibles and m'zuzos to carry with them the following day in combat. It was interesting to inquire why so many boys, who hadn't asked for either a Bible or a m'zuzo before, now wanted both. Most of the reasons given fell into one of the following groups:

1. "I want a Bible and a m'zuzo to protect me against injury or death. It's not that I'm superstitious, and I have no guarantee they'll help—but what can I lose? My Christian buddy said the crucifix he wears around his neck will save him from harm, so why shouldn't I try the same thing?" (Incidentally, there was one curious case of a Christian boy who tried to get "double-insurance" by wearing around his neck both a crucifix and a m'zuzo!)

2. "I don't expect the Bible or the m'zuzo to turn aside a bullet or shell that may be headed in my direction. But I want them because they can help me in other ways. The m'zuzo will identify me as a Jew. Wherever I am—whatever happens—whether I'm conscious or not—I want to be known immediately as a Jew. As far as the Bible is concerned, I know that it contains passages that have given inspiration and comfort for centuries to people who were worried or frightened. Maybe I'll be able to find in my Bible some of the help I'll need."

In the proper place of your workbook compare these two attitudes. Which is more modern? Why? Is either of them completely unacceptable? Why? If you were the chaplain, would you have given Bibles and m'zuzos to both groups? Would you have stopped to discuss the matter with either? If not, why? If so, what would you have said? Of what value do you think wearing a crucifix would be to a modern Christian in combat?

Here is an interesting clipping from the *New York Times* of March 12, 1953:

SAVED BY POCKET BIBLE

Soldier Carried Book in Jacket—It Deflected Shrapnel

SEOUL, SOUTH KOREA (Reuters)—Pvt. Paul Montelongo of San Angelo, Tex., tucked a pocket-sized edition of the Bible into the left pocket of his field jacket when he went on duty in the front line. A short while later he was hit in the chest by shrapnel.

A piece of jagged metal ripped through one cover and all the pages of the little testament, but stopped at the inner cover—a few inches from Private Montelongo's heart.

How would you explain this strange occurrence? Did God protect Private Montelongo because he had a Bible in his pocket? Would his life have been saved if any other book the same size had been there? Explain your answer.

In the last chapter you were asked to rate the importance or value of a number of things for which a person might pray in illness. It should be interesting to do the same thing here with a list of requests a man might make if he were praying in combat. Here are a number of them for you to think about; there will be space for your answers in the workbook.

1. Help me get out of this alive and uninjured.
2. I pray that we may win this war.
3. May my dear ones at home find strength not to worry too much about me.
4. I hope my comrades and friends will all survive this.
5. Please keep any bullets from hitting me.
6. May we be able to build a world of peace, based on the ideals for which we are fighting this war.
7. Please help me kill more Japs.
8. I pray that I may find courage to set a good example to others who are near me.

Close to Home

George L., a high school student in his junior year, doesn't pray much. When he was a child he prayed every night before falling asleep, but he hasn't done that now for several years. There is one time, however, when he still prays; that's before any important exam at school. Exams have always bothered George. He would be afraid to tackle one unless he had prayed the night before that God would help him pass.

> What do you think of George's prayers to pass his exams? Do they show him to be religious or superstitious? Could they really help him pass? Does God have anything to do with passing an exam? For what might George properly pray before an exam? For what might it be improper or foolish for him to pray?

"I Can Pray Anywhere!"

"Can you? . . . can you pray in a boiler room? . . . Can you pray in a crowded trolley-car or subway during the rush hour when you are packed in with other people like sardines? . . ."

"Oh, now, wait a minute, please. . . . Don't take advantage of me; that's not fair. Sure, there are some places where it's harder to pray than others, and maybe even some places where I couldn't pray at all. . . . But you know what I mean. I mean you don't have to be in a synagogue or church in order to pray. I'm perfectly willing to agree to most of your conclusions about prayer, but I can't for the life of me see why we have to go to so much bother and fuss to provide special buildings and prayer books."

Does this imaginary conversation express some of your own feelings about prayer? We wouldn't be surprised, since it consists of remarks which have actually been made to the writer by members of previous Confirmation classes he has taught. There are really three questions asked in this conversation; we want to deal with them now, before concluding our discussion on prayer.

1. Why do we need a set *time* for praying?
2. Is it necessary to build a special *place* for prayer?
3. Why must we print special *prayer books?*

First—the question about a set time. Why is it necessary for churches to set aside special hours on Sunday morning and synagogues on Friday night and Saturday morning for services of prayer? Wouldn't the same purpose be served if religious institutions simply remained open all day, every day, and invited people to come in individually when they felt like praying? Perhaps the best way to answer that question is with another: If synagogues and churches did that, how often do you suppose the average person would stop in to pray? How often would you? We're very much afraid the answer wouldn't be too complimentary for any of us. Not that we're bad people, or that we wouldn't agree regular prayer is important; but we'd just never—or almost never—seem to get around to it. We live such busy lives, now even more than in past centuries. Unless we establish definite, scheduled times to do the things we want to get done, we keep pushing them aside and before we know it, a week, a month, then a year has passed.

You know very well that if you or your parents want to visit an art exhibit or see a good show or hear a concert, you have to plan in advance when you expect to go. Otherwise, without really intending it, you either forget or find yourself at the last minute with no time. In the same way, a musician must set aside certain definite times for practice; he can't just say he'll practice whenever the spirit moves him. A person who wants to take weight off through regular exercise must schedule the days and hours for such exercise or he just talks about it, without actually accomplishing anything. So with prayer in these busy times; we need to know when to schedule it.

In a way prayer becomes a habit in our lives. The longer a person goes without it, the harder it becomes to start praying again. The person who prays regularly, however, finds it easy to continue praying. In this respect praying is no different from any other experience in life. When a professional baseball player hasn't played through the winter months, he's a little "rusty"; he has to go through spring training to get "back in the groove." If a musician goes for months without practice, some of his skill at least temporarily leaves him. If you were to tie your right arm tightly to your side, so that you couldn't move it for a long period, you wouldn't be able at first to move it at all at the end of that period. Your muscles, because they hadn't been used for so long, would temporarily have lost their usefulness. Continual, regular exercise or practice is needed for the muscles, the musician or the baseball player to keep operating at top skill. The same thing is true of prayer, which is another reason we need regular times for worship.

The suggestion is nevertheless a good one that synagogues and churches should have at least a small chapel which remains open throughout the day, so that anyone who feels the urge or need to pray may have an appropriate place available. But this should be in addition to regularly scheduled public services, not in place of them.

Before leaving this first question, it would be well to add that all this applies also to daily or nightly prayer. Some people pray each night before falling asleep, others each morning upon awakening, and still others at both times. Our Jewish tradition includes special prayers for the individual both on retiring at night and awakening in the morning.

> Which do you yourself prefer, night or morning prayers? Why? Do you yourself pray regularly? Whether you do or not, what value can you see in such regular daily worship? What good might it do? Could such prayer help you live each day of your life as a better person? What are some of the things you would think it important to include in such a regular prayer? Should it be the same every day? Should some part or parts of it be the same? Why? Write a prayer which you yourself would think important and valuable as a morning or evening prayer for yourself.

Second—why do we need a special place for prayer? Do you remember the description given in an earlier chapter of the Cathedral of the Pines in New Hampshire? People who have worshipped there say they were never so thoroughly inspired, nor have they ever felt so religious in any synagogue or church, as they do sitting out under the pine trees, with a roof of blue sky visible through the branches, looking out over endless miles of natural beauty. Others have said, "I can worship on a mountain top just as well as in a synagogue."

No one would want to quarrel with such opinions. There is no question about it: we certainly *can* worship God in the midst of His natural beauty, and many of us do whenever we have the opportunity. But the proper reply to the person who says he *can* pray out under the trees is to ask how often he actually *does*. Most of us don't have a chance very frequently to pray in a place like the Cathedral of the Pines or on a mountain top.

But can't we pray, then, in our own homes or wherever we happen to be? Yes, of course we can—just as we can enjoy great music or art in our own homes. But that doesn't prevent us from building concert halls and art museums. A great concert hall like Carnegie Hall in New York or Severance Hall in Cleveland is a place built especially to add to our enjoyment of music. The seats are comfortable, the lighting, decorations, acoustic effects, etc., are all planned to increase our enjoyment of music.

A great painting is equally great whether we see it on the wall of an art museum or in our basement. But we enjoy it more in the museum, where the lighting and general environment are especially arranged to add to our appreciation of art. In other words, certain kinds of buildings are constructed with a special purpose in mind.

A synagogue or church is a building planned to enhance our prayers. Everything—the seats, soft lights, colored windows, gentle organ music—puts us in a mood for prayer. We *can* pray anywhere, but we're more apt to feel like praying either in the midst of great natural beauty or in a building planned and arranged for that purpose.

There is another reason why a special place for prayer is important, and that is to give us a chance to pray all together. There are occasions when each of us would rather pray alone. But it is also good to know there are others praying, too, and to pray together with them. We can secure our exercise individually too, can't we? And there are times when each of us prefers to be alone, to walk or run or row by himself. But for the most part it is better to get our exercise by participating in sports together with others.

It is even truer in religion that we gain a great deal by worshipping in a community, together with others. That is why the great Rabbi Hillel, who lived about two thousand years ago, said, Al tifrosh min hatsibur, אַל תִּפְרשׁ מִן הַצִּבּוּר, "do not separate thyself from the congregation." To which the Talmud adds: "Whoever has a Synagogue in his town and does not enter in to pray, is called an evil neighbor!" And finally, Maimonides expressed the same opinion in these words: "It is necessary . . . for every person to affiliate with a congregation and not pray alone so long as there is an opportunity to join in group worship."

Reading Selection K deals with this question of public worship. What advantages does the author of that selection see in group prayer?

Which leaves us now with this question: *Why do we need a printed prayer book and a set service?* Couldn't each person just compose his own prayers in his own words? As a matter of fact, some people think a regular ritual from the prayer book takes much of the life out of a religious service. They feel that our worship would mean very much more and would be fresher if each of us spoke out in his own heart the prayers he felt within himself at the moment.

There is no question that the prayers we compose or speak ourselves are apt to be the most meaningful ones for each of us. The trouble is, however, that so few of us are actually skilled enough either in writing or speaking to find the words through which to express our thoughts about God. The prayer book collects for us in one anthology a variety of ways in which great poets and writers have already expressed very beautifully the emotions and thoughts which we too feel from time to time. Every service, however, ought to have room and time for at least a few moments of silent prayer, during which, stimulated by the beautiful words of others, we also have an opportunity to voice our own feelings.

One of the Rabbis quoted in the Talmud said, "If a man prays only according to the exact text of the prayer and adds nothing from his own mind, his prayer is not proper imploration."

Not every prayer in our prayer book will suit or please every worshipper. As a matter of fact, a prayer which may express exactly the way you feel on one occasion may have little or no meaning for you some other time. Furthermore, since a prayer book is intended for use by many people with different ideas about God and religion, it must contain different kinds of prayers. Some of them will express ideas which to us may seem ancient or childish; so long as they help anyone in the congregation, they belong in the prayer book. Other prayers, which seem acceptable and expressive to us, may be of little value to a person who does not share our own interpretation of religion.

Putting Our Conclusions to Work

Our final—and most important—task on the subject of prayer will be actually to examine some of the prayers in our own prayer book, to decide which of them we like and which not. For that purpose we shall use the newly revised edition, Volume I, of the *Union Prayerbook*. If this happens not to be the prayer book used in your congregation, your rabbi or teacher will assign other prayers for your class. Whichever book you use, however, it will first be necessary to determine how to decide whether a given prayer is good or not. We would suggest the following three questions for this purpose:

1. Does the prayer express a modern concept of God and religion? Does it use language about God which makes us think of Him as a physical person or as a creative power?

2. Does it ask for something which is impossible?

3. Does it deal with something we ourselves can help achieve, and does it make us want to do something active to help answer it?

There may well be other questions too which we ought to use in judging our prayers. If you can think of any now, add them to the list; then proceed to your final assignment on prayer.

Unless your rabbi or teacher prefers to give each member of the class a definite assignment, each of you will be expected to write an evaluation of three prayers: (1) the prayer which appears as Reading Selection A at the end of this chapter; (2) any one of the prayers listed under Group I below; and (3) any one of those listed under Group II. In each case, answer all the questions listed above, plus any you may have added. Indicate in general whether or not you like the prayer about which you are writing, and tell specifically what you do and do not like about each.

GROUP I

UNION PRAYERBOOK, PAGE	PRAYER BEGINNING WITH THE WORDS:
14	*"Thou shalt love the Lord . . ."*
22	*"Grant us peace . . ."*
38	*"God and Father . . ."*
39	*"O Lord, how can we know Thee?"*
45	*"O Lord, though we are prone . . ."*
46	*"In this moment . . ."*
68	*"O Lord our God . . ."*
71	*"May the time not be distant . . ."*

GROUP II

18	*"Praised be Thou . . ."*
56	*"Cause us, O Lord our God . . ."*
69	*"God be gracious unto us . . ."*

SOMETHING FOR YOU TO READ

A. Once more do we gather in the House of God for the observance of our Sabbath. Here in our quiet hour of worship we pause to reflect upon the meaning and purpose of our lives. Solemnly we recall the ever-living message of religion; that life is real and earnest; that not without wise purpose were we placed here, and not without wise purpose can we live.

At this moment we reflect on that purpose. We feel once more that our most cherished aim in life must be to fulfill ourselves. Each of us is a reservoir of possibilities. Each of us is a dynamo of potential good. And each of us carries within him a vision of his own highest self, a glimpse of that which he can and should become. If we would truly give life meaning, then we must seek actually to become like that vision; we must ever fulfill the noblest and highest and finest that in us lies.

But it is not easy to live such a life of discipline and purpose. Our fathers were wise enough to know that. And so they decreed that once each week we must pause to refresh our spirits, to renew within us the vision of our highest selves.

Ofttimes in the pursuit of our daily tasks we forget it. We are so busy with a number of things—providing for our loved ones, caring for our children, entertaining our friends—these and a whole host of details so fill our days and hours that now more than ever do we need the Sabbath in order to take stock of ourselves and our lives.

Let us remember that even an artist must sometimes pause as he paints, must sometimes lay aside his brush, look away from his canvas, and seek new inspiration. If only we understood that living a life is like painting a picture. Our life is a canvas. Everything we do —every word we speak, every thought we think—is a stroke of the brush. And ours is the power to make that picture beautiful or ugly, meaningful or vain.

On this Sabbath eve, then, let us pause to see what we have painted in the week now gone. Let us close our eyes for a moment that we may see once again the vision we would follow. Then, renewed and refreshed, inspired by this hour of challenge, let us return to the canvas and paint—each of us—the portrait of a life filled with beauty, with goodness, and with truth.

It is this vision of our highest selves, a vision of perfection, that we call by the name of God. And we rise now, as our fathers have done for centuries, to praise God and to glorify His name.—Supplementary Song and Service Booklet, Central Synagogue of Nassau County, Rockville Centre, Long Island, N. Y.

B. Often, . . . when troubled in spirit and restless in mind, I have gone into the woods surrounding the old farm where I am writing these words, and seating myself upon a fallen log have just "let go." I have not tried to wrestle with my problems, nor have I tried to clarify my mind. I have just allowed the quiet and the stillness to creep in. Never have I known it to fail that I have left the woods at peace with myself and the world. On other occasions I have seated myself at the keyboard of a piano or organ, allowing my fingers to wander "idly over the noisy keys." But the effect has been the same.

Others have had similar experiences when wandering on an ocean beach or when standing upon the top of a hill overlooking the valley below.

Judging by results, these are forms of prayer; though of course the idea of prayer may not even enter the mind. What takes place on such occasions is almost impossible to put into words, but none who reflects upon the experience can fail to conclude, that Power greater than oneself has crept into heart and mind bringing its benediction and renewal.—Horace Westwood, *And So You Never Pray!* The Beacon Press.

C. "The answer to the prayer," C. G. Montefiore writes, "may be in the prayer; the effect upon the man who prays may, in one sense, be produced by the man; but if so, that is only because the man himself is not *alone,* or because (in other words) prayer may make him receptive to mysterious influences, or strengthen and make vivid within him a part of him which is Divine."—Quoted by Samuel S. Cohon, in *Judaism—A Way of Life*, Union of American Hebrew Congregations.

D. (The German-Jewish dramatist, Richard Beer-Hoffman, has written a poetic drama based on the story of Jacob in the Bible. It is entitled, "Jacob's Dream." The following selection is from one of the prayers he puts into the mouth and mind of Jacob):

O Thou, Unknown—Unseen—
God of my fathers—dost Thou hear me now?
Know'st Thou of me? And is my trembling more to Thee,
  Lord, than a grass blade shaking in the wind?
Hear'st Thou my words more than the murmuring sound of
  yonder spring now falling towards the vale?

The tree may think it rustles up to Thee,
And yet 'tis but Thy stormwind sweeping through it—
So through my lips Thou to Thyself—may be—
Dost speak, my prayer is but a discourse
That goes—from Thee to Thee!

—Beer-Hoffman, *Jacob's Dream*, Jewish Publication Society of America, by special permission of Johannespresse.

E. (The following is the famous Twenty-third Psalm):

The Lord is my shepherd; I shall not want.
He maketh me to lie down in green pastures;
He leadeth me beside the still waters.
He restoreth my soul;
He guideth me in straight paths for His name's sake.
Yea, though I walk through the valley of the shadow
of death,
I will fear no evil,
For Thou art with me;
Thy rod and Thy staff, they comfort me.
Thou preparest a table before me in the presence
of mine enemies;
Thou hast anointed my head with oil; my cup
runneth over.
Surely goodness and mercy shall follow me all the days
of my life;
And I shall dwell in the house of the Lord for ever.

F. . . . if someone comes to you and asks your help, you shall not turn him off with pious words, saying: "Have faith and take your troubles to God!" You shall act as though there were no God, as though there were only one person in all the world who could help this man—only yourself.—Martin Buber, *Ten Rungs*, Schocken Books, Inc.

G. Congregational prayer is always heeded, and even if there are sinners in the congregation, the Holy One, blessed be He, does not reject the prayer of the group. Therefore, a man should join a congregation, and not pray alone if he can pray with a group.—Maimonides.

Two men carrying a load would not be able to carry it as well separately as together. Two men raising their voices are more apt to be heard than if they cry separately. So it is with Yom Kippur; because all folk, great and small, afflict themselves together, even if a few have sinned, the many do not lose the good that has been decreed for them. . . .—Sefer Hasidim (13th century). Both the above quoted in Agnon, *Days of Awe*, Schocken Books, Inc.

H. When you pray, pray in the synagogue of your city; if you are unable to pray in the synagogue, pray in your field; if you are unable to pray in your field, pray in your home; if you are unable to pray in your home, pray on your couch; and if you are unable to pray on your couch, meditate in your heart. This is the meaning of the verse: "Commune with your own heart upon your bed, and be still."—Midrash.

I. The fact that even the petitions are also praises of God and therefore, not exclusively or even predominantly petitional in mood, clearly reveals a significant attitude toward prayer itself. This attitude has been specifically stated in the following rabbinic statement, "A man should always utter the praises of God before he offers his petitions." Judging by this mood . . . prayer is primarily the achievement of an affirmative relationship to God, a sense of gratitude and appreciation for the blessings we have received. If our faith can succeed in curing us of the mood of constant discontent and can teach us to find joyous gratitude in whatever happiness we already have, however small it may be, then it will engender [cause] a healthy-mindedness within us that makes for a happy life, itself the answer to most of our prayers. This habit of praising God rather than begging from Him has become, through centuries of this type of prayer, a prevalent state of mind which enabled our fathers to find joy even in minor blessings and thus played its part in preserving Israel through the vicissitudes [changes] of history. A poverty-stricken, forlorn, exiled Jew, raising his last crust of bread to his mouth, might perhaps be justified in cursing his lot and denouncing God, but instead it would not enter his mind to partake of this bit of bread without first saying, "Praised be Thou O Lord who bringest forth food from the earth.". . . Prayer in Israel teaches man to overcome bitterness and self-pity; to think not of what the world owes him, but what he owes the world and God.—Freehof, *The Small Sanctuary*, Union of American Hebrew Congregations.

J. A musician must practice by prearranged schedule, regardless of his inclination at the moment. So with the devout soul. It may not rely on caprice or put its hope in chance. It must work. The man on the other hand who folds his hands, waiting for the spirit to move him to think of God—who postpones worship for the right mood and the perfect setting, a forest or mountain peak, for example—will do little of meditating or praying. After all, how often does one find himself in a "cathedral of nature," and when he does who shall say that he will be in a worshipful temper?—Milton Steinberg, *Basic Judaism*, Harcourt, Brace and Co.

K. When we pray together with others we help ourselves become aware of many facets of our faith. Among those is the realization that we are not alone in this wide world; that in our efforts for the good life others are joined with us. Thus, prayer offered in a group reaffirms within us the essential unity of all mankind and the unity of Israel. Even as our prayers of adoration and integration help us realize that the laws of God and the laws of nature are with us when our own wishes are in harmony with the universe, so does prayer experienced with our fellow men affirm within us that our wishes can be realized insofar as they are in harmony with the needs and the welfare of others. When we pray "b'tzibur" [in a group], we are helped to rid ourselves of self-centered aspirations and selfish petitions. Group worship thus becomes an expression of group interest and social solidarity, a pledging of loyalty to the general welfare. When we see each other, when we hear each other, we become one with the other. . . .

Group worship also provides technical help in praying. Some people have difficulty in verbalizing [expressing] their feelings. Public prayer, in which one shares either as a participant, observer or listener, provides for him the instruments of articulation [expression] which he may not have been able to articulate on his own. The group experience also helps to break down inhibitions to the prayer process by the very contagion of the group situation.—Ernst M. Lorge, in *The Teaching of Prayer*, Chicago Board of Jewish Education.

L. We need also to do more basic thinking on how we pray in our services of worship. Too often our prayers are petitionary [asking for something] and expressions of praise for special blessings. We ask God to help us, to give us strength when we know that we have far more power already available to us than we are using. We ask God to bring peace when we know that we are the ones who have brought on our wars, and must be the ones to bring peace. We ask God to grant us his special blessings, to protect us from harm and tragedy, when we know that we can expect no special favors in such a universe as ours. We ask God to forgive us, when we ourselves harbor distrust and hate toward those who need our forgiveness. We ask God to search us and know our hearts, to try us and know our thoughts, and to see if there be any wicked way in us, when we know that it is we ourselves who must do the searching.—Fahs, *Today's Children & Yesterday's Heritage*, The Beacon Press.

M. And I remembered the chaplain who would get together with the boys before they took off. One morning a new crew, fresh from the States, was going up. The chaplain let them have it straight from the shoulder. I remember just how he put it: "Prayers won't hold your planes up, boys. Only aerodynamics will."

A scared young pilot said, "You mean we shouldn't pray? You mean prayers aren't worth a hoot?"

"I don't mean that at all, Lieutenant," said the chaplain. "Prayer has brought many a plane home safely. Not because it gave magical immunity—but because it gave the crew peace and calm and courage, and enabled *them* to bring the plane home safely!

"Prayer isn't a rabbit's foot, Lieutenant. It won't draw a magic ring around your plane and post a sign in the sky, 'All flak detour here.' But prayer will give you inner peace—another name for courage—and you'll handle that plane right. You'll make the right decisions, you'll take the right evasive action, you'll be alert, you'll do right by your instruments. There's no better way to get aerodynamics on your side."—From: *A Reporter in Search of God*, by Howard Whitman. Copyright 1951, 1952, 1953 by Howard Whitman, reprinted by permission of Doubleday and Co., Inc.

WAY OF LIFE
THEN AND NOW (See page *260*)

REMEMBER THE SABBATH DAY—

—TO KEEP IT HOLY (See page *267*)

WE LIVE THROUGH OUR CHILDREN (See page 288)

15. *Way of Life: Then and Now*

Throughout our discussions thus far we have emphasized again and again that our Jewish religion is a "way of life," not just a way of thinking or believing about things. To be sure, thinking and belief are important parts of Judaism or of any religion, but the more important part by far is the conduct to which our beliefs direct us. In the course of countless centuries, the great teachers and leaders of Judaism have formulated many laws and codes to guide their followers toward proper conduct. The greatest of these codes are to be found in our Bible, in the Talmud, and in the writings of such great Jews as Maimonides. We wish there were time here to consider all of them. Since that would obviously be impossible, and since we nevertheless do want to talk about at least some of these essential laws, we're going to devote this chapter to the heart and core of all Jewish laws of conduct, namely, the Ten Commandments.

You're familiar with at least some of these commandments, of course. Every intelligent person has read them. You may even know all or some of them by heart. Our purpose here, however, isn't to have you memorize the Ten Commandments if you don't already know them; we want rather to discuss them in such manner that you will thoroughly understand them and see their proper application to modern life.

First, a few words of introduction. It would be a mistake to think these ten directives constitute all of Jewish ethical law. The Bible itself, immediately upon stating these commandments, proceeds to list a number of additional laws which, in a sense, are the specific application to practical problems of the spirit and intention established by the Ten Commandments. But these laws do give us the foundation, so to speak, not only for all subsequent Jewish law, but indeed, for most kinds of law later developed by civilized mankind. One who knows and understands the Ten Commandments has grasped the most important ethical truths of Jewish religion. By the same token, a society established upon the basis of these commandments would be a society well on its way toward what we have called the Messianic Age.

These ten laws are stated simply, perhaps too simply. Because it seems easy to understand them, there is a temptation merely to read each, to grasp at once its obvious surface meaning, and to go on at once to the next. This is the mistake made by most people when they read these laws. We shall try to avoid that mistake here. You remember, we hope, our earlier discussion about the *Truths* which are to be found beneath the surface of Bible words if we dig for them. The same is true of the Ten Commandments. In our discussion here, we want to discover not only what each commandment seems to say on the surface, but also what its real, deep meaning is.

We want also to compare its meaning today to the original intention of Moses in stating it. You recall, of course, the story of Moses receiving the Ten Commandments on Mt. Sinai, and we hope you remember the interpretation given a chapter or two back (page 181) according to which Moses ascended the mountain alone in order to commune with the best within himself and with God in order to give his people a charter or constitution which would guide them. To this we must now add that the people who received these laws from Moses consisted of a group which had lived in Egyptian slavery for generations.

Now slavery does something to any people. It weakens them. It makes them dependent upon others. It drains their energies, and makes them more like a herd or flock of animals than a society of free, creative human beings. If Moses were to lead this band of slaves, or their descendants, into Palestine, and make of them there a free, creative nation, he would have to begin the long process of education which alone could build them into a society. The Ten Commandments were his blue-print for this education. They consisted of the laws which he thought to be most important for the children of Israel to survive and to fulfill the mission he saw for them.

Our first concern, therefore, as we look at each of the commandments, will be to inquire why it was so important in those days, at that time. Then we want to ask whether it is still equally important for us today, whether it requires any additional interpretation for us, or whether it has outlived its usefulness and is no longer needed. These, then, are the questions we shall have in mind for each:

1. Stated in our own words, just what does it say or mean?
2. Why was it so important in the time of Moses?
3. Is it still important for us today?
4. What does it mean for our modern society?

Actually, the Ten Commandments were considered so important that they appear, with minor differences, twice in our Bible. The wording we shall use in this chapter is taken from the twentieth chapter of Exodus; a slightly different version may be found in the fifth chapter of Deuteronomy. Some Christian sects divide these commandments somewhat differently; we shall of course use here our usual Jewish division. If you are interested in observing the differences between the two Jewish versions, compare Deuteronomy 5:6–18 to the wording of Exodus, used here.

1. I AM THE LORD THY GOD, WHO BROUGHT THEE OUT OF THE LAND OF EGYPT, OUT OF THE HOUSE OF BONDAGE.

What strikes you at once as strange about this first commandment? If you're like most people and you haven't just skipped over the tops of the words, you must have noticed immediately that it somehow doesn't sound like a commandment at all, does it? It doesn't direct us, or even ask us to do anything. It just announces that our God is the one who brought us out of Egypt. One author, telling how these words impressed him as a child, writes: "The First Commandment seemed to be just something put in there to confuse everybody. So I quit bothering about that. It didn't mean anything, so far as I was concerned."

Before agreeing with this comment, let's have another look at the words of the First Commandment, a good "digging" look rather than a quick glance. Why do you suppose they were put there, as the beginning of the ten laws? They really constitute an introduction, don't they? They tell us that all the laws which are to follow come from God, and furthermore, from the God who had just delivered the children of Israel from slavery. To a people which had just escaped from Egypt, that was the best possible way of attracting immediate attention for the commandments which were to follow. It was equivalent to saying: Look here, these aren't just casual statements I am about to give you; these words come from God Himself, so you'd better pay close attention.

But we aren't the ancient children of Israel and we haven't just escaped from Egypt. Do we still need this introduction, or can we dispense with it? What do the words mean for us? At least two things. First, that the commandments to follow are the product of man's cooperation with the power of God in the past, and that they point the way toward greater cooperation in the future; that these laws weren't just jotted down in a hurry by a man with a pencil; they came out of a great prophet's struggle with his own conscience, out of his thinking about man's purpose in life, out of his listening to the voice of God within his own heart and mind.

To discover the second modern meaning of these introductory words, it is important to notice with which ethical ideal this first commandment immediately associates the word *God.* "Who brought thee out of the land of Egypt, out of the house of bondage." Freedom! The greatest and most important of the many ideals contained in our inspiring master-ideal is freedom! Unless a man is free, there is no point to going on with the other nine laws. If a person is slave to a state which orders him not to worship God, what use is there in telling him the opposite? If a man is subservient to a government which orders him to kill, what point to telling him he shouldn't kill? In order to follow the Ten Commandments, a person needs freedom to choose between good and evil, freedom to live his own life, gradually striving to reach upward toward the goal—God.

"It didn't mean anything, so far as I was concerned." No, this commandment isn't apt to mean much if we just skim over the surface of the words. But if we read it carefully and think about it conscientiously, we'll find that for us, as for the Jews of ancient times, it sets the mood, it establishes a framework, so to speak, for the specific laws which are to follow. Within that framework, we are ready now to consider the rest.

2. THOU SHALT HAVE NO OTHER GODS BEFORE ME. THOU SHALT NOT MAKE UNTO THEE A GRAVEN IMAGE, NOR ANY MANNER OF LIKENESS, OF ANY THING THAT IS IN HEAVEN ABOVE, OR THAT IS IN THE EARTH BENEATH, OR THAT IS IN THE WATER UNDER THE EARTH: THOU SHALT NOT BOW DOWN UNTO THEM, NOR SERVE THEM; FOR I THE LORD THY GOD AM A JEALOUS GOD, VISITING THE INIQUITY OF THE FATHERS UPON THE CHILDREN UNTO THE

THIRD AND FOURTH GENERATION OF THEM THAT HATE ME; AND SHOWING MERCY UNTO THE THOUSANDTH GENERATION OF THEM THAT LOVE ME AND KEEP MY COMMANDMENTS.

We shouldn't have any difficulty either in understanding what these words mean or in recognizing their enormous importance at the time when Moses first spoke them. Remember that generations of slave-life in Egypt must have resulted in the children of Israel carrying with them many of the Egyptian religious customs, including the making of idols. Remember also that all the peoples with whom they were to have contact for centuries and among whom they were to live worshipped images of one kind or another. Moses realized that a people praying to images could never learn either that God is One, or that God is purely spiritual, not physical. Therefore it was important for him, at the immediate beginning, to insist that Jews must not worship idols. Then they must not make idols either, for once made, images would find their way into religious usage and worship.

Is there any danger of idolatry today? Isn't this one lesson the world has learned pretty well through the centuries, so that we could dispense with the Second Commandment? Not so fast! Let's have one of those "deep looks" before deciding. Aren't there still churches and shrines, even among civilized, advanced people today, in which men and women bow down to images and idols? And doesn't that still lead to confusion between a purely spiritual God, who can't be seen or represented in any tangible form, and the physical statues that are used to represent Him? Perhaps there is still need for this ancient Jewish teaching, even in a literal sense, today.

But there is another sense in which the Second Commandment is even more important for our time. What it really says is: only God is worthy of our highest devotion. Only the power and force responsible for life and the goal or master-ideal which is the purpose of life are important enough to become the theme of our whole existence. Someone once said that anything to which a person devotes his most precious time and gives his greatest energy and attention is, in a sense, that person's God. There is much truth to that. You and I know people today—do we not?—who base their whole lives on making money. Everything they do or plan or think is devoted to the single goal of increasing their wealth. Money has become the theme and purpose of their lives—not a means to be used for greater and more important ends, but the very end of life itself. There are others who live only for success, or power, or fame. These have become the little gods or idols of their lives.

The Second Commandment tells us that no such gods as these are worthy. That only the One God whom we have tried to understand and recognize is worth our highest loyalty, our deepest devotion. "Thou shalt have no other gods before Me." Still mighty important words, don't you think so?

We wouldn't want to leave this second commandment without commenting on its final portion. Read carelessly, the idea of "visiting the iniquity of the fathers upon the children" seems both unfortunate and unfair. But if you will repeat these words thoughtfully, particularly remembering our earlier reference to them during our discussion of moral law in Chapter Eight, you will understand that whether we prefer it that way or not, they describe something which actually exists. It is true that children often do have to suffer because of the sins of their fathers; that's something fathers who are wise keep in mind. (See Reading Selection C on page 277.)

The word "jealous" in this commandment has bothered a great many modern people. It is hardly consistent with our Jewish idea of God to think of Him as possessing a petty human trait such as jealousy. Actually, however, the Hebrew word for "jealous" may be translated "zealous." If translated thus, God is interpreted as being anxious and eager for human beings to live ethically. For modern Jews this is a far better translation.

3. THOU SHALT NOT TAKE THE NAME OF THE LORD THY GOD IN VAIN: FOR THE LORD WILL NOT HOLD HIM GUILTLESS THAT TAKETH HIS NAME IN VAIN.

That sounds like an easy one to understand, doesn't it? "Thou shalt not take the name of the Lord thy God in vain" means we shouldn't use the word *God* in cursing and when we swear to anything using God's name we should be sure to tell the truth. Very true—but this is only part of what the commandment says. These simple, obvious meanings are important, but as in the two preceding commandments, let's see whether there aren't deeper meanings which are even more important.

First, however, a word about the importance of the Third Commandment when it was originally pronounced. Moses realized that if his people were to take seriously the new religion he was beginning to teach them, they would have to take the idea of God seriously. They couldn't afford to accept God just lightly, or to use His name flippantly in daily conversation. Nor could they diminish His importance by using profanely an idea or a word which was holy.

And now, for our own day: what other ways are there to take the name of God in vain? Well, for one thing, certainly the person who professes to believe in God, who calls himself religious, but then neglects or ignores the practice of a religious life, would be violating this commandment. In some ways people who claim to be religious, but don't do much about it, are more to be condemned than those who openly consider themselves atheists. There are millions of Americans—both Jewish and Christian—who would emphatically deny they are atheists but who are not to be found normally in synagogue or church, who seldom if ever pray, and whose homes are empty of the religious celebration and observance of important holidays. Such people have clearly taken the name of God in vain.

An even more dangerous way of taking God's name in vain, however, is to claim belief in Him but to ignore the ethical principles and conduct which alone can justify religion. Men like Daniel Drew and John D. Rockefeller, Sr., took God's name very much in vain when they made huge fortunes by treating their fellow men unfairly, yet gave the impression of being active, generous members of the church. Men who call themselves religious, who support and attend services, but who pay their workers inadequately or treat their competitors unfairly or in any other way violate these Ten Commandments, have taken God's name in vain in a far more serious and unforgivable way than if they had occasionally used it improperly in cursing.

We hope that by now you recognize there is more than merely one simple meaning to each of these commandments, so that in those to follow you will be searching beneath the surface for their deeper importance.

4. REMEMBER THE SABBATH DAY, TO KEEP IT HOLY. SIX DAYS SHALT THOU LABOUR, AND DO ALL THY WORK: BUT THE SEVENTH DAY IS A SABBATH UNTO THE LORD THY GOD, IN IT THOU SHALT NOT DO ANY MANNER OF WORK, THOU, NOR THY SON, NOR THY DAUGHTER, NOR THY MAN-SERVANT, NOR THY MAID-SERVANT, NOR THY CATTLE, NOR THY STRANGER THAT IS WITHIN THY GATES; FOR IN SIX DAYS THE LORD MADE HEAVEN AND EARTH, THE SEA, AND ALL THAT IN THEM IS, AND RESTED ON THE SEVENTH DAY; WHEREFORE THE LORD BLESSED THE SABBATH DAY, AND HALLOWED IT.

Because most of us today take the idea of a day of rest for granted, the words of this commandment may not seem so striking. But to a nation of slaves, who were accustomed for generations to the hardest, harshest kind of labor without any rest, this fourth commandment must have sounded almost revolutionary. Moses knew how important it was to teach his people the difference between slave-labor which destroys a person and the dignified labor of a free man. So he included, among these ten most important laws, an order to rest one day each week, and to allow all who lived with them—animal as well as human—a day of rest.

We can understand the whole importance of the Fourth Commandment for today only if we think about the real meaning of rest. In one sense, of course, it means merely abstaining from all physical exertion. Even in that respect, however, our ideas of rest and therefore of Sabbath observance have changed through the centuries. Originally Jews were not allowed to have any light on the Sabbath, because making a light involved building and maintaining a fire, which was hard work. Most American Jews today, however, no longer consider it wrong to have a light on the Sabbath, when all that is involved is the flick of a finger.

But this is only the simplest, most elementary meaning of rest. It also means a chance to cease doing the regular work of the week, and to seek new inspiration and encouragement toward a truly religious life. Sabbath rest really goes back to the original meaning of the word recreation (re-creation). It gives us an opportunity to become acquainted again with the high ideals of our faith, and to rededicate ourselves to the right kind of living. That is why observant Jews, after spending the Sabbath morning worshipping in their synagogues, usually devoted the afternoon to study or reading or listening to a traveling preacher speak on an ethical theme. In short, going back to our recent discussions on the meaning and importance of regular prayers, the Sabbath is our principal time for inventory, for taking stock of ourselves, for "tuning in" once again on God.

In a more literal and direct sense, this fourth commandment has another significance. This lies in the fact that it doesn't just offer a day of rest and inspiration to the man who works for himself. It includes "thy man-servant" and "thy maid-servant" and even "thy stranger that is within thy gates"! This implies the right of every human being to a decent job, and once he has such employment, to proper time for rest, limited hours of labor, and a salary on which he and his family not only can have enough to eat, but also enjoy some of life's pleasures and luxuries. In this sense, the Fourth Commandment is the foundation of all those laws passed by our government to protect the human rights of workers and farmers throughout the land. "Remember the Sabbath day, to keep it holy!"

5. HONOUR THY FATHER AND THY MOTHER, THAT THY DAYS MAY BE LONG UPON THE LAND WHICH THE LORD THY GOD GIVETH THEE.

While they were slaves in Egypt our ancestors had very little chance to develop strong home or family life. As a free people, however, it would be important for them to learn strong family loyalty and love. This was Moses' purpose in including a law concerning the family among the Ten Commandments. He realized also that he could not possibly teach every individual Jew himself. Therefore, he ordered everyone to honor his parents, so that the parents, who would learn the important principles of their religion from Moses, would then be able to instruct their children. It is easy to see how important this was in ancient days.

It should be easy also to see its importance now. The most important lessons a child learns—the foundations for his later happiness and success—come from his parents. An old Jewish tradition says that God, knowing He couldn't be everywhere to take care of everything at the same time Himself, created parents to be, so to speak, His representatives. To which the Talmud adds: "There are three partners in man: God, father, and mother. When men honor their parents, God says: 'I account it unto them as if I were dwelling among them and they honored Me.' "

We today interpret these thoughts to mean that children are

first introduced to God through their parents. It is from our parents that all of us received our earliest instruction in the ethical rules of religion. When we were very little children, our mothers and fathers were our goals of conduct. Whatever they did was right; our highest aim was to copy them. Later, as we developed and matured, we acquired even higher and loftier patterns of conduct, until now we realize that only God is the master-ideal, the vision of perfection we must seek. But our first glimpse of a goal and a pattern of ideals to follow was the conduct of our parents. It is by honoring them and the ideals they taught us that we develop religiously.

Having said this, however, we must in all fairness say one thing more. Parents must deserve and earn the respect of their children. One of your readings for this chapter will describe how confused one boy was when he realized that not all the parents of his friends were people whom he could honor. If the chief distinction of parents is that they introduce us to the ideals of God, it follows that only parents who consistently and conscientiously represent those ideals throughout their lives are entitled to the respect commanded by Moses. This does not mean that our parents are supposed to be perfect; we have already become familiar with the major Jewish teaching that no human being can ever be really perfect. It does mean, however, that parents must constantly and consciously strive by their own conduct to set a high ethical example for their children. Unfortunately, there are parents whose conduct could scarcely be used as a pattern by their children. They have not earned the obedience of their children to the Fifth Commandment.

What is true of parents is at least equally true of children. The relationship between human parents and children is considerably different from that between animals and their offspring. Even a dog or cat demonstrates a certain kind of physical love toward its pups or kittens. It takes care of them and feeds them until they are able to care for themselves: up to that time it will protect them against all danger. The kittens and pups, in turn, remain close and devoted to their parents so long as they need them. But because human beings have developed spiritually as well as physically, the relationship between human parents and children is also a spiritual relationship. Each must deserve and continually earn the respect, the honor and the love of the other. (See Reading Selections A, D, and E.)

6. THOU SHALT NOT MURDER!

It would hardly seem necessary to explain such strong and simple words as these. We are tempted just to say they mean what they obviously say, and to go on with the next commandment. But there have been different ways of interpreting even these seemingly simple words. Some people, for example, applying the prohibition against killing literally and everywhere, say it is wrong to kill animals for use as food for humans; therefore they are vegetarians, refusing to eat any meat. Most of us, however, interpret the Sixth Commandment to express the sanctity and value of life, especially of human life. We say, therefore, that while no animal should be killed needlessly, yet if meat is required for human nutrition and health, it is not a violation of the commandment to slaughter beasts for this purpose.

How about war? Isn't the bombing and shooting of enemy soldiers murder? And aren't those enemy soldiers human beings? In that case, every soldier, sailor or marine who ever participated in combat has violated this commandment, hasn't he? Indeed, there are people called *conscientious objectors* who say exactly that, and who refuse, therefore, to wage war or to serve in the armed forces. Even the government respects the right of individuals who object to war on grounds of religious principle and adherence to the Sixth Commandment. Most of us, however, would say again that the purpose of this law is to protect human life, and that sometimes it becomes necessary to destroy some human lives in order to protect and preserve a great many others. For example, what about the lives of the six million Jews who were butchered by the Nazis before and during World War II? Which is the way to obey the Sixth Commandment—to wage war in order to save the lives of additional victims, or to abstain from war because we refuse to kill their tormentors?

This isn't an easy question to answer. Many great and good men have gone through the torture and turmoil of struggling with conscience in search of an answer. We have no right to criticize or to blame an honest person who differs from our own conclusion. The important thing to recognize, however, is that this commandment sets human life up as the greatest good on earth. It insists that anything which needlessly destroys human life is evil; that which protects and preserves human life is good.

Are these, then, the only ways in which people can be guilty of murder? Not by any means! It is possible that some highly respectable and apparently religious people among us have been guilty of violating this commandment. The owners of factories and mines, who, in the name of lowered expense or increased profit, refuse to install every possible mechanism or device for safeguarding the health and safety of their employees, are as guilty of murder as the man who fires a gun at his fellow man! Likewise, any human being who tries to dominate another—to do all his thinking for him and dictate all his decisions—has in a sense killed something fine and important in that other person. The same is true of one who murders the best in himself by failing to use all his ability to its utmost, for the good of others and of himself. So there are many methods of murder. The Sixth Commandment, properly interpreted and understood, prohibits them all. (See Reading Selections B, F, G and H.)

Abraham ibn Ezra, one of the great medieval Jewish poets and thinkers, said, " 'Thou shalt not murder' includes 'by poison of the tongue.' "

> What do you think he meant? Is this really a form of murder? Is there any other of the Ten Commandments to which this belongs more properly than to the Sixth? Why?

7. THOU SHALT NOT COMMIT ADULTERY!

Do you remember the first questions you asked about this Seventh Commandment—how the adults you asked talked all around it without actually saying what it meant, while you probably knew all the while? There really isn't any excuse for that, and we don't intend to hide anything from you here. The dictionary gives this definition of the word *adultery:* "Sexual unfaithfulness of a married person; voluntary sexual intercourse by a married man with another than his wife or by a married woman with another than her husband."

What Moses was actually saying, then, was that a man should have sexual intercourse only with his wife, and a woman only with her husband. His reasons should be obvious. Violations of this law would mean the break-up of families, constant jealousy and suspicion among families and between members of the same family, feuds leading to murder, children of uncertain parentage, and many other serious evils.

Every reason for this commandment in the time of Moses is equally valid today. Plus many more. The differences we have many times noted between human beings and animals are true especially in the field of sex. With animals, sex is purely and entirely a physical experience. There is nothing either spiritual or lasting about it. A male dog, feeling a sexual urge, experiences sexual intercourse with a female dog who happens to be near. When they have satisfied their respective urges, that is the end of the whole experience; they may never even see each other again; the whole thing has been limited to physical pleasure. With human beings it is different. Though sex, like most phases of human life, is admittedly a physical experience, it rises out of the purely physical to become a spiritual experience, too.

The sexual attraction between a man and a woman, unlike that of animals, forms the basis for the lasting affection they feel for each other. When a human male has intercourse with a female whom he does not love, he is cheapening sex by living it on the animal level. When he experiences intercourse with the one woman whom he loves above all others, sexual experience increases the spiritual love between them also, while the deeper their spiritual love, the more attracted they are to each other sexually.

This is a choice every one of us has as a human being. We can, if we like, get our nourishment the animal way by eating wild plants and fruits and by tearing the meat off beasts with our bare hands. Or, if we prefer, we can be nourished the human way, at a table set with china and linen, with the proper utensils used politely, enjoying conversation, and learning from each other as we eat. We can live altogether on the physical level of eating, sleeping, and enjoying ourselves. Or we can reach a higher, more human kind of life, anticipating the future of evolution, by sharing the pleasures of great art, music, poetry, etc. We can reduce our sex experience also to the animal level of merely momentary physical pleasure. Or we can wait for sexual intercourse until we have found the one person with whom we want to share life's highest joys, then enjoy our sex life with that person only.

There are few human experiences in which the God within us is more clearly or beautifully evident than in the deep love which husband and wife feel for each other. And the one, single moment when human beings come closest to sharing the creative power of God in the universe is when two of them who are in love with each other unite to create a new life as the fruit of their love. The Seventh Commandment says a great deal more than its obvious simple meaning. It tells us that in sex, as in everything else in human life, that which helps man live his life on the highest possible level, most like God and most unlike animals, is good. Anything else, though much easier, is cheapening and therefore wrong. Reading Selection M should make this clearer for you.

A word should be said about the difference between the attitude of Judaism toward sex and that of many other religions. A great number of Christian churches, for example, look upon sex as a necessary evil. Naturally, without sex it would be impossible for the human race to survive; therefore they cannot altogether oppose it. But they believe that even between husband and wife the practice of sex relations is a source of evil.

The Catholic church carries this attitude to the point of proclaiming that the highest level of human existence is celibacy, that is to say, living without any sexual intercourse. This is why Catholic priests and nuns are not allowed to marry. Catholics also believe that in marriage sex relations between husband and wife must be limited only to those occasions when a child is wanted.

While Judaism agrees that the most sacred privilege of a man and woman who love each other is to become parents, it does not agree that this is the only justification for sexual intercourse between husband and wife. We believe this experience is also legitimate as an expression of the deep love a married couple should have for one another, as well as a stimulant for the further development of their love. In Judaism, therefore, sexual relations in marriage are considered a good thing.

8. THOU SHALT NOT STEAL!

One way of determining how well you have absorbed our discussion of the commandments thus far will be to let you do the interpreting yourself for the final three. In your workbook, you will be expected to answer for each of the remaining commandments the four questions asked on page 261. Since they won't be repeated again in the workbook, it would be well for you to keep that page of your text before you as you do this part of the work. In addition to the four general questions for each of these commandments, there may be specific inquiries about each.

> For example, in connection with the Eighth Commandment, you should ask yourself: What ways are there for one man to steal from another, besides taking money out of his pocket or his house? What meaning can I discover by digging down under the words instead of just sailing over the top? In what ways may I myself ever have been guilty of stealing? What meanings might "stealing" have today, in our world of modern business and industry, which it did not have in the time of Moses? (See Reading Selection I.)

9. THOU SHALT NOT BEAR FALSE WITNESS AGAINST THY NEIGHBOUR!

A few extra questions to consider here, in addition to those on page 261. What is the meaning here of the word *neighbour?* Is this commandment more or less important today than in the time of Moses? How can we state this negative commandment in a positive way, that is, instead of saying *Thou shalt not*, to commence with *Thou shalt?* Would this commandment apply only to the relationship between individuals, or also to those between societies and nations? (See Reading Selections J and K.)

10. THOU SHALT NOT COVET THY NEIGHBOUR'S HOUSE; THOU SHALT NOT COVET THY NEIGHBOUR'S WIFE, NOR HIS MAN-SERVANT, NOR HIS MAID-SERVANT, NOR HIS OX, NOR HIS ASS, NOR ANY THING THAT IS THY NEIGHBOUR'S.

Additional questions: What does the word *covet* mean? Doesn't this commandment seem comparatively less important than the other nine? Does it really belong here among the ten most important laws Moses could possibly have given his people? What is its relationship, if any, to the other nine commandments? To which of them is it most closely connected? If it is to be kept among the ten, is this the most logical place for it? Why? Does it apply only to individuals, or also to nations?

A Word in Conclusion

Though this has been a long chapter, we have done little more than *introduce* the discussion of the Ten Commandments. There is much more that could have been said. When you have completed this chapter and its readings, however, and have done the workbook assignment, you should be better able than before to appreciate why these ten laws have quite properly been called the foundation of religion and religious behavior. They are the blue-print of Judaism as a way of life. Properly understood, they mean more, not less, and are needed more, not less, than 3,200 years ago when they were first written, through the cooperation of God and a man named Moses.

SOMETHING FOR YOU TO READ

A. I used to wonder what it would be like if my father and mother had been bad people, if they had been cruel and dishonest and stupid. I began to see that there were fathers and mothers who were these things . . . the Bible itself, both in the Old and the New Testaments, teaches that we should not honor unworthy people. No, it didn't make any sense to say flatly, like that, "honor thy father and mother" without stopping to find out whether the father and mother were worthy of honor. I could honor mine easily enough, but I knew that there were many boys and girls who couldn't possibly honor theirs without being fools. . . .—Robert O. Ballou, *This I Believe*, The Viking Press.

B. I didn't ever want to kill, but I had killed many times, because my mother had told me to. Every Sunday, on the farm, we used to have a chicken dinner, and every Saturday someone had to kill the chicken. Often I had to do it, even though I hated it. . . .

But apparently the sixth commandment didn't mean that one shouldn't kill chickens or cows, or other animals to eat. Or rats or mice or mosquitoes. Everybody killed these. It must mean only that we shouldn't kill men and women.

But even this was confusing. For nations which call themselves Christian killed people in war. And states which called themselves Christian killed, by hanging or electrocution, men and women who had committed murder. And the steel mills run by Elbert H. Gary (the good Christian man who had given Wheaton its fine stone and concrete and oak and stained glass church) killed men by making them so sick they could not live, and by accidents. . . .—Robert O. Ballou, *This I Believe*, The Viking Press.

C. The worship of anything but God is idolatry and brings a train of evil consequences such as the second commandment describes. The worship of money or power or fame—how dismal their effects! Some of us make a god of pleasure. Some bow down to their own beauty or cleverness or to their social standing or their achievements. Our own self sometimes becomes our God. A troubled heart, a confused mind, a tainted conscience are the results of such worship. . . .

It is also true that when parents do wrong, the children are likely to suffer. This is not because God is unjust, punishing the children for what the parents have done; the great prophets, Jeremiah and Ezekiel, protested eloquently against such a thought. It is merely a law of nature that parents who would have good and happy children must themselves live good and wholesome lives. How careful we should be of our conduct, perceiving that not we alone but countless others are affected thereby!—Abraham Cronbach, *Service for Confirmation*, Bloch Publishing Co.

D. Learning the Torah is a greater thing than honoring father and mother.

Should his father tell him to transgress the words of the Torah, whether they be mandatory [positive] or prohibitory [negative] laws, or even only commandments according to the words of the sages, he shall not obey him.—Joseph Karo (16th century), quoted in Glatzer, *In Time and Eternity*, Schocken Books, Inc.

E. In what does reverence for a father consist? In not sitting in his presence, and in not speaking in his presence, and in not contradicting him. Of what does honour for parents consist? In providing for them food and drink, in clothing them, in giving them shoes for their feet, in helping them to enter or leave the house. Rabbi Eliezer said: Even if his father order him to throw a purse of gold into the sea, he should obey him.—Talmud.

A man may feed his father on fattened chickens and inherit hell, and another may put his father to treading the mill, and inherit Paradise. In the first case, a son gave his father fattened chickens to eat, and the father said, "My son, whence did you get these?" The son said, "Old man, old man, eat and be silent; so the dogs eat and are silent." He feeds his father on fattened chickens and inherits hell. The other man grinds in his mill; there comes an ordinance for millers to go and grind for the government. The son says, "Father, come and grind here instead of me; if any ill-treatment should happen, better that it befall me and not you; if there should be scourgings [whipping], better that they come to me and not to you." Such a one makes his father grind the mill, and will inherit Paradise. —Talmud. Both the above quoted in Montefiore and Loewe, *A Rabbinic Anthology*, Macmillan and Co. (London).

F. He who aids a fellow-man to do a wicked thing is as if he had murdered him.—Midrash, quoted in Newman, *The Talmudic Anthology*, Behrman House.

G. There are many ways of killing people. We can kill people by vexing them to death, worrying them to death, working them to death or letting them starve to death. Through coldness or neglect, we can render people so unhappy that they will wish for death, lose their health or, in some instances, take their own lives. Many a wayward son or daughter has brought a parent's gray hairs in sorrow to the grave. Overworking and underpaying those whom we employ is not the least of the ways in which the sixth commandment is violated.

Would we be guiltless of shedding human blood? Then must kindness be the law of our lives, fairness the rule of our lives and justice the principle of our lives. Otherwise, great is the peril that we break the commandment, "Thou shalt not kill."—Cronbach, *Service for Confirmation*, Bloch Publishing Co.

H. Certainly it is not possible to avoid moral difficulties by the simple expedient [device] of never taking life. . . . This is no solution, because we are faced frequently with a choice of *which* life is to be taken. Will you kill the lice which carry the typhus germs or will you let the typhus germs kill the people? On the highest grounds, a person who *can* kill the lice, and refuses to do so, is terribly evil. He seems to be avoiding the issue, but his very avoidance is really taking sides. He is valuing lice rather than men. For this reason the sensitized conscience realizes that lower forms of life must frequently be sacrificed for the sake of higher forms of life. . . .

The only practical solution of the problem of the sacredness of life is the cultivation of the uneasy conscience. Animals must die to feed humans or to save them from disease. We must deliberately give them infantile paralysis if we are to save boys and girls from this dread malady. *But* we must never do this wantonly or easily or gladly.—Trueblood, *Foundations for Reconstruction*, Harper and Bros.

I. . . . Just as there may be forms of idolatry and forms of killing that we do not suspect, so there are forms of stealing that we do not suspect. Oppression of the laborer and exploitation of the poor are forms of stealing. Overcharging in business and underpaying those who work for us are forms of stealing.

When we are unfaithful at our work, we are also stealing. We are stealing from those for whom we are working. . . . To do poor and careless work when we are paid to do good and careful work is surely a form of stealing.

Again, it is possible to steal people's time. The disorderly pupil in the class room thus commits stealing. That pupil steals not only the time of the teacher but also the time of all the others in the class.

Do we not often steal from our mothers and fathers? Not money, to be sure, but the time and the strength that are more than money. The unruly, disobedient son or daughter who gives his or her parents needless trouble, work or care is thus a violator of the eighth commandment, "Thou shalt not steal."—Cronbach, *Service for Confirmation*, Bloch Publishing Co.

J. He who is suspicious of innocent people says in his heart, I am committing no sin, because (he says), what harm have I done to him? I only suspect him; perhaps he is guilty, and perhaps he is not. This man does not realize that thinking of an innocent person as a possible transgressor is an iniquity.—Maimonides, quoted in Agnon, *Days of Awe*, Schocken Books, Inc.

K. He who slanders, who listens to slander, and who testifies falsely, deserves to be thrown to the dogs.—Talmud, quoted in Newman, *The Talmudic Anthology*, Behrman House.

L. What immature minds have done to the Decalogue has been, in the second place, to give it so narrow and literal an interpretation that it has been largely robbed of its power to encourage man toward moral maturity. "Thou shalt not steal" has been chiefly interpreted to mean that you must not overtly take what obviously belongs to somebody else. Most of the subtler [less obvious] forms of stealing, however—through the adulteration [corruption] of goods, for example; through financial manipulations [tricks] of the market; through imperialism—have been given other names than stealing and have been largely ignored.

The same has been true in the case of admonitions [warnings] against lying, killing, committing adultery, coveting. Arthur Hugh Clough, in his new Decalogue, has pointedly suggested how the narrow, literal interpretation of these moral commands has failed to reach the full-scale immoralities that are part of the going concern we call civilization:

Thou shalt not covet, but tradition
Approves all forms of competition;

Thou shalt not kill, but needst not strive
Officiously [obligingly] to keep alive.
—H. A. Overstreet, *The Mature Mind*, W. W. Norton and Co., Inc., New York.

M. Sex is a part of life. It can be fine and full and very beautiful. It can be painful, restricting, and shameful. Like every other source of power, it must be harnessed or it runs wild and becomes destructive. Electricity wired into your home will light your house, cook your meals, warm your feet, and perform all kinds of miracles. Left unleashed, as lightning, it can destroy everything you care about in one burning holocaust. So it is with sex. It can be the basis of the fullest friendships, the finest love, the happiest marriage, and the supreme satisfaction of home and parenthood. Or it can, if left to run wild, hurt and destroy and leave forever scarred all that you hold dear.

Your sex life is yours to choose. More than ever before in history young people are given the freedom to work out their own behavior and to run their own lives. Your sex worries, your difficulties with sex are yours to work out with all the help that modern science and religion can offer. Your fulfillment of the sex side of life is yours to achieve, too, with the benediction [blessing] of all who find life good.—Duvall, *Facts of Life and Love*, Association Press, 1950.

16. *When Life Is Sad*

SEVERAL times in the chapters already finished we have referred to the problems of people who have had to suffer unhappiness in life. Though we don't like to talk about things so unpleasant, we propose to devote this sixteenth chapter to a discussion of such unhappiness, because it is one of the most important problems religion must face. If our course in Jewish religion does not prepare you for the unhappy as well as the happy experiences of life, we shall have failed in one of our most essential purposes.

People won't hold to any religion which doesn't help them over the bumps of life. Sometimes they give up religion altogether because they feel it has failed them in such circumstances. On the other hand, intelligent modern men and women can't be satisfied either with a superstitious explanation of their suffering or with a "religion" which closes its eyes to all evil and sorrow, simply denying that they exist.

This isn't just a world of simple happiness and pleasure. There is much happiness in human life, but there is suffering and sorrow too. Even so deeply religious a man as Albert Schweitzer has been so impressed by the sad side of life that he wrote: "Unrest, disappointment, and pain are our lot. . . . All life is suffering." This, of course, is taking into consideration only one side of life. It would be just as tragic a mistake to see only the sadness as it would be to recognize only the joy of life. We need to accept both, and our religion must help us explain both. When we are afflicted—as all of us must be from time to time—by pain, by illness, by the death of our loved ones and the disappointment of ambitions and hopes, how does our modern Jewish religion help us explain these experiences and survive them?

The first and most honest thing to say is: there is no one simple answer. Human experience includes many different kinds of trouble, for which we must seek different types of explanation. For some of the burdens we must carry, there just is no adequate answer, not yet; some day there may be. For the time being, after all our searching and seeking we must conclude: we just don't know. No truly religious person can afford to be smug either in thinking he knows all the answers or in minimizing someone else's trouble or sorrow. But we do have a number of ways, based on our religious convictions and beliefs, of explaining and enduring some of life's sadness. What are these ways?

A. How Little We Know

Perhaps we ought to begin by acknowledging that sometimes, because of our very limited knowledge, what seems to be a tragic misfortune is actually for our own ultimate good. The Talmud tells a story about Rabbi Akiba which illustrates this. Once when Akiba was traveling he came to a certain town after dark. His request for hospitality was refused, so he had no choice but to spend the night in the forest. He lit his lantern and tried to make himself comfortable. When a gust of wind blew the lamp out and he had no means of lighting it again, he considered that a grave stroke of misfortune. He felt the same way when a lion, prowling nearby, killed his mule, and when a cat made off with his rooster. The next morning he discovered that during the night a band of robbers had attacked the city in which he had unsuccessfully sought hospitality, stealing its wealth and carrying off many of its inhabitants. On their way to the city, the robbers had passed through the very woods in which Akiba had spent the night. Had he been granted lodging in the town, or had either his mule or his rooster been on hand to make noise, he would himself have been one of the victims. What had seemed at the time to be a series of tragedies turned out to be the best thing that could have happened to him.

The attitude illustrated by this story has become so much a part of our Jewish approach to life that we have adopted a fine Hebrew saying, Gam zu l'tovo, גַם זוּ לְטוֹבָה, meaning "this too is for good." When a Jew suffers tragedy or unhappiness, he often consoles himself by saying, "Gam zu l'tovo." In ways that we may not be in a position to appreciate until much later, even the sad things that happen to us may be blessings in disguise. We don't always see the whole picture.

Most of us have heard stories of individuals who missed a plane or train which it was extremely important for them to catch, only to learn later that by the "misfortune" of being late they had been saved from death in a tragic accident or crash. This is a simple, yet instructive example of how little we sometimes know about what really is good or bad for us.

The story has been told of the time when the future of England for centuries depended on Wellington's success in his battle against Napoleon. There being no telegraph or telephone in those days, the people of London had arranged for the outcome of the struggle to be signaled to them from the top of a cathedral spire. After hours of waiting, at last they saw a light beginning to flash from the tower. It spelled out slowly: "Wellington Defeated". . . and then a dense fog settled over the city. Its inhabitants were oppressed by thick gloom; their cause had apparently been lost. It was only later, when the fog had lifted and the light in the tower could resume its signals, that they saw the completed message: "Wellington Defeated the Enemy!" Sometimes that happens to us also as we face the problems of life. We see only part of the picture, which looks tragic. Later when we are able to see more, tragedy turns to blessing.

It would be both unfair and dishonest to pretend that this is always true, or that all sadness is only apparent or temporary. The death of a young person is often a tragedy which neither this nor any other explanation can soften; but there is also the possibility that it saved both the victim and his dear ones from even greater pain in the future. The college student who is denied admission to a medical school may indeed be suffering a permanent blow, from which he will never fully recover; but it is also possible, in some cases, that he would never have been happy as a physician anyway, and that this lesser sorrow now has saved him from greater unhappiness later. We don't always know; we can only use our past experience as a guide, showing us that sometimes it is our own limited knowledge and understanding which makes the blows of life seem greater than they are.

B. God Is a Convenient Scapegoat

At other times we ourselves are to blame for the unhappiness we attribute to God. Generally, you know, people don't like to accept blame for the things they do wrong. Most of us would much rather think someone or something else was at fault when we fail or feel disappointment. It's much easier to say the teacher wasn't fair than to admit we didn't do our best work; more comfortable by far to pretend someone else got the prize we wanted because he cheated or had influence than to admit that maybe we just didn't deserve it. We have already seen in this course how people—especially people with an ancient or childish concept of God—are inclined to "pass the buck" to God, using God as a scapegoat for their own failings.

Don't misunderstand: this doesn't mean that individuals are always guilty of some wrong when they suffer sorrow of any kind. We want to repeat what was said earlier in our discussion about moral law. The tragedies and blows of life aren't by any means portioned out only to those who deserve punishment. Innocent, decent, righteous people suffer too. The book of Job in our Bible, about which we shall say more later, makes that clear.

What we do mean to say here is that much of life's sadness could be avoided, and that very often a given tragedy is due not to God's deficiency but rather to our failure as human beings to cooperate fully with God. For example, the intense suffering which is caused by war is our fault, not God's. War comes because we human beings fail to live according to the ethical principles we know. If we were to do our share in the partnership between man and God, war, with all its sorrow and pain, could be abolished. If we are honest, therefore, we will accept the blame for this type of unhappiness ourselves.

More types of sorrow than you would at first suppose can be explained this way. Take even so apparently unrelated a case as death caused by cancer. Surely we human beings don't create cancer as we do war. How, then, can any of the blame be directed against us? How, indeed! Is it unreasonable or far-fetched to suppose that if there had been no wars in the world over the last fifty years, that if our bullets and bombs had not killed off some of the finest minds that might have been devoted to medical science, that if we had spent as many billions of dollars on cancer research as we have devoted to experiments in new and more fiendish ways of killing each other—is it unreasonable to suppose we might now be very much closer to an understanding of cancer and a cure for it? Even in suffering from diseases which we human beings didn't originate or cause, we can't entirely escape all blame ourselves and direct it all to God.

The Talmud tells the story of a king who invited many guests to his palace for a party. He told them in advance, however, that each should bring his own mattress or pillow on which to rest. Some of his guests refused to take him seriously. Wouldn't a king have enough resting places in his palace for all? On the night of the party those who had brought nothing found themselves with only logs and stones to lie on. So they turned in anger against their host, the king. Are we not often like this too—taking the easy way of explaining all our troubles instead of more honestly accepting at least part of the blame ourselves? Several of your readings for this chapter will have more to say along this line.

Many people, even some who are not consciously aware of it themselves, are willing to believe in God only so long as things go well with them. As soon as misfortune occurs in their lives, they "punish" God by no longer believing in Him. One such incident is reported in the Bible. When Jacob was on his way to Paddan-aram to find a wife for himself, he made a "bargain," so to speak, with God. He said, "If God will be with me, and will keep me in this way that I go, and will give me bread to eat, and raiment [clothing] to put on, so that I come back to my father's house in peace, then shall the Lord be my God." In other words, Jacob seemed willing to acknowledge God only if he were fortunate in life and received everything he wanted. That's the way many people are even today.

Judaism, however, has never approved this kind of religion. Our rabbis and teachers have always insisted that even at times of sadness and disappointment we must recognize God in all our experiences. The great creative power or force of God is present in the beauty and order of the universe, in the power, not ourselves, that makes for righteousness, in our goal of ethical perfection and within ourselves, even when things go wrong. Two of the many statements in which our rabbis expressed this thought are the following: "Let a man love God with a perfect love, whether it go well with him or ill," and "Man is bound to bless God for the evil, even as he blesses God for the good."

C. Humanity Is a Team

In this connection it should also be said that sometimes an individual suffers tragedy not because of anything he himself did wrong, but because of someone else's evil or mistake. Twice we have explained the phrase "visiting the iniquities of the fathers upon the children" by saying that often one generation suffers because of the sins of an earlier generation. That is true in a wider sense than just within families. Whether we like it or not, each of us belongs to a team—a human team consisting of all our fellow men. When one member of a football team fumbles, all his team-mates suffer for his error. When one member makes a brilliant run, all the others benefit. An end may play the most brilliant, flawless game of his career, yet lose because of his quarterback's mistakes. So in life at large we share the benefits of belonging to the human team, and we must also be prepared to share the costs.

How much more drab and dreary our lives would be if each of us had to accomplish everything for himself and could receive none of the benefits created by others. We live longer because of the scientific research of others; we thrill to great art and music because of the creative achievements of others; we feel the beauty of God within us due to the love of others. We must expect, then, also sometimes to suffer because of the evil done by others. This obviously applies in the case of war, already discussed above, where millions of innocent people must suffer along with those who may, directly or indirectly, have caused the war. Cain tried to escape responsibility for murdering his brother by asking, "Am I my brother's keeper?" We cannot explain or understand a large part of the suffering we meet in life unless we are ready to answer his question in the affirmative. We are—all of us—each other's keepers; we can all bring either greater happiness or deeper sorrow into the lives of others.

Our rabbinic ancestors showed that they understood this truth when they made a statement like the following, "When God judges the world, He judges it according to the merits of the majority of the population."

D. No Miracles Today

On a mountainside in New Hampshire is a tablet commemorating a landslide some years ago which wiped out an entire family. Visiting tourists are told that the family had constructed a shelter some yards from their home, anticipating that if a landslide should ever start, they would all run to the shelter and be saved. One night they heard rumblings which unmistakably announced the realization of their fears. Together they rushed out into the darkness to reach their place of safety. There were only a few yards to be traveled, but tons of earth came down upon them in an instant, and all were killed in the space between shelter and house. The next morning neighbors who had survived discovered that a huge boulder directly above their house had so divided the falling earth and rocks that the house itself hadn't even been touched. Had they remained there, they would have been saved. Rushing out for certain protection, all of them had been killed!

Obviously this tragedy can't be explained by any of the suggestions given so far in this chapter. It would be a little far-fetched, to say the least, to claim that the instant death of an entire family just seemed to be a tragedy, but was actually for their good. Likewise, the landslide couldn't very well be blamed either on their own or someone else's wrong-doing. The only explanation we can give is that somehow, by operation of the laws of nature, the wind and rain and soil erosion had created a condition whereby the earth and rocks began to fall down the mountainside. Once that had started, the force of gravity kept the slide falling and everything except the one spot which happened to be protected by the boulder was covered. Now then, if God were what primitive and ancient men supposed Him to be —an all-powerful supreme being who could do anything He wanted to do—then it would be quite proper and fair to blame the landslide and the resultant deaths on God.

But if God is the force or power which is responsible for the laws of nature and which must itself operate according to those rules, if God doesn't possess the power to work miracles, then we cannot intelligently expect Him to have saved this family. Furthermore, we must ask ourselves: What kind of world would this be if God *could* interrupt the laws of nature whenever He felt like it or whenever someone asked Him to in prayer? We can't have it both ways, you know. We can't rely on the benefits of a world which always operates by law, yet at the same time complain about its dangers.

If this were the kind of world in which God could at will make rocks fall upward or sideward instead of downward, then it would also be the kind of world in which other innocent people would be killed or in which we could never count on when or where the sun would shine or how long our earth could exist without colliding with some other planet. It shouldn't be hard to see that, tragic as life can sometimes be now, it would be filled with far more heartache and sorrow if nature's laws did not operate as they do. So another explanation for certain kinds of suffering is that it is the price we must pay for living in a universe on which we can always depend because it is operated by God.

> But how shall we explain the fact that the house from which the family escaped stood safely, while they were killed on their way to the shelter? Coincidence? Because they didn't live righteous lives? Because they weren't religious or didn't pray? What would your explanation be?

E. The Cost of Being Human

There is one further explanation which may help us understand some kinds of suffering or sorrow. The higher a creature is on the scale of evolution, the greater are its joys in life, and the more numerous also are the types of tragedy it can feel. A dog has the advantage over a tree in that it can move around freely, but the dog can also feel sharper pain than the tree when it is hurt. A human being has the advantage of appreciating music and art, of creating beauty and consciously advancing the development of evolution; but a human being, in addition to the physical pain he shares with the dog, can also suffer anxiety and anguish, grief and pain, worry and tension which the dog never knows. An eel never has to suffer the torment of separation from its loved ones or the frustration of disappointed ambitions. But then an eel can never enjoy love or a symphony or a poem either.

It's the old story once more: we cannot expect to enjoy the benefits of standing at the pinnacle of evolution without at the same time paying a price.

Life is so constituted that there is no progress without pain. Before the chicken can hatch, the egg must be broken. Before a human child can be born, its mother must feel the pain of giving birth. If the advance of evolution had stopped somewhere along the line—let us say, with the shellfish—we would have been spared much of the pain and suffering we now know. But then we would be shellfish, not human beings, partners with God. If no one had ever felt pain, either physical or emotional, doctors and clergymen and psychiatrists would never have been stimulated to work as they have for discoveries and truths which have hastened the progress of evolution on its way toward forms of life far more wonderful than any we know today, including ourselves.

The story has been told of an amateur naturalist who happened one day to watch the struggle of an emperor moth in the chrysalis stage to get out of the narrow opening of its cocoon. Impressed by the difficult struggle, the man decided to help by cutting the cocoon, thus immediately releasing the moth. The moth escaped all right, but it was never able to fly. The struggle was necessary to strengthen its wings. Because its growth from one stage to the next had been too easy, the wings were imperfect; it could only flutter to the ground, not fly. With human beings too, it often seems that the finest and noblest characters are those who have themselves suffered sorrow and misfortune.

Sometimes people wonder, as the Roman governor did when he questioned Rabbi Akiba about the poor, why God didn't create a world in which all these problems had been solved and all suffering eliminated. In the first place, such a question indicates at once that the questioner has very little understanding of our modern concept of God. But even beyond that, a world created perfect from the beginning would have meant that we human beings would have had no part at all in the awe-inspiring adventure of evolution—that we, like the rocks and stones of earth, would merely have been objects to be acted upon by God and nature, not creative, active, thinking *partners* of God, sharing with Him the joy of working upward toward perfection. One of your readings at the end of this chapter, which expresses something of this thought, is especially noteworthy since it comes from Harold Wilkie, the minister we mentioned some chapters back, who was born without arms. Few people on earth have a better right to speak of the achievements made possible by our suffering and pain.

But When All Is Said and Done . . .

. . . We must never forget how far we are from knowing all the answers or being able to explain every tragedy which mars human existence. Some day in the distant future men may know much more about these things than we do now. It is possible that some of us in this class may be able to think our way closer to a solution than anyone has yet. For that matter, you may be able right now to think out explanations of certain tragedies that we haven't given here.

Perhaps the most important thing to be remembered is this: We may have very little choice over the sadness we must face, but we and we alone can determine what that sadness will do to us—whether it will *make* us or *break* us. People react very differently to suffering. Some fathers become bitter against God and humanity when their sons or daughters die in early childhood. When that happened to Nathan Strauss, he devoted the rest of his life and much of his fortune to providing fresh, pasteurized milk for other children in New York City. Countless thousands of other parents were spared their children because one father was determined to *use* his grief instead of allowing it to *use him.*

Some men are deterred from further effort when they suffer a single disappointment. A man named LaGuardia, however, in a single year was defeated in his bid for nomination as mayor of New York, suffered a major surgical operation, and lost both his wife and one-year-old daughter. All within twelve months! Whereupon he proceeded to rebuild his life both personally and politically, to become a distinguished Congressman and eventually mayor of New York, and to bring healing and health into the lives of millions.

Shortly after the close of World War II the writer of this book met two fathers whose sons he had buried during combat on Iwo Jima. Both were good men; both missed their sons terribly and mourned them deeply. But the difference between them was almost unbelievable. The first father was literally a broken man. His grief was morbid. When the writer saw him again four years later his eyes still filled with tears whenever the boy's name was mentioned. He had been totally unable to "snap out of it" or to regain control of himself in all that time.

The second father, mourning no less than the first, reacted altogether differently. Almost immediately after hearing of his son's death, he had taken the money being saved for his boy's college education, had used it to bring to this country a Polish-Jewish orphan boy whom he was sending to college and medical school in place of his own son. Whenever he thought of the dead boy, along with his sadness was a strength and a feeling of rich accomplishment in that he was doing something his son would have wanted and was perpetuating his memory in a wonderful way.

In an earlier chapter of this book you were given another example of parents who used their own loss to help others by building the Cathedral of the Pines. Their story and the two told here illustrate our meaning when we say that we can choose whether or not to grow personally through our sufferings and to make them sources of blessing for others.

Our Rabbis in the Midrash called attention to the fact that gold becomes purified when heated in fire, while baser metals are melted. One of them also said, "The flax worker does not beat the hard flax much, because it would split; but the good flax, the more he beats it, the better it grows." In much the same way, genuine human character is strengthened by suffering. This is another of the important choices we face as human beings. We can use our misfortunes, or be used by them.

Getting Down to Cases

One of the real tests of religion is whether it helps us face specific trouble in life. We are going to close this chapter by describing several imaginary experiences—imaginary only because the people we are describing are fictitious; their experiences could be very real. In your workbook you will be asked to tell exactly what you would say to each of the individuals being described if he came to you for help.

Look back over the explanations discussed in this chapter, think over the important religious concepts with which this whole course has dealt; then indicate what you would say to help each person understand what had happened to him, to show him how his religion as a modern Jew might help him. Don't be satisfied with giving the same general answer to each. These are individual cases, requiring individual answers to suit the particular circumstances. By the time you complete the five of them, you should have used all the explanations of tragedy given in this chapter.

Case A—Mrs. L.'s three children were playing one day on the sidewalk in front of their apartment house. They were six, four, and three years old respectively. Mrs. L. had gone into the house to answer the telephone, when a police car pursuing a band of thieves came speeding up the street. Just before they reached the apartment the two cars commenced firing at each other. The children, not even understanding what was happening, stood still, too frightened even to move. By the time Mrs. L. returned, her three-year-old and six-year-old were both lying on the sidewalk—dead—shot by bullets intended for the speeding gangsters. Mrs. L. has been grief-stricken beyond description or relief. She cannot understand why this happened, or how she can believe in a God who would allow it.

Case B—Imagine that the father described in Reading Selection B of this chapter had come to you for help. What would you say to him?

Case C—John R. has been quite beyond consolation since his mother died. It isn't that he expected her to live forever, he keeps on repeating. But she was only fifty-four years old—far too young to die. And what bothers him even more: her passing came as such a terrible shock. She had never been seriously ill in her life. She fell ill on Saturday. The doctor came the following day and diagnosed her trouble as a stroke due to high blood pressure. He doubted whether she would regain consciousness. He was right; she died in her sleep Monday night. It's the suddenness of her death to which John can't reconcile himself.

Case D—Carl was one of the most promising students in his high school and college graduating classes and ranked first when he graduated from medical school. What people liked most about him was that with all his brilliance, he was sweet and considerate of others. Everyone predicted a career of distinction and success for him in his chosen profession. War broke out a month before Carl completed his hospital residency. He became a medical officer in the navy, was assigned to a marine division, and was killed in the landing on Iwo Jima. His mother has never been able to set foot inside the synagogue since that happened. She says that her husband was killed in a drowning accident when Carl was a baby, and with this second tragedy blighting her life, she just can't accept religion any more.

Case E—Even though two years have passed, Mrs. M. has never been able to accept understandingly the sudden death of her husband, a prominent clergyman. What makes it especially hard for her to become reconciled is that he did so much good in the world and had so much more to offer his fellow man. A busy man, he was never too busy to help others. At almost any hour of the day or night people in trouble knew they could count on him. His average work day for years had been anywhere from twelve to eighteen hours; how he managed to get so much work done and to help so many people was a mystery to his friends. His widow cannot understand the sense in such a man, with so much to give, dying at a relatively young age.

So much of the suffering and sorrow of human experience is due to death that we shall devote the next chapter to that subject exclusively. These aren't very pleasant subjects to spend so much time on, are they? Yet surely you must recognize how important they are. It is easy for a person to accept life and to believe it worth while when he is happy. It is in moments of sorrow and grief, however, that we need religion most. That is why our course could not be completed without this and the next chapter.

SOMETHING FOR YOU TO READ

A. When we look about us in the world, we see many terrible conditions: war, sickness, poverty and so on. How are we to understand the presence of these conditions? In this way: the godliness in men has not yet been exercised to the full. We have not yet made use of *all* the power that is in us. It is as though we were to see a horse car and wonder why that car has to be drawn by horses and not by electricity. The answer is: we have not yet gotten around to electrifying this particular car. It does not mean that electricity does not apply to this car; it means merely that whoever is in charge of that car has not yet realized that it could be moved by electric power.

Thus (when) we see evil in the world, it is (sometimes) because the people who are responsible for that evil have not yet applied their godliness to it; they have failed to make use of that goodness which would correct the evil. To believe in God is to believe that this goodness is endless, that its power can never be exhausted, and that if it were applied properly on all occasions, it would help us to bring about a perfect world, one which would be completely worth while living in.—Ira Eisenstein, *What We Mean by Religion*, Behrman House.

B. A sixteen-year-old, attractive Swedish boy was brought to the hospital suffering from a brain tumor. After opening the boy's skull the doctors found he had a highly malignant tumor which could not be removed. When the father was told of the boy's condition he said little. Later, as the father talked with a minister, he burst out, "There is no God. There could not be if this is true. I have been a fool to believe there was!"—Cabot and Dicks, *The Art of Ministering to the Sick,* copyright, 1936 by The MacMillan Co. and used with their permission.

C. One can choose protection at the price of growth, or growth at the price of pain. Admittedly, the pain does not guarantee growth; but neither does the protection which sometimes comes from the sacrifice of so great a value as growth offer sure and lasting peace of mind.—Harold Wilkie, *Greet the Man,* Christian Education Press.

D. Most of the evil that befalls individuals comes from the imperfections within themselves. Out of these imperfections of ours we cry out demands. The evil we inflict upon ourselves, of our own volition, and which pains us, this evil we ascribe to God.—Maimonides, quoted in Glatzer, *In Time and Eternity,* Schocken Books, Inc.

E. I heard from some of the elders who came out of Spain that one of the boats was infested with the plague, and the captain of the boat put the passengers ashore at some uninhabited place. And there most of them died of starvation, while some of them gathered up all their strength to set out on foot in search of some settlement.

There was one Jew among them who struggled on afoot together with his wife and two children. The wife grew faint and died, because she was not accustomed to so much difficult walking. The husband carried his children along until both he and they fainted from hunger. When he regained consciousness, he found that his two children had died.

In great grief he rose to his feet and said, "O Lord of all the universe, you are doing a great deal that I might even desert my faith. But know you of a certainty that—even against the will of heaven —a Jew I am and a Jew I shall remain! And neither that which you have brought upon me nor that which you will yet bring upon me will be of any avail."

Thereupon he gathered some earth and some grass, and covered the boys, and went forth in search of a settlement.—Solomon ibn Verga (16th century), quoted in Glatzer, *In Time and Eternity,* Schocken Books, Inc.

F. Why was the Confession (for Yom Kippur) composed in the plural, so that we say, We have sinned, rather than, I have sinned?

Because all Israel is one body and every one of Israel is a limb of that body; that is why we are all responsible for one another when we sin. So, if one's fellow should sin, it is as though one has sinned oneself; therefore, despite the fact that one has not committed that iniquity, one must confess to it. For when one's fellow has sinned, it is as though one has sinned oneself.—Isaac Luria, quoted in Agnon, *Days of Awe*, Schocken Books, Inc.

G. Moses said to God, "I am one, and Israel is six hundred thousand. Often have they sinned, and I have prayed for them, and thou hast forgiven them: thou hast had regard for the six hundred thousand, wilt thou not have regard to me?" God replied, "The doom of a community cannot be compared with the doom of an individual."—Talmudic literature, quoted in Montefiore and Loewe, *A Rabbinic Anthology*, Macmillan and Co. (London).

H. The description of tragic accidents, high rate of infant mortality, and raging epidemics as "acts of God" is an alibi for human negligence and ignorance.—Mordecai M. Kaplan, in *The Reconstructionist*, April 21, 1950.

I. God is not to be the valet for my private wishes; He is not to disrupt for human ends the order of Nature established by Him for the foundation of the world.—William Ernest Hocking, *Science and the Idea of God*, University of North Carolina Press.

J. I deny that God is responsible for the social tragedies of our century. I deny this because I believe it is neither fair nor just to make God the scapegoat for our own man-created suffering and evil. Certainly if there is one experience which we Jews know more intimately than any other people, it is the experience of being a scapegoat. What is a scapegoat? An innocent object of the wrath and the anger of a people who are not mature enough to assume responsibility for their own deeds and misdeeds. What is happening today, however, is that so many men everywhere are performing the same psychological trick and using the same shabby device in relation to God. God is being made the cosmic scapegoat for man's failure.

For if mankind had achieved peace and justice and equity and all human beings were living together as brothers, if human life were itself filled with the divine quality and if suddenly earthquakes would erupt upon our planet and great hurricanes and storms were to uproot city after city, and if every year some new disease were to descend from the clouds upon the human race, I could then understand cosmic atheism. The fault and the tragedy would obviously be non-human in its origin. But the situation is just the reverse today. The planets are moving in their orbits in silent order. No catastrophic meteors are winging their way through the clouds to rip open the earth and to make empty craters yawn where the cities of men once sent their spires into the horizon. It is man and man alone that is transforming the garden of the earth into a wasteland. What logic is there then in saying, "I cannot believe in God today"? Let us say rather, "It is difficult to believe in man today."

We Jews should recall then that at the very heart of our religion is this conviction that man should be mature enough to assume responsibility for the way that his world turns out. When we turn upon God and blame Him for the social and the economic calamities of our times we really talk as though man were the slave of the divine dictator. Now, most of the time we do not act as though we had no freedom of will. We do not really think of ourselves as impotent putty in the hands of a master potter. Our whole political democracy is based upon the theory that men are both free enough and intelligent enough to make responsible choices. Indeed, we do take responsibility for every good thing that we do. We pride ourselves upon every achievement that we make. We rejoice in every song that we sing, every painting that we paint, every business that we develop, every friendship that we nurture. We do not say in these moments that God is responsible; we take the credit for the good things we achieve. Why then suddenly when we are confronted with the evil consequences of human action, do we act like children and say, "It is God's fault." Why should we flee from the burden of our own guilt and attribute human tragedy to divine intervention?

Let Jews and Christians in the Western world work together for that kind of society when men will no longer have to ask the bitter question, "My God, my God, why hast Thou forsaken me?" and work for the coming of that day when God will not have to ask the human race a bitterer question, "Man, man, why hast thou forsaken Me?"—"How I Can Believe in God Now," by Rabbi Joshua Loth Liebman (from a radio address in 1940).

K. (David Nieto, rabbi of the Spanish-Portuguese congregation in London 250 years ago, wrote the following parable in explanation of human suffering):

Imagine a great pool full of sweet and pure water which never ceases. From it several channels conduct the water for the irrigation of surrounding fields.

One day the water stopped coming to some of the fields. The

farmers thereupon complained to the owner of the pool, saying that he had stopped the water for their fields in order to harm them, and to let them die of starvation and thirst. But the owner of the pool answered and said: "I am supplying water for all the fields, as usual. If there is no water for your fields, this can only be due to the state of disrepair in which you have left the channels and the conduits. Your complaints are therefore not against me but against your own laziness which has caused this damage. Go, then, and clear the way of the water, and remove the stones from it, and the water will return to you as at first. Understand, moreover, that I am not holding back for my own use the water which is meant for you. But, as is its nature, it continues to flow through such openings as it can find." —Translated by Rabbi Jakob J. Petuchowski, *Commentary Magazine*, July, 1954.

L. Our bodies, just because they are capable of thought, accomplishment, joy, beauty, love, are likewise susceptible to disease, distortion, dementia [mental illness], despair. Our capabilities require complexity of structure; and the greater the complexity, the greater the possibility of disorder and agony. Animals suffer less than human beings, plants less than animals, and rocks and metals suffer not at all; the less the complexity, the less the pain. We might truthfully assert that everything bad in the world is but the price we pay for everything good in the world.—Cronbach, *Judaism for Today*, Bookman Associates.

17. *What Happens to Us When We Die?*

OF ALL the important questions about religion which we have thought and talked about this year, none has been asked more frequently or persistently through the ages than the title of this chapter. There isn't a member of our class, in fact, there isn't an intelligent human being above the age of earliest childhood who hasn't wondered and asked about death and what happens to us after we die. There are several reasons why this question has occupied the attention of so many people. One is *curiosity*. Just because no one is able to give a definite, positive answer, because no one has ever come back to life on this earth after he died to tell of his experiences, our desire to know what follows this life is increased. But curiosity is far from the only or even the chief reason.

A greater reason is *fear*. Primitive man, living an active, robust life, became frightened when he saw that his companion, who fished and hunted with him yesterday, lay lifeless and motionless today. When his friend was asleep, he could arouse him by shaking him or making a loud noise. But this was a different kind of sleep. From this sleep there didn't seem to be any way of awakening his friend. And just as primitive man feared thunder and wind and everything else in the world of nature which he could neither understand nor explain, so he feared death, which he knew would some day carry him off also. Because he feared it, he wanted all the more desperately to know about it; hence his many questions.

There is probably less fear of death today than in the time of very early men, just as there is less fear of thunder. We understand better today that death is part of life, an experience which comes sooner or later to all of us. Yet there are people in modern times who still fear death, just as some still are afraid of thunder and lightning.

A third and more personal reason is our deep sense of sorrow and chagrin when someone we love dearly passes away. It is not easy to accept such losses calmly. When we have been deprived of a person who has been very dear to us, it is only natural that we should want to know what has happened to him and whether he still lives.

A fourth reason for our intense interest in death is our very deep *love of life*. If our existence on this earth consisted mostly of suffering and pain, more of us might anticipate death as a welcome release. There are some individuals, of course, who suffer so much on earth that they do indeed hope for an early death. But we all recognize such people to be exceptions. More remarkable is the fact that sometimes the very people who are suffering the greatest amount of pain and sorrow are the ones who cling most frantically to life and do not want it to end. For most of us, life, even with its trials and tribulations, is a series of fascinating experiences in a setting of vast and wonderful beauty. As God did after each day of creation in the Genesis story, we look around us at life and see that it is good. It is, therefore, our great love of life which makes us wonder all the more about what happens when it ends.

A fifth and final reason is *our anxiety that good shall prevail over evil,* that righteousness must win out over injustice, and that mankind's upward path in evolution toward God shall be continued. In the total pattern of our universe—on a planet which has existed for billions of years and on which some form of human life goes back about a million years—the life even of the oldest human being is but an instant of time. Man lives, at the very most, to be about a hundred years old. But, in the words of our ancient literature, "a thousand years in Thy sight are but as yesterday when it is past, and as a watch in the night."

Because our individual lives are so short compared to the total picture of the universe, we sometimes become discouraged over the possibility of progress. We may happen to live during one of those periods of temporary setback which we noticed when we drew a line depicting man's ethical progress and development. We notice that a particular individual or society which disobeys the moral law nevertheless seems to succeed. And we are anxious to see the outcome, to witness with our own eyes that in the long run such disobedience cannot prevail and that the line of mankind's progress does indeed turn upward again. No human being lives long enough to have all his discouragements and doubts reassured. Therefore it is but natural for us to project ourselves beyond the end of our individual lives on this earth, and to hope that all the things in which we believe, all the good causes for which we sacrifice and labor will in the end triumph and prevail.

For all these reasons, then, it is only natural for us to wonder, *What happens to us when we die?* Your first Reading Selection at the end of this chapter will show that even the writers of our

Bible were known to express their fears and doubts about life after death. Some people living today, on the other hand, seem absolutely sure they know the answer. Several years ago many newspapers carried the picture of a five-months-old baby girl under the caption, "They Seek Her Immortality." Under the picture was this explanation:

> Here is Baby Jean, the five-months-old baby adopted by James B. Schafer . . . who predicts that if plans work out Jean will live forever. Plans call for Baby Jean to refrain from meats (including eggs, milk and butter) and never to hear the words "sickness" or "death."

At about the same time, the following item, sent out by the Associated Press, appeared in a number of other papers:

CULTISTS SAY WOMAN WILL RETURN TO LIFE

But Utah Health Commissioner Demands Death Certificate for Missing Body

SALT LAKE CITY, April 24 (AP)—Dr. J. L. Jones, State Health commissioner, demanded a death certificate today for a long-dead woman who, fellow cultists insist, is coming back to life. . . .

Local authorities investigated when word spread that the woman's body had not been buried. It was reported found in a state of preservation and tourists flocked there. Later the body disappeared and sceptics declared that the colonists had secretly disposed of it.

Mrs. Ogden (leader of the cult) said: "I am in communication with Mrs. Peshak (the dead woman). We not only expect her to be restored to us in physical life, but we expect her to be recognized by others."

Closely related to this is another newspaper clipping on a subject about which we often joke—haunted houses and ghosts! This one is from the *New York Herald-Tribune*, issue of January 26, 1950.

2 BRITONS SLEEP WITH LIGHTS ON, HEAR NO GHOST

Wife Keeps Bedclothes Over Head on Return to House Where Vicar Exorcised

BRISTOL, ENGLAND, Jan. 25 (AP)—A Church of England vicar—and plenty of electric lights—appear to have chased the ghost from 13 Highworth Road. Mr. and Mrs. William Baber, who appealed for use of an ancient Christian rite to rid their home of the faint form of a little old woman with a halo, slept there last night for the first time in a week.

They did so after the Rev. Francis J. Maddock visited every room in the house, intoning the words of a ghost-dispersing rite called exorcism. The Babers backed the ancient religious ceremony with plenty of light—a strong one burning in every room.

SEE NO SIGN OF OLD FIGURE

They said today they saw no sign of the old figure walking sorrowfully through the house, which previously had disturbed them repeatedly. The couple originally planned to stay away from the house until daylight, but finally decided there was no use waiting.

"I slept with the bedclothes over my head and heard nothing," Mrs. Baber said.

The Babers said the ghost first walked six months ago. It talked, as well, they said. It took the form of a little old woman in black, who, in their words: "Just comes along, says 'Ah, hah' in an accusing voice, then goes away again. . . ."

The Babers say the ghost may be that of the former owner of the house. Its first appearance came after Mrs. Baber opened the door to the room in which the woman died, locked for more than eighteen years.

The Babers plan to continue sleeping with all the lights on for a while.

In these items we see immediately two quite different ideas of what happens to us when we die. Though neither can really be called modern, there are people living today who still believe in both. One is a belief that there is a way to keep human beings alive forever here on this earth—to avoid death altogether. The other is a faith that after a person dies, he can somehow be brought back to this earth again. We shall say more about this in a moment.

Despite the apparent assurance of people like these, no one

really knows the answer to our question. As in the case of our earlier discussions about God, religion and prayer, we shall find widely varying answers proposed by different groups of people. You may or may not find one of them satisfactory to you. Perhaps this chapter will leave you still with no answer, but if it stimulates and helps you to think about death and immortality, your thinking will some day bring you closer to an answer.

With this in mind, let's look at a few of the answers that have been suggested.

Address Unknown

First, there is the belief that after we die our lives are continued somewhere else—no one knows exactly where—pretty much as they were on this earth. We look the same, act the same, do the same things and feel the same emotions; only our address has changed. Because the ancient Egyptians believed this, when they buried a man they placed in his tomb all the things they thought he would need or want in his next life. His favorite horse, his clothes and weapons, food enough to sustain him on his journey from one life to the next—all these and many other objects were buried with him. As recently as 1942 a man was buried in Indiana with his radio, shaving utensils, mirror, wine glass, magazines, and a bed cover! He must have had ancient Egyptian blood in him.

The belief that a human body will leave its grave after death and continue its physical existence is often referred to as *resurrection*. Most Christians believe this is exactly what happened to Jesus. Good Friday is observed in Christian churches as the day on which Jesus died. Easter Sunday is the remembrance of the third day after his death, the day on which he is supposed to have been resurrected to live forever.

There have been Jews too at various times who believed in resurrection. For a long time there was a legend current among some Jews that when the Messiah would come, all righteous Jews who had ever died in the past would be resurrected from their graves to live again in Palestine.

On Call

No doubt you have heard of "spiritualists." They believe that after a person dies, his spirit or soul not only lives on, but it can be called back to this earth by someone who knows the proper technique, to give information and advice to the living. "Spiritualists" call the sessions at which they endeavor to call back the spirit of a dead person *seances.* In every case where scientific investigations have been held, it has been discovered that magic tricks of one kind or another were used at such seances to fool people. There are no known cases in which a person who had died was actually brought back to speak with those who remained alive.

In ancient times there were more people than there are now who believed this sort of thing. In our Bible, for example, I Samuel 28:3-20 tells how Saul, even though he had himself ordered all those who pretended to bring back the spirits of the dead to be banished, nevertheless asked a woman to bring Samuel back to advise him when he was frightened before one of his battles with the Philistines. It would be a good idea for you to read this story in the Bible before going on with this chapter.

Over and Over Again

A somewhat different type of belief holds that the spirits or souls of the departed are born again into other bodies. People who believe this would say that the soul which belongs to each of us existed before on this earth in some other body—either of an animal or another human being. When that other body died, its soul was reborn in us; when we die, it will in turn be born into another body. Thus souls go on living indefinitely, even though the bodies which temporarily house them may perish.

There is a Chasidic belief—never accepted by Jews or Judaism officially, but interesting none the less—that if a soul fails to achieve a sufficiently high ethical life in its first earthly appearance, it must be born over, and if necessary over again and again until it does. The soul which reaches a high ethical standard the first time, however, need not be born again.

Heaven and Hell

Even more common than any of these beliefs is the notion that after we die, we go either to heaven or to hell. Those who are good are believed to go to a place called heaven, where they continue living and are rewarded for the good they did on earth. Those, on the other hand, who were wicked, are believed to go to hell, where they are punished. In some cases the belief is that they remain forever in hell; others think the wicked must suffer punishment in hell only until they have paid for the evil they did during life on this earth. According to some beliefs, it is actually our bodies which go either to heaven or to hell, while others would say it is only our souls. Reading Selections B, C, and I for this chapter are based on this or similar beliefs.

The four tentative theories of immortality described above may all be considered together. In a moment, we shall suggest certain other explanations. First, however, think about those already given. The following questions should guide your thinking:

> What have these four theories in common? Wherein do they differ? Do any of them appeal to you? Why? Do any of them seem to you quite inadequate for modern Jews? Why? Which of them would you find comforting or encouraging? Why? Is the concept of the soul which is assumed by these beliefs similar to the idea of the soul we have presented in these discussions? What do you find lacking in these beliefs?

When you have carefully considered these questions and have compared the ideas presented thus far, we shall be ready to consider a second and somewhat different group of explanations answering the question, *What happens to us when we die?*

No Room

Many people, thinking about life and death, have reached the conclusion that death is a very necessary part of the whole picture, making life possible. If there were no such thing as death, they say, soon there would be no room for further births on this earth. The seas would be so filled with fish no more fish could be hatched, the forests so overcrowded with beasts that any infant beasts would be stifled and starved, the earth so densely packed with human beings that its resources couldn't possibly feed and sustain them all. The Midrash anticipated something like this when it said: "The great ones of each generation must die to make room for the greatness of successors." In other words, only if one generation dies can there be room enough on this earth for future generations to be born and to live.

To show how true this is, someone has figured out that if only one kind of insect—the locust—were unaffected by death, very soon there could be no plant or animal life left on this earth—at least not land life acquiring oxygen via lungs. The locusts alone, if they lived forever and continued to breed, would soon crowd every green plant and vegetable off the face of the earth. The result obviously would be that even the locusts themselves would have no food and could not live.

It follows further from this that if there were no death, the course of evolution could not continue its upward progress. For it is chiefly in the birth of a new generation that those changes occur which eventually lead to new life forms. So if we who are now alive could live forever, after a while no new generations could be born and no further development through evolution could be expected.

Indeed, it has been suggested that death is a price we must pay to make evolution possible. Certain animals and trees live far longer than do human beings—in some cases for many hundreds of years. It is even possible that the lowest, simplest forms of life can live forever. But it is only through those species of life where death occurs that enough mutations appear to make evolution possible.

> Well, what do you think of this explanation? Is it likely to calm any of man's fears about death? Would it be apt to comfort a human being who faces the death of a loved one? Would it help him accept that death? Does it make sense to you?

Sunshine and Rain

Somewhat related to this thought, though by no means the same, is the idea suggested by others that it is precisely the certainty that life must one day end which increases our enjoyment and appreciation of the experiences that come to us. When we have a vacation, these people would say, or when we enjoy any kind of pleasant experience, the thought that it must come to its proper end makes us appreciate every minute of it all the more. So it is with life. If we knew we could live forever, we would waste a great deal of time and would not capture the greatest possible benefit from each experience. Because we know there will be an end to all this—at least as far as earthly physical life is concerned—we enjoy that much more the years we have here. You have probably noticed yourself that on a day which is crowded with activity you get much more done than on another day when you have but little to do. The average human being, knowing that he has more than enough time to accomplish the day's work, is apt to sit around until night falls, with little or nothing done. When the same person faces a very crowded schedule, he works at a pace which enables him to complete a great deal. So with life itself, the fact that we know our time on this earth to be limited, with much work to be accomplished, enables us to achieve much more.

Rabbi Joshua Loth Liebman must have had this thought in mind when he wrote: "I often feel that death is not the enemy of life, but its friend, for it is the knowledge that our years are limited which makes them so precious."

We are also reminded that most of our enjoyment and pleasure in life comes through opposites. That may at first sound rather strange, but we shall try to explain. If all our days were filled only with brilliant sunshine, we would soon come to take sunlight for granted and would no longer thrill to it. Our days of cloudiness and rain make us appreciate the sunshine more. Similarly our knowledge that life on earth is not endless makes us enjoy our years here more than we otherwise might.

> Do you agree or disagree? Why? Would you call this a belief in immortality? Why? Is it at all comforting or helpful? Is it enough?

Part of Nature

Frequently in the early chapters of this book we referred to the fact that we human beings are part of the larger world of nature. You will recall our mentioning not only our relationship to other life-forms through evolution, but also the fact that the chemical elements to be found in our bodies are the same as those in the universe around us. Based on a recognition of our relationship to the world of nature, some people have suggested that it is through the rest of nature that we achieve our immortality. It is true, they say, that our bodies no longer live after death, but they then are transformed into other forms of life in nature. The energy and chemical elements from our bodies go into the soil, where they help make flowers grow and directly or indirectly provide food for plants and perhaps even for other animals and human beings. Thus we, who came from nature, return to nature. In a sense, nature loaned each of us a certain amount of its energy, which we used during our lives on earth, then returned to nature when we died, to be used in some other form.

> Is this a form of immortality? Does it appeal to you? Why? Would it be as helpful in facing the thought of death as any of the four beliefs described in the first part of the chapter. Why?

We Live through Our Children

Still another theory about life and death is that we live on only or chiefly through our children. We might almost call this a belief in the immortality of families rather than of individuals. Before we were born, the genes which were to determine the color of our eyes and hair, for example, existed in the body-cells of our parents, and before they were born, in those of our grandparents, our great-grandparents, and so on. Something like this is true in a spiritual as well as a biological sense. Almost from the day you were first able to understand, your parents have tried to teach you the kind of life which is most important to them—the causes in which they believe, the work they think it important to accomplish. When you become a parent, you in turn will try to transmit all that to your own children. Thus, when each generation dies, the most important ideals and goals in which it believed live on through the next generation.

> What is your opinion of this belief? Would you call it immortality? Is it comforting or satisfying? How about people who have no children? According to this theory, would there be any immortality for them?

We Live through Our Group

An extension of the belief in immortality through our children is the idea that the individual man or woman achieves a certain kind of immortality through the continued life of the group to which he belongs. Something of this belief is to be found both in the Chinese and the Jewish attitudes toward life. A great surgeon, Dr. William Osler, for example, once wrote about the Chinese: ". . . the educated Chinaman looks for no personal immortality, but the generations past and the generations to come form with those that are alive one single whole; all live eternally, though it is only some that happen at any given moment to live upon earth."

A similar view is expressed in an old Jewish legend about the death of Moses. When Moses was about to die on Mt. Neboh without entering the Promised Land, he begged God to let him live longer. After much pleading, God finally said to him that His intention was to allow Moses to die then so that the people of Israel might live. If Moses preferred, however, He would reverse His original intention, allowing Moses to live forever, but bringing the life of Israel to a close. Moses, of course, saw the wisdom and necessity of his own death, and complained no more.

As far as Judaism is concerned, it isn't just the biological survival of the group which is important. It is rather the ideals in which the group believes and for which it stands which must go on living. The individual, during his lifetime on earth, must add all he can to the significance of his group and to the contribution it makes to civilization. Then, when he dies, in a sense, the most important part of him lives on through what he has added to the life of his people. In this spirit the Talmud says: "Whoever leaves a son after him studying Torah is considered as if he had never died." And one of the great Chasidic Rabbis said, "One is immortal if his descendants study the Torah."

> Ask yourself now the same questions about this belief as you already have concerning the others. Is it really a form of immortality? Which is more important, the individual or the group? Does the individual live for the group or the group for the individual? What difference is there between the thought of Achad Ha-am, expressed in your readings for this chapter, and that of the Nazis, who killed countless thousands of individuals because they said each person lived for the sake of the State? According to the quotation from the Talmud above, would an ignorant man have any immortality?

It may help you answer the last question if we give here a quotation from one of the ancient Rabbis who said, "The amei ho-orets, עַמֵּי הָאָרֶץ (ignorant people), will not live again. Whoever is slack about Torah will not live again. Whoever makes use of the light of Torah, the light of Torah will revive him (after death); . . ."

We Live in the Good We Do

Somewhat similar to this last idea is the thought that each of us continues to live on this earth in the good he accomplishes during his lifetime. According to this view, a great composer like Beethoven is more alive today, in that his music is still played and still thrills millions, than a person who may be biologically living now but who has never created anything worth while or brought any goodness into the lives of others. A man like Theodor Herzl is more alive today in the realization of his dream in Israel than another person who lives only for himself.

People who hold this belief would say that our ideas of immortality depend very much on what we think is most important about a human being or a human life. Those to whom our physical, material existence is most important require a concept of immortality which tells them the body itself lives on in some other life. Those, on the other hand, who appreciate the far greater importance of man's spiritual life, will find the comfort and assurance they need in a belief which tells them that the most important things man creates and the values he holds most precious will surely endure forever.

A Canadian soldier in World War I saw his best friend blown to bits before his very eyes. Stunned for a moment, he regained his composure, was silent for a time, then said, "It will take more than that to stop you." What do you think he may have meant? What concept of immortality did he probably have?

Edgar Arlington Robinson, in a poem about John Brown, says of him, "he will not sleep in history." Later in the same poem he has John Brown remarking, "I shall have more to say when I am dead."

Is it possible for a man to have more to say after he has died than others say while still alive? Would this be a form of immortality? What examples can you give?

Another martyr is reputed to have said, just before being shot to death by a firing squad, "Your bullets, my friends, will have no effect on the thoughts in my humble head. They will continue in other humble heads." One more quotation—this time from our own Jewish tradition, expresses the same basic thought: ". . . the righteous, even after their death, may be called living, whereas the wicked, both in life and in death, may be called dead."

In an earlier chapter we mentioned the novel and motion picture, *Grapes of Wrath*, which told the story of the "Okies," the miserably impoverished migrant farm workers in the far west. Tom, the son of such a family, expressed this idea of immortality with simple eloquence to his mother, when he said, ". . . I'll be all aroun' in the dark. I'll be ever'where—wherever you look. Wherever they's a fight so hungry people can eat, I'll be there. Wherever they's a cop beating up a guy, I'll be there . . . why, I'll be in the way guys yell when they're mad an' I'll be in the way kids laugh when they're hungry an' they know supper's ready. An' when our folks eat the stuff they raise an' live in the houses they build—why I'll be there."

Not everyone, of course, can be a creative artist or contribute significantly to great causes and ideals. But every human being without exception can bring love and goodness into the lives of others if he tries. According to the theory we are considering now, even the simple, unlearned individual can count on the immortality of whatever good he does to others. Whoever did a kindness for any young, struggling artist or composer, whoever spoke a word of inspiration or encouragement to any great man or woman, shares in every major achievement of that man or woman. Even the shoe-shine boy who cheers up the people whose shoes he cleans has a share in the immortality they may earn in part because of their contact with him. It is obvious, however, that this isn't just an easy, automatic kind of immortality on which everyone can depend. This is a kind of immortality each of us must earn.

In this connection we want to mention another theory which is sufficiently similar to be considered together with this one. We have suggested before that God is the soul of the universe, just as each of us has a soul within himself. Your soul is the non-physical, spiritual part of you which has developed through long centuries of evolution out of the physical body; it is the margin of difference and superiority which distinguishes you from animals. God, who is the soul of the universe, is the non-physical, spiritual power or force which we have seen working time and time again.

Now then, it has been suggested that in a sense, the soul of each of us is a kind of "loan" from the great *oversoul* which is God. Each of us at birth is given a quantity of this soul to care for and develop during his years on earth. At death, the soul originally given to us is returned to its source. If we have lived life richly and well, we return more soul than we originally received; in that increase we find our immortality. If we have failed to realize our fullest potentialities, we return at life's end only as much or perhaps even less soul than we received in the beginning. In that case, we have lost our chance at immortality.

> How does this type of immortality compare with the others already considered? Would it help a man live a better life? Would it comfort or reassure him in facing death? Is this a type of immortality available to everyone, or only to a few? What examples can you give of men and women who will live forever in the sense discussed here? What type of person would be apt to find this concept of immortality satisfying? What type of person would find more encouragement in the idea of heaven and hell? Why the difference?

Through Others Too

Our final theory of immortality is very similar to the one we have just considered. It agrees that we live in the good we accomplish, and adds that our lives are also continued in the additional good which others who follow us are able to achieve because of us. The writer of this book had a young friend who was killed in World War II. He happened to be one of the most intelligent, idealistic young men one could possibly meet. Since his death, not only has the writer been completely unable to forget him, but many times, in moments of discouragement and doubt, when the temptation was to take the easy way and overlook some evil or injustice, the memory of that young boy and how he would have felt and acted has served as an inspiration to his older friend and has motivated him to accept a challenge he might otherwise have shirked. It would be foolish—would it not?—to say that the life of such a boy has permanently ended, when his soul still lives in the hearts of others who are contributing good to the world because of their friend whom they can see no more but who still influences them almost daily.

There are, to be sure, other theories and ideas of immortality. But the suggestions we have covered in this chapter include a sufficient variety for our purposes. Look them over again, and try to decide which theory or combination of theories strikes you as being closest to your own ideas. If none of them seems satisfactory to you, try to explain what is lacking in them and what sort of belief in immortality would suit you better. If you think any of them are not justified by the facts and are therefore unreasonable beliefs, say so and explain why. You will be given an opportunity to answer these questions and to evaluate our various theories in your workbook.

Judaism on Life and Death

Before concluding this chapter it is important to say an additional word about the distinctive attitude of Judaism toward life and death. Throughout this course we have noticed at many points where Jewish religion differs from the attitudes or creeds of other faiths. The Jewish approach to death is also a unique one. It expresses itself especially in two ways. One is in the simple, yet eloquent statement from the Book of Job which we include in our Jewish funeral service: "The Lord giveth—the Lord taketh away; blessed be the name of the Lord." And the other is our traditional memorial prayer, the Kaddish, one of the most unique prayers in all the liturgies of the world.

Though the Kaddish is a prayer recited especially by mourners in memory of their loved ones who have died, strangely and significantly enough, it does not contain a single word either about death or about the dead! The English references to death in the so-called translation to be found in our prayer books are not translations of the original at all. The Kaddish itself is a prayer affirming with mighty eloquence that God is to be praised and His name sanctified everywhere—on the earth and in the heavens.

A moment's thought will show you how deeply significant this really is. Our Jewish faith bids us concentrate on life more than on death. The Kaddish is, in a sense, a pledge to take up the burden of life from those who have laid it down, and to go on living for the ideals they held dear. The Kaddish is our way of saying that death and life alike are the results of a great force or power working through us. The death of one person is as truly a manifestation of God as is the birth of another. Even when we face the tragedy of parting from our loved ones, therefore, it is our obligation as Jews to express our gratitude for the power we see in our lives and to go on living with confidence and hope.

What happens to us when we die? We do not know. No one really knows. This is another of the many questions about religion which have disturbed men for many centuries and for which they have sought answers. The search continues in our time and beyond. Perhaps we or our children will reach closer than others have to the answer. Meanwhile, our Jewish religion tells us that with so much purpose and meaning to everything we see in human life, there must be a meaning to death also, though we can only guess at it now. Our hearts and minds together give us confidence that the great creative power of God, on which we can depend and through which we can live life at its highest and best, is working out its purposes in death as in life. That which is most important about us, that for which we were born and given a chance to live on this earth, will endure forever and will triumph.

You have probably wondered and thought a great deal about death. Perhaps this chapter has clarified your thinking on this subject; perhaps, on the other hand, it has only added to your confusion. In either event, before concluding this part of our discussion it would be well for you to set down in writing some of your own thoughts on death. In your workbook you will find place for a brief essay on *one* of the following topics:

1. Why I Would Like to Live Forever.
2. Why I Would Not Like to Live Forever.
3. My Thoughts about Death.

SOMETHING FOR YOU TO READ

A. (Our first reading selection for this chapter is Job 14:7–12):

For there is hope of a tree,
If it be cut down, that it will sprout again,
And that the tender branch thereof will not cease.
Though the root thereof wax old in the earth,
And the stock thereof die in the ground;
Yet through the scent of water it will bud,
And put forth boughs like a plant.

But man dieth, and lieth low;
Yea, man perisheth, and where is he?
As the waters fail from the sea,
And the river is drained dry;
So man lieth down and riseth not;
Till the heavens be no more, they shall not awake,
Nor be roused out of their sleep.

B. (The following description of heaven and hell is taken from the writings of a Swedish statesman and philosopher named Swedenborg):

In heaven the angels are men who live in society as men do on earth. They have houses and gardens, flower-beds and fields. There are cities with roads, streets and squares. Habitations, ever so beautiful, contain drawing-rooms and bed-chambers too! Beautiful garments, that are so very real that they can be seen and felt, are worn by these inhabitants. But in the other place, to which the wicked are consigned, a raging fire exists, and in this furnace the denizens [inhabitants] of the pit—clothed, it is true, but in ragged, filthy garments—pass their spiritual lives. Every child in heaven goes to school and becomes an angel; and all angels have mouths and tongues and ears just like men.—Edward Lawrence, *Spiritualism Among Civilized and Savage Races*, copyright by The MacMillan Co. and used with their permission.

C. *Epitaph Found in Chiswick Churchyard, England*

Her last words on earth were, Dear friends, I am going
Where washing ain't done, neither sweeping nor sewing.
But everything there is exact to my wishes,
For where they don't eat, there's no washing of dishes.
I'll be where loud anthems will always be ringing.
But having no voice, I'll be out of the singing.
Don't mourn for me now; don't mourn for me never;
I'm going to do nothing for ever and ever.

Young, *Social Psychology*, Crofts.

D. Let us then try to imagine for ourselves what our world would be like if we all lived on and on forever on the earth. If no one died, the time would soon come when the world would be full of people and then there would be no more room for new-born babies. What a queer lot of old folks we should be after a few centuries! A world filled with old people who could boast of thousands of birthdays! No babies born! No children learning and growing! No lovers courting! No brides and grooms! Everybody old together! What a dull world it would be! What joy we all should miss! How our love would shrivel up!

No—a thousand times no! We would rather die when we are old than to give up the joy of growing up, or the thrill of watching the newly born.—Fahs and Spoerl, *Beginnings of Life and Death*, The Beacon Press.

E. (The following quotation is from the writings of the great modern Jewish philosopher who used the pen-name, Achad Ha-am, meaning "one of the people"):

I live for the sake of the perpetuation and happiness of the community of which I am a member; I die to make room for new individuals who will mold the community afresh and not allow it to stagnate and remain forever in one position. When the individual thus values the community as his own life and strives after its happiness as though it were his individual well-being, he finds satisfaction and no longer feels so keenly the bitterness of his individual existence, because he sees the end for which he lives and suffers.

F. Our living immortality is found more concretely in our children, in our children's children. We may not be sculptors, able to hew immortal statues out of immobile rock. Most of us, however, have the infinitely greater privilege (which we take too much for granted) of molding the spiritual life and destiny of the generations that come after us. Men and women whom we influence by the example of our lives, the children who are touched by the flame of our spirits—it is in them that we live on and find our eternal significance.—Joshua Loth Liebman, *Peace of Mind*, Simon and Schuster.

G. *On Going*

A grave is all too weak a thing
To hold my fancy long;
I'll bear a blossom with the spring,
Or be a blackbird's song.

I think that I shall fade with ease,
Melt into the earth like snow,
Be food for hungry, growing trees,
Or help the lilies blow.

And if my love should lonely walk,
Quite of my nearness fain,
I may come back to her and talk
In liquid words of rain.

—from *Color* by Countee Cullen, copyright 1925 by Harper and Bros.

H. *The Choir Invisible*

Oh, may I join the choir invisible
Of those immortal dead who live again
In minds made better by their presence; live
In pulses stirred to generosity,

In deeds of daring rectitude [righteousness], in scorn
Of miserable aims that end with self,
In thoughts sublime that pierce the night like stars,
And with their mild persistence urge men's search
To vaster issues. . . . May I reach
That purest heaven—be to other souls
The cup of strength in some great agony,
Enkindle generous ardor, feed pure love,
Beget the smiles that have no cruelty,
Be the sweet presence of a good diffused,
And in diffusion ever more intense!
So shall I join the choir invisible,
Whose music is the gladness of the world.

—George Eliot.

I. To believe so (in a heaven where everything is physically perfect) is to be a schoolboy who expects nuts and sweetmeats as compensation for his studies. Celestial [heavenly] pleasures can be neither measured nor comprehended [understood] by a mortal being, any more than the blind can distinguish colors or the deaf appreciate music.—Maimonides.

J. First of all, we can obviously accept what may be called biological immortality. From the standpoint of biology, you are not in any sense a self-made man or woman. Through a hereditary process, you are the product of innumerable generations before you. You have your Uncle Elmer's ears, your father's physique, your Grandmother Jones' hair, and possibly your Great Grandfather Smith has bequeathed to you that special heart condition you suffer from. And what is more, this bundle of hereditary traits, characteristics and tendencies, received from your progenitors [ancestors], will be passed on from you to your children, and from them on down the line indefinitely. Biologically speaking, you are not a separate entity floating freely in time and space, but are a part of a continuing, living chain, the beginning and the end of which no man can see. —Argow, *What Do Religious Liberals Believe?* The Beacon Press.

K. Who would be so insensitive to history as to say that Abraham Lincoln is dead? With every passing year Lincoln becomes more truly alive through the increasing influence his memory and example have on the peoples of the world. When, in simple eulogy of his dead president, Secretary of War Stanton declared, "Now he belongs to the ages," he was simply testifying to the immortality of

Abraham Lincoln.—Argow, *What Do Religious Liberals Believe?* The Beacon Press.

L. When King David had completed the Book of Psalms, he felt exceedingly proud, and said: "Lord of the Universe, hast Thou a creature that proclaimeth more praises of Thee than I?"

God thereupon sent to him a frog, which said: "David, take not such pride in thyself. I chant the praises of my Creator more than dost thou. Moreover, I am performing a great Mitzvah [good deed]. For when my time to expire [die] is at hand, I go to the shore of the sea, and permit myself to be swallowed up by one of its creatures. Thus even my death is a deed of kindness."—Talmud.

The Rabbis ask: "Why does the Bible in recording David's death say: And David slept with his fathers. Why does it not say: And David died."

"Because," replied the Sages, "David left a son who walked in the good ways of his father, and who continued his noble deeds; therefore, David was really not dead, but lived on through the good deeds of his son."—Talmud, both the above quoted in Newman, *The Talmudic Anthology*, Behrman House.

M. We need a new doctrine of immortality and several have been proposed. There are those who say that a man lives after death in his children and should be satisfied to find in them his immortality. Others point out that matter is indestructible and that the chemical elements of a man's body live on forever in altered forms. Poets have rung the changes upon this thought, but few men are imaginative enough to derive any great satisfaction from the possibility that their ashes may some day fertilize the greensward. Still others talk of the immortality of influence and long to join the choir invisible of those whose memory makes future generations happier. And a fourth theory dwells upon the idea that he who helps to establish an institution which lives on through the years and renders social service is thereby himself immortal.—Charles Francis Potter, *Creative Personality*, Funk and Wagnalls.

N. The late Rufus Jones had only one son, Lowell, who died at the age of eleven, but the boy continued, for forty-five more years, to be a dominant influence in the great man's life. The Jones' study at Haverford included many photographs of the learned and famous, but the central place, over the mantel, was always occupied by the portrait of this boy. Rufus Jones felt that he had to live for both himself and his boy, and in this he succeeded, to a remarkable degree. Writing more than forty years after the occasion of his sorrow, Rufus Jones told of the boy as follows: "I overheard him once talking to a group of playmates, when each one was telling what he wanted to be when grown up, and Lowell said when his turn came, 'I want to grow up and be a man like my daddy.' Few things in my life have ever touched me as those words did, or have given me a greater impulse to dedication. What kind of a man was I going to be, if I was to be the pattern for my boy!"—Trueblood, *The Life We Prize*, Harper and Bros.

18. *A Book with No Conclusion*

So WE end our year together.

You know by now what we meant in the beginning when we said that in these pages we would be discussing some of the most everlastingly important questions that have ever challenged the minds of men. We hope that these chapters, and our class discussions based on them, have not only been interesting for you, but even more that they have stimulated you to do a great deal of honest thinking.

Ordinarily, you would expect a book of this kind, particularly one which asks so many questions, to end with a chapter of final conclusions, summarizing the answers at which we have arrived. In that sense at least, this is a book without any conclusion. There will, indeed, never be a final conclusion to the kind of discussion and speculation we have had here. Human beings will never cease to ask the kind of questions which have concerned us in this book; and no generation will be completely satisfied with the answers given by its predecessors. Furthermore, no one individual or group of individuals will ever be able to suggest a system of answers which will be perfectly acceptable and helpful to everyone.

To whatever extent a summary may be possible at the end of this volume, it will be of far greater benefit for you to write it yourself. We have shared each other's deepest thoughts on such subjects as God, religion, prayer, human suffering, immortality, and the Ten Commandments. What have these discussions meant to you? To what extent and how have you benefited from them? How have your ideas about these matters changed? Your summary is to consist of answers to such questions as these. Specifically, in the final assignment of your workbook, answer these questions:

1. What is the most valuable thing you have learned from our course? Has this course helped you? If so, in what way?
2. What is the greatest change this book has caused in your thinking?
3. What is your biggest disappointment in the course? What do you think was the weakest point in our discussions? What did you find most difficult to grasp, or what ideas presented here are you unable to accept?

Aside from your general answers to the second question above, you will have a clear measure of the changes caused by this course after you have marked the "true and false" statements in Section IV of your workbook. These are the same statements given in Chapter One; a comparison of the answers given there with your opinions now as the year ends will show where and how your attitudes have changed. Remember, however, that there are no "right" or "wrong" answers to these statements and that your grade in the course will not be affected by the opinions you express. The "right" answer in each case is your own honest opinion at this moment, without regard to how you felt at the beginning of the year.

Finally, you will be expected to write an essay on the subject, "The Purpose of Human Life." Using as many of the ideas covered in this book as you wish, you are to describe at length and in your own words what you now believe to be the purpose an individual should seek to achieve in the course of his life on earth. Try to avoid mere generalities; be as specific and as concrete as you can. While nearly every chapter and page we have covered during the year can aid you in writing this essay, the following chapters should be particularly helpful: Four, Five, Eight, Nine, Ten, Thirteen, Fifteen, and Seventeen.

While we are not adding the usual Reading Selections to this final chapter, the following statement by the eminent zoologist, Julian Huxley, may aid you in working out this essay: "Each time you enjoy a sunset or a symphony, each time you understand an interesting fact or idea, each time you find satisfaction in making something, or in disciplined activity like sport, evolution has brought another of its possibilities to fruition."

> What other types of activity might Mr. Huxley have included in this statement?

Our Hope—

We had two over-all aims at the beginning of our course. For fear of unduly influencing your thinking, we hesitated even to mention them until this final chapter. First, we have hoped throughout that you would "catch" something of the endless adventure of Jewish religious thinking and that you would come to feel yourself part of a long, long process, of a challenging quest for answers to these eternal questions. This course will have succeeded to the fullest extent of our hopes if you feel that way now, and if in addition you recognize your own role in the working out of God's plan for the universe and for human life.

If you have even just begun to feel yourself a part of God, and God a very real part of you, so that neither is conceivable without the other, then a major hope of all this effort will have been amply realized.

Last, but very far indeed from least, we have been guided by the prayer that through these discussions you would come to feel increased pride in the fact that you are Jewish. There are many ways in which one can be a "proud Jew." One way, which is far from desirable, is to believe unthinkingly that everything Jewish must necessarily be better than anything which is not Jewish. Another is to swell up boastfully every time a Jewish athlete scores some success or a Jewish scientist achieves a discovery. Yet another way is to become belligerent whenever we hear a disparaging remark about Jews. None of these is the best or the most intelligent way of feeling Jewish pride. None of these is the way we have kept constantly in mind during this course.

What we mean here by Jewish pride is that you will see yourself as part of a people which has made a greater contribution than any other group to the religious thinking of mankind, and which has yet more to give in future days than it has already given in the past. And even more, that you begin to think of our Jewish religion as an important, functioning part of your own personal life. Not just as something others felt, nor as something we learn about only from a book—the way we study Greek history or the Spanish language—but rather as an outlook on life, an interpretation of human existence, which actually *works within yourself*, which inspires you to be a better, more decent kind of person than you might otherwise be, and which—in every crisis of your life—will give you strength to meet the problems you must face and to turn each disaster or sorrow into a triumph which will enrich your own life and the lives of all who know you.

May you keep these pages always, and look back upon this year as the beginning of a process of serious thought which will never end, to the final day of your life. May you find comfort and challenge in the asking of such questions as these. And in religion, as in all other aspects of your life, may you never grow fearful of new ideas or of change. For change can mean growth. And growth means progress. And progress means that we have moved one little step forward and upward in our yearning to reach God.

Index

A

B

C

D

UNION GRADED SERIES

EDITED BY

EMANUEL GAMORAN, PH.D., *Director of Education*
Union of American Hebrew Congregations